A Text Book of

# PHARMACEUTICAL CHEMISTRY - I

**FIRST YEAR DIPLOMA IN PHARMACY**
As Per E.R. 1991

**Dr. A. V. KASTURE**
Professor of Pharmaceutical Chemistry,
Department of Pharmaceutical Sciences,
Nagpur University, NAGPUR 400 010.

**Late Dr. S. G. WADODKAR**
Reader in Pharmaceutical Chemistry,
Department of Pharmaceutical Sciences,
Nagpur University, NAGPUR 400 010.

| PHARMACEUTICAL CHEMISTRY – I | ISBN 978-81-85790-12-1 |
|---|---|

**Thirteenth Edition** : July 2015
© : Authors

The text of this publication, or any part thereof, should not be reproduced or transmitted in any form or stored in any computer storage system or device for distribution including photocopy, recording, taping or information retrieval system or reproduced on any disc, tape, perforated media or other information storage device etc., without the written permission of Authors with whom the rights are reserved. Breach of this condition is liable for legal action.

Every effort has been made to avoid errors or omissions in this publication. In spite of this, errors may have crept in. Any mistake, error or discrepancy so noted and shall be brought to our notice shall be taken care of in the next edition. It is notified that neither the publisher nor the authors or seller shall be responsible for any damage or loss of action to any one, of any kind, in any manner, therefrom.

**Published By :**
**NIRALI PRAKASHAN**
Abhyudaya Pragati, 1312, Shivaji Nagar
Off J.M. Road, Pune – 411005
Tel - (020) 25512336/37/39, Fax - (020) 25511379
Email : niralipune@pragationline.com

**Printed By:**
Repro Knowledgecast Limited,
Thane

☞ **DISTRIBUTION CENTRES**

**PUNE**
Nirali Prakashan : 119, Budhwar Peth, Jogeshwari Mandir Lane, Pune 411002, Maharashtra
Tel : (020) 2445 2044, 66022708, Fax : (020) 2445 1538
Email : bookorder@pragationline.com, nirallocal@pragationline.com

Nirali Prakashan : S. No. 28/27, Dhyari, Near Pari Company, Pune 411041
Tel : (020) 24690204 Fax : (020) 24690316
Email : dhyari@pragationline.com, bookorder@pragationline.com

**MUMBAI**
Nirali Prakashan : 385, S.V.P. Road, Rasdhara Co-op. Hsg. Society Ltd.,
Girgaum, Mumbai 400004, Maharashtra
Tel : (022) 2385 6339 / 2386 9976, Fax : (022) 2386 9976
Email : niralimumbai@pragationline.com

☞ **DISTRIBUTION BRANCHES**

**JALGAON**
Nirali Prakashan : 34, V. V. Golani Market, Navi Peth, Jalgaon 425001,
Maharashtra, Tel : (0257) 222 0395, Mob : 94234 91860

**KOLHAPUR**
Nirali Prakashan : New Mahadvar Road, Kedar Plaza, 1st Floor Opp. IDBI Bank
Kolhapur 416 012, Maharashtra. Mob : 9850046155

**NAGPUR**
Pratibha Book Distributors : Above Maratha Mandir, Shop No. 3, First Floor,
Rani Jhanshi Square, Sitabuldi, Nagpur 440012, Maharashtra
Tel : (0712) 254 7129

**DELHI**
Nirali Prakashan : 4593/21, Basement, Aggarwal Lane 15, Ansari Road, Daryaganj
Near Times of India Building, New Delhi 110002
Mob : 08505972553

**BENGALURU**
Pragati Book House : House No. 1, Sanjeevappa Lane, Avenue Road Cross,
Opp. Rice Church, Bengaluru – 560002.
Tel : (080) 64513344, 64513355,Mob : 9880582331, 9845021552
Email:bharatsavla@yahoo.com

**CHENNAI**
Pragati Books : 9/1, Montieth Road, Behind Taas Mahal, Egmore,
Chennai 600008 Tamil Nadu, Tel : (044) 6518 3535,
Mob : 94440 01782 / 98450 21552 / 98805 82331,
Email : bharatsavla@yahoo.com

niralipune@pragationline.com | www.pragationline.com
Also find us on www.facebook.com/niralibooks

# PREFACE

The present book on 'Pharmaceutical Chemistry, Part I (Inorganic) has been written with a view to cover revised syllabus framed by the Pharmacy Council of India as per Education Regulations 1991. The new syllabus has been drawn considering the eligibility criteria and academic standards for the students to be admitted to Diploma Course in Pharmacy.

A few books are available for the course content in inorganic pharmaceutical chemistry. The inorganic compounds referred in Indian Pharmacopoea needed more discussion from teaching point of view. These are some of the points that prompted us to undertake the present endeavour.

The book has been divided into respective chapters with a view to match the P. C. I. syllabus. Not only the compounds therein are included but some more related compounds have also been discussed to present a more clear picture. While attempt has been made to cover all the essential topics, due care has been taken to avoid the details not expected at diploma level.

We hope this book will prove useful not only to the students and, teachers of Diploma In Pharmacy but also the students of B. Pharm. course.

We express our sincere thanks to Mr. Dineshbhai Furia, Publisher of Nirali Prakashan, Pune for his encouragement and having brought this book out in a short period. We will be glad to receive comments and criticism for the improvement of this book.

**AUTHORS**

# Salient features of this issue

Apart from the study of inorganic pharmaceutical compounds mentioned in the syllabus, this provides valuable information in respect of :

1. Definitions of commonly used chemical terms.

2. Atomic weights of some important elements.

3. Identification tests for Anions and Cations.

4. Antidotes in poisoning.

5. Importance and uses of Intra and Extracellular electrolytes.

6. Relevant information on Radiopharmaceuticals.

7. Sources of impurities in Pharmaceutical Substances.

•••

# SYLLABUS

1. General discussion on the following inorganic compounds including important physical and chemical properties, medicinal and pharmaceutical uses, storage conditions and chemica incompatibility.
   - **(A) Acids, Bases and Buffers :** Boric acid, Hydrochloric acid, Strong ammonium hydroxide, Calcium hydroxide, Sodium hydroxide and Official buffers.
   - **(B) Antioxidants :** Hypophosphorous acid, Sulphur dioxide, Sodium bisulphite, Sodium meta-bisulphite, Sodium thiosulphate, Nitrogen and Sodium Nitrite.
   - **(C) Gastrointestinal Agents :**
     - **(a) Acidifying Agents :** Dilute hydrochloric acid.
     - **(b) Antacids :** Sodium bicarbonate, Aluminium hydroxide gel, Aluminium phosphate. Calcium carbonate, Magnesium carbonate, Magnesium trisilicate, Magnesium oxide, Combinations of antacid preparations.
     - **(c) Protectives and Absorbents :** Bismuth subcarbonate and Kaolin.
     - **(d) Saline Cathartics :** Sodium potassium tartrate and Magnesium sulphate.
   - **(D) Topical Agents**
     - **(a) Protectives :** Talc, Zinc oxide, Calamine, Zinc stearate, Titanium dioxide, Silicone polymers.
     - **(b) Antimicrobials and Astringents :** Hydrogen peroxide, Potassium permanganate, Chlorinated lime, Iodine, Solutions of iodine, Povidone - iodine, Boric acid, Borax, Silver nitrate, Mild silver protein, Mercury, Yellow mercuric oxide, Ammoniated mercury.
     - **(c) Sulphur and its Compounds :** Sublimed sulphur, Precipitated sulphur, Selenium sulphide.
     - **(d) Astringents :** Alum and Zinc Sulphate.
   - **(E) Dental Products :** Sodium fluoride, Stannous fluoride, Calcium carbonate, Sodium meta phosphate, Dicalcium phosphate, Strontium chloride, Zinc chloride.
   - **(F) Inhalants :** Oxygen, Carbon dioxide, Nitrous oxide.
   - **(G) Respiratory Stimulants :** Ammonium carbonate.
   - **(H) Expectorants and Emetics :** Ammonium chloride, Potassium iodide, Antimony potassium tartrate.
   - **(I) Antidotes :** Sodium nitrite.
2. **Major Intra and Extracellular Electrolytes :**
   - **(A) Electrolytes used for Replacement Therapy :** Sodium chloride and its preparations, Potassium chloride and its preparations.
   - **(B) Physiological Acid-base Balance and Electrolytes used :** Sodium acetate, Potassium acetate, Sodium bicarbonate injection, Sodium citrate, Potassium citrate, Sodium lactate injection, Ammonium chloride and its injection.
   - **(C)** Combination of oral electrolytes powders and solutions.
3. Inorganic Official Compounds of Iron, Iodine and Calcium, Ferrous Sulphate and Calcium Gluconate.
4. **Radiopharmaceuticals and Contract Media :** Radioactivity, Alpha, Beta and Gamma Radiations, Biological Effects of Radiations, Measurement of Radioactivity, G. M. Counter - Radio Isotopes - their uses, Storage and Precautions with Special Reference to the Official Preparations.
   Radio-opaque Contrast Media - Barium sulphate.
5. **Quality Control of Drugs and Pharmaceutical :** Importance of Quality Control, Significant Errors, Methods used for Quality Control, Sources of Impurities in Pharmaceuticals. Limit Tests for Arsenic, Chloride, Sulfate, Iron and Heavy Metals.
   Identification Tests for Cations and Anions as per Indian Pharmacopoeia.

•••

# CONTENTS

| | | |
|---|---|---|
| 1. Quality Control in Pharmacy | 1.1 | – 1.2 |
| 2. Errors in Analysis | 2.1 | – 2.6 |
| 3. Impurities in Pharmaceutical Substances and Limit Tests | 3.1 | – 3.12 |
| 4. Water | 4.1 | – 4.8 |
| 5. Solubility of Pharmaceuticals | 5.1 | – 5.6 |
| 6. Acids, Bases and Buffers | 6.1 | – 6.14 |
| 7. Antioxidants | 7.1 | – 7.8 |
| 8. Gastrointestinal Agents | 8.1 | – 8.18 |
| 9. Topical Agents | 9.1 | – 9.30 |
| 10. Dental Products | 10.1 | – 10.4 |
| 11. Inhalants | 11.1 | – 11.6 |
| 12. Expectorants, Emetics and Respiratory Stimulants | 12.1 | – 12.6 |
| 13. Major Intra and Extracellular Electrolytes | 13.1 | – 13.16 |
| 14. Official Compounds of Iron | 14.1 | – 14.8 |
| 15. Official Compounds of Iodine | 15.1 | – 15.6 |
| 16. Official Compounds of Calcium | 16.1 | – 16.14 |
| 17. Radiopharmaceuticals and Contrast Media | 17.1 | – 17.8 |
| 18. Antidotes in Poisoning | 18.1 | – 18.4 |
| 19. Identification Tests for Ions and Radicals | 19.1 | – 19.18 |
| Appendix | A.1 | – A.3 |
| Index | I.1 | – I.4 |
| Bibliography | B.1 | – B.1 |

•••

# 1

# QUALITY CONTROL IN PHARMACY

The term 'Quality Control' has assumed vast importance in pharmaceutical field. Since it is necessary that a good quality product should be available to the doctors to treat patients or for the users; the responsibility of pharmacist and those of pharmaceutical industry has increased considerably. The basis for maintaining the quality of a product could be seen through the following Good Manufacturing Practices.

The term quality, as applied to drugs and drug products, includes all those factors which contribute directly or indirectly to the safety, effectiveness and reliability of the product. In order to have the above referred properties in a drug it is necessary to have a quality control. To achieve 'Quality Control', a concept of 'Total Quality Control' has to be appreciated. Total quality control will include all those aspects starting with the procurement of raw material to the finished product available at the drug store and till it is consumed by the customer. Thus, it will include not only the parameters of GMP but also to the storage; handling and preserving the sample till ultimate use.

The major areas of quality control include all those steps to determine, within reasonable limits, that (i) drug is of a genuine good quality and nature, (ii) it is physically and chemically pure, (iii) it contains all the ingredients stated on the label in the right amount (iv) it is rendered in such a form as to be effective after administration and (v) it retains quality in terms of shelf-life or stability.

Now, in order to maintain 'Quality', the quality control is effected in the pharmaceutical industry. The job of quality control is to test a drug for quality and quantity. In order to ascertain both these parameters of qualitative identification and quantitative determination, the procedures and standards laid down by various agencies are followed. In every country, the standards for drug quality are set by state, center or by a committee. The quality set for a drug, is after consideration of recommendations of various expert bodies and these standards are published in the form of books (compondiums) like pharmacopoeias, pharmacopoeial codex, etc. Furthermore, the compondiums are revised periodically and supplements are issued between revisions, to keep them up-to-date with respect to matters pertaining to drug quality.

One of the important areas of quality control is to analyse a drug for quality and quantity. Various tests and procedures for analysis, including finding and determining impurities, are laid down in the official books. This applies both to the drug as raw material as well as in the form of finished product. The pharmacopoeial monograph gives details about this.

In the quantitative analysis, depending upon the characteristic of drug and its formulation various analytical methods are followed. These include, Physicochemical methods - which are based upon some specific physical or chemical property of a substance being analysed. This will include determinations of specific gravity, density, viscosity, surface tension, refractive index, optical rotation, etc. and all the types of volumetric analysis. While utilizing the physicochemical properties, use of instrumental methods like pH-potentiometry, conductometry, polarography, colorimetry, spectrophotometry, fluorimetry, flame photometry, etc. is made.

The other methods for quantitative determination will include the separational techniques like chromatographic, gravimetric, precipitation and complex formation, proximate assays and special methods which require distinct type of apparatus like, volatile oil determination, alcohol determination, technique of oxygen flask method, etc.

Besides the usual qualitative and quantitative determinations, pharmaceutical products are also evaluated for their quality. The studies and tests like disintegration, hardness, friability, dissolution for tablets and related preparations, bioavailability studies, absorption-elimination studies, pharmacokinetic studies, biological and microbiological studies are also carried out.

The basis of all the studies and tests of quality control is to ensure that quality drug is available to the consumer and patient.

## EXERCISE

*1. What is 'Quality Control' ? Discuss its importance in the pharmaceutical industry.*

*2. What are the quantitative methods for ascertaining quality in pharmacy ?*

■■■

# 2

# ERRORS IN ANALYSIS

It is not very uncommon in analytical work to get different results; and no analysis is complete until the results have been calculated and properly reported. Since the ultimate result of analysis is important from accuracy and reliability point of view, is essential to understand, the various terms involved in analysis.

The term accuracy refers to the agreement of experimental result with the true value and it is usually expressed in terms of error. In scientific experiments, it is often found that true value is not known. It is simply the value that has been 'Accepted' and is generally a mean calculated from the results of several determinations from many laboratories using different techniques.

The difference between the experimental mean and a true value is known as 'Absolute Error'. Often a term 'Relative Error' is used. The relative error is the value found by dividing the absolute error by the true value.

Thus,  Relative error = $\dfrac{\text{Measured mean value} - \text{True value}}{\text{True value}}$

The relative error is generally reported as percent by multiplying the relative error by 100 or by expressing it as parts per thousand by multiplying the relative error by 1000.

Precision is defined as the degree of agreement between various results of the same quantity. That is, it is the reproducibility of a result. Good precision is not necessarily accurate. A constant error may always give reproducible results yet deviating from accuracy. An analytical chemist always attempts to get reproducible results (i.e. precision) to assure the highest possible accuracy.

**Source and Nature of Errors**

In any scientific work, the result of measurement seldom agrees. It is generally accepted also that result of analysis are subject to errors. The discrepancies in the results are caused by various sources of errors. There are two main classes of errors which affect the accuracy or precision of a measured quantity.

**1. Determinate errors :** These are those errors, as the name indicates, which are determinable and can be either avoided or corrected. The error may be constant as in case of weighing with uncalibrated weights, in measuring a volume using uncorrelated burette or pipette. Such measurable determinate errors are categorised as systematic errors. The determinate errors arise due to :

    **(a) Instrumental errors :** Those occurring due to use of faulty equipment or instrument.

(b) **Operative errors :** Those errors which are made by persons operating or doing analysis. This error is called personal error also.

(c) **Chemical errors :** This error is due to impurities in chemicals, solvents, reagents, etc.

(d) **Errors in the methodology :** This is a most serious error in analysis, as the error arises due to faulty method, e.g. coprecipitation of impurities, slight solubility of precipitate, incomplete reactions, etc.

Errors of this category are usually detectable and can be eliminated to a large extent.

**2. Indeterminate errors :** The indeterminate errors are often called accidental or random errors. They are revealed by small differences in series of measurements made by the same analyst under identical conditions. They cannot be predicted and hence cannot be eliminated.

The random distribution of indeterminate errors of various magnitudes is shown in a graph.

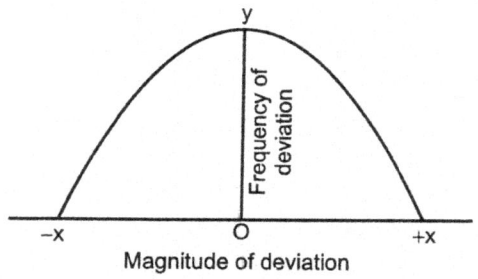

Fig. 2.1

The magnitude of error (abscissa) and the frequency of deviation (ordinate) has the shape of a normal frequency distribution curve or probability curve. This graph is also called 'Curve of Error'. From the graph it will be seen that (i) very large errors are unlikely to occur, (ii) smaller errors occur with greater frequency than large errors and (iii) The errors on positive and negative side occur with equal probability.

It is customary to find out whether the results of experiments or of analysis are true and accurate. This is done by expressing them in different ways. The data of analysis is subjected to some mathematical treatment in the following way :

Mean = $\bar{X}$    which is an average of all readings.

Range = R    This is the difference between the largest and smallest readings in a series of measurements.

**Average deviation (d)** : This is determined by finding the differences between individual result and mean, without regard to the sign, summation of these differences and dividing by the number of determinations.

$$d = \Sigma \frac{[X_1 - \bar{X}]}{N}$$

where, $\bar{X}$ = mean
$X_1$ = individual reading
and $N$ = number of measurements

**Relative Average Deviation** is found by dividing the average deviation 'd' by the mean $\bar{X} = d/\bar{X}$.

**Standard Deviation (S)** is found by formula (also called variance).

$$S = \sqrt{\frac{\Sigma(X_1 - \bar{X})^2}{N}}$$

If the number of measurements or readings is less than ten, the equation is

$$S = \sqrt{\frac{\Sigma(X_1 - \bar{X})^2}{(N-1)}}$$

**Relative Standard Deviation** (also called coefficient of variation) is found by dividing the standard deviation by the mean and multiplying by 100 thus,

$$\text{Coefficient of variation} = \frac{S}{\bar{X}} \times 100$$

**Standard Error (S.E.)** : It is calculated by dividing standard deviation by root of N.

$$SE = \frac{S}{\sqrt{N}}$$

**Rejection of Result :**

Frequently, it is observed that one of the results appears to differ markedly from the others. A decision will have to be taken whether to reject the result or retain it. Unfortunately, there is no uniform criteria to know and to decide if a suspect result can be due to accidental error or by a chance variation. Some statistical tests are used to determine whether the result is to be rejected or not. In these tests a range is established within which statistically significant observations should fall. One of such test is 'Q' test.

The 'Q' test is most satisfactory for small number of samples or results. The ratio Q is calculated by arranging the data in decreasing order of number. The difference between the suspect value and its nearest is divided by the range. This ratio is compared with tabulated values of Q (Refer table 2.1). The tabulated values of Q at 90% confidence level are recorded in books.

If the observed value of Q is greater than the tabulated value, the suspect observation or result is rejected. The following example will elucidate this point.

$$Q = \frac{\text{Suspect Value} - \text{Previous Value}}{\text{Range}}$$

In a standardisation of an acid, following values of normality were recorded : 0.1067, 0.1070, 0.1066, 0.1050. Can one of the results be discarded as accidental error ?

In the above example, suspect value is 0.1050. It differs from its nearest neighbour 0.1066 by 0.0016. The range is 0.1070 − 0.1050 i.e., 0.0020.

$$Q = \frac{0.0016}{0.0020} = 0.8$$

The tabulated value for four observations is 0.76. Since the calculated value is more than the tabulated, the suspect value is rejected.

**Table 2.1 : Rejection 'Q' values at 90% confidence limit**

| No. of samples | Q |
|---|---|
| 2 | – |
| 3 | 0.94 |
| 4 | 0.76 |
| 5 | 0.64 |
| 6 | 0.56 |
| 7 | 0.51 |
| 8 | 0.47 |
| 9 | 0.44 |
| 10 | 0.41 |

**Significant Figures :**

In recording observations or measurements, it is essential to know about the significance of figures. Some errors do creep in when figures are not properly recorded. The proper manner of expressing a result or observation is to retain such number of figures, that all, except the last, are known with certainty.

The number of significant figures can be defined as the number of digits necessary to express the results of a measurement consistant with the measured precision. Each digit denotes the actual quantity that it specifies.

It should be clear that zeros are employed to denote the significant part of measurement (to denote tens, hundreds, thousands, etc.) or merely to locate the decimal point. Thus, zeros within a number like 25.05 and 1350 are significant as they express the exact quantity, while zero before the decimal in figures, like 0.0234, only show the magnitude of other digits.

In quantities 1.267 g and 1.0056 g the zeros are significant numbers, but in the quantity 0.0035 kg the zeros even though significant, can be eliminated. The zeros in 0.0035 kg serve only to locate decimal point and can be omitted by use of proper units e.g. 3.5 g. In the first two numbers there are five significant figures but in 0.0035 there are only two significant figures.

The digits of a number which are needed to express the precision of measurement must be retained. Thus when a volume is between 15.7 ml and 15.9 ml, it should be written as 15.80 is same as 15.8, after 15.79 comes 15.80 i.e. 15.8 only, since the latter would indicate that the value is between 15.79 ml and 15.81 ml. If a weight is to the nearest 0.1 mg (e.g. 3.2800 g), it should not be written as 3.280 g or 3.28 g.

**Rounding of Figures :**

In rounding of the quantities, the correct number of significant figure should be retained e.g. in addition of

$$128.12 + 6.018 + 0.2678$$

it should be written as

$$128.12 + 6.02 + 0.27$$

Similarly, in multiplication or division, similar rounding of the figures is carried out, as in multiplication of $1.12 \times 2.301 \times 0.578$ the values used are

$$1.12 \times 2.30 \times 0.58.$$

The rounding of the figures thus is essential to curtail lengthy and tedious calculations.

## EXERCISE

1. Differentiate between accuracy and precision. Discuss the ways of determining accuracy.

2. Explain in brief : (i) confidence limit, (ii) 'Q' test and (iii) frequency distribution giving examples.

3. What is determinate error and indeterminate error ? How is relative error found out ?

4. In determination of aluminium % in a coin, following values were obtained : 24.92%, 25.07%, 25.15%, 24.85%, 24.98% and 25.35%. Should any of these result be discarded ?

5. What do you understand by the term "Significant figure". How many significant figures are there in the following : (a) $1.8 \times 10^{-6}$, (b) $4.58 \times 10^{-2}$, (c) 180.01, (d) 0.0057.

6. Following are the values of % nitrogen in a samnple :

   15.01, 14.84, 14.79, 15.32, 15.85. Calculate (a) mean (b) mean deviation (c) standard deviation and (d) coefficient of variation.

■■■

# 3

# IMPURITIES IN PHARMACEUTICAL SUBSTANCES AND LIMIT TESTS

## INTRODUCTION

The substances that are used in the pharmaceutical field, should be almost pure so that they can be safe to use. It is rather difficult to obtain an almost pure substance. We find substances and chemicals, with varying degrees of purity. For example, substances like cane-sugar (sucrose), dextrose, common salt and many inorganic salts, are found with over 99% purity while many others only contain traces of impurities. The purity of substance depends upon several factors, such as their methods of manufacture and types of crystallisation or purification process. In the pharmaceutical field, one deals with a large number of drugs, chemicals and other substances which are used in formulations. All such materials need to be pure. However, it is almost impossible to get an absolutely pure material, as impurities get incorporated into them either during manufacture, purification or storage.

## SOURCES OF IMPURITIES

The type and amount of impurity present in the chemicals or pharmaceutical substances depends upon several factors. Some such factors are discussed below.

**Raw Materials Employed in Manufacture :**

When substances or chemicals are manufactured, the raw materials from which these are prepared, often contain impurities. These impurities get incorporated into the final product. Impurities like arsenic, lead, heavy metal, etc., are present in raw materials, and are hence found in substances. It is, therefore, necessary to employ pure chemicals and substances as raw materials, for the manufacturing process.

**Method or the Process used in Manufacture :**

There are a number of drugs and chemicals (especially organic), which are manufactured from different raw materials by adopting different methods or processes. Some impurities get incorporated into the materials during the manufacturing process. The type and amount of impurity present in the drugs or chemicals varies. Furthermore, for certain drugs a multiple-step-synthesis procedure is involved, which produces intermediate compounds. The purification of the intermediates is also essential, otherwise impurities present in the intermediates, will get into the final compound. Often, side reactions take place during the synthesis. Impurities of the side reaction product are also found in the substances.

## Chemical Processes and Plant Materials Employed in the Processes :

In the synthesis of drugs, many chemical reactions like nitration, halogenation, oxidation, reduction, hydrolysis, etc. are involved. In these chemical processes, different solvents, chemicals, etc. are used. When chemical reactions are carried out in vessels or containers, the materials of these vessels (like iron, copper, tin, aluminium etc.) are reacted upon by the solvents and chemicals and reaction products are formed. These reaction products that are derived from the plant material occur as impurities in the final product. Thus, impurities of iron, lead, heavy metals, copper, etc. in substances are due to the above mentioned reasons.

## Storage Conditions :

The chemicals or substances, when prepared, are stored in different types of containers, depending upon the nature of the material, batch size and the quantity. Various types of materials are used for storage purpose. These may be plastic, polythene, iron, stainless steel, aluminium and copper vessels, etc. Reaction of these substances with the material of the storage vessel may take place and the products formed, occur as impurities in the stored material. The reaction may take place directly or by the leaching out effect on the storage vessel. Alkalies stored in ordinary glass containers, extract lead from it, which occurs in the final product. Similarly, strong chemicals react with iron containers, and extract iron.

## Decomposition :

Some substances decompose on keeping and the decomposition is greater in the presence of light, air or oxygen. The result of decomposition causes contamination of the final product. Many substances lose water of crystallisation when kept open, while deliquescent substances absorb water from the atmosphere, and get liquified. Crude vegetable drugs are especially susceptible to decomposition. A number of organic substances get spoiled, because of decomposition on exposure to the atmosphere e.g., amines, phenols, potent drugs, etc. The decomposition products thus appear as an impurity in the substances.

## EFFECT OF IMPURITIES

It can be seen that almost pure substances are difficult to get and some amount of impurity is always present in the material. The impurities present in the substances may have the following effects :

(a) Impurities which have a toxic effect, can be injurious when present above certain limits.

(b) Impurities, even when present in traces, may show a cumulative toxic effect after a certain period.

(c) Impurities are sometimes harmless, but are present in such large proportions, that the active strength of the substance is lowered. Thus therapeutic effect of drug is decreased.

(d) Impurities may bring about a change in the physical and chemical properties of the substance, thus making it medically useless.

(e) Impurities may cause technical difficulties in the formulation and use of the substances.

(f) Impurities may bring about an incompatibility, with other substances.

(g) Impurities may lower the shelf life of the substance.

(h) Impurities, though harmless in nature, may bring about changes in odour, colour, taste, etc., thus making the use of the substance unethical, as well as unhygienic.

**Permissible Impurities in Pharmaceutical Substances :**

Since it is not possible to avoid impurities, it is necessary to have substances that are reasonably pure. The pharmacopoeial committee takes the following points into consideration with respect to the problem caused by impurities in substances.

(a) For impurities which are of a harmful type e.g. lead, arsenic etc. a low permissible limit is prescribed. This is based upon, how much of these can be tolerated. Which itself is based upon, how much of the impurity is harmful.

(b) For impurities that are harmless the aim is to fix their limit so that, their presence does not interfere in the therapeutic usefulness of the drug. Here, again, the limits are prescribed and fixed. This is done depending upon the nature of the impurity, the type of substance, use of the substance, etc.

(c) Another consideration is the practicability of obtaining substances without impurities, at reasonable costs. It may be possible to prepare substances (through a series of steps of purification) without any impurity, but this may be achieved at an exorbitant cost. Considering this aspect, limits of various impurities are fixed.

(d) Deliberate adulteration using materials that have similar qualities also accounts for the presence of impurities in the substance, e.g. adulteration of sodium salt with potassium salts, calcium salts with magnesium salts etc. Such adulteration which brings impurities into substances, need not exhibit less therapeutic activity but it is reasonable to expect unadulterated material from an ethical point of view. Pharmacopoeias guard against this type of impurity by employing tests for identification.

## TEST FOR PURITY

Pharmacopoeias of various countries prescribe 'Tests for Purity', for substances which are to be used for medicinal purposes. The so called 'Tests for Purity', are as a matter of fact tests for detecting impurities in the substances and pharmacopoeias fix the limits of tolerance for these impurities. The governing factor for these tests, is to determine how much impurity is likely to be harmful, or to bring about technical and other difficulties, when the substance is used.

Pharmacopoeias do not aim at ensuring freedom from every possible impurity in a substance, but to test for few major impurities, which are likely to interfere in their use. Certain tests which are carried out on the substances are :

**Colour, Odour and Taste :**

Along with other tests for purity, description of taste odour, colour etc. are given in the pharmacopoeias. Though they have limited value, they are useful in determining whether the substance is reasonably pure, hygienic, etc.

### Physico-chemical Constants :

Solubility of the substance in various solvents, determination of melting and boiling points for organic substances, optical rotation for optically active substances and refractive index for liquids, are some values which tell us about the purity of substance. Determination of the acid value, iodine value, saponification value, acetyl value, ester value, etc., for vegetable oils are generally constants and a variation in their value, signifies the presence of impurities. The extent of the variation in these values, usually depend upon the nature and extent of impurities present in the substances. However, a very low concentration of impurities, may fail to alter these constants, and thus remain undetected, unless tested specifically, by special tests.

### Acidity, Alkalinity and pH :

Substances that are prepared from chemical reactions involving acids and alkalies often contain considerable amounts of the acid or alkali, as an impurity. Thus, the tests for acidity or alkalinity are of a great help to estimate the extent of the impurity. Furthermore, solutions of certain substances have a definite pH at a given concentration. The presence of an impurity will bring about a change in the pH and thus it can be detected.

### Anions and Cations :

A large number of synthetic drugs both inorganic and organic are prepared using strong acids like hydrochloric, sulphuric, nitric etc. The presence of chloride and sulphate ions are thus common impurities. Test, for these ions (anions) is thus generally carried out. Similarly, tests for sodium, ammonium (cations) are often carried out to detect impurities in inorganic compounds (test for sodium in potassium salt and vice-versa, calcium in magnesium salts, etc. Tests for heavy metals, like lead, iron, copper and mercury are also carried out as these are very common impurities in substances.

### Insoluble Residue :

Pure substance give a clear solution in a given solvent. When insoluble impurities are present in a substance then the solution appears cloudy, or shows opalescence. The measurement of turbidity or opalescence helps to determine the amount of insoluble impurity present in the substance. If the insoluble residue is high, then this can be determined by filtering and weighing the insoluble residue.

### Ash, Water-insoluble Ash :

Determination of ash in crude vegetable drugs, organic compounds and some inorganic compounds, gives a good indication about the extent of impurities of heavy metals or minerals in nature. This determination is therefore commonly employed for a number of substances. In certain cases, water-insoluble ash is also determined to find water-insoluble heavy metals or mineral types of impurity.

It is thus clear that depending upon the type of material or substance, pharmacopoeias prescribe tests for purity of particular nature e.g., salicylic acid in acetyl salicylic acid, phenatidine in phenacetin, acraldehyde in glycerine, paminophenol in paracetamol etc.

In general, it could be said that, impurities of chloride, sulphate, iron, heavy metals, lead and arsenic, are common in drugs and chemicals. Pharmacopoeias of various countries, therefore prescribe limit tests for these to be carried out by a particular method.

## LIMIT TESTS FOR CHLORIDES AND SULPHATES

The principle of the limit tests for chlorides and sulphates is based upon the measurement of opalescence or turbidity produced in the known amount of substance (by addition of reagent), and comparing it with the standard opalescence or turbidity. For comparison of turbidity for different substances with varying amount of impurity, the amount of substance to be used is varied, and not the standard turbidity. Pharmacopoeias do not give a numerical value to the limits, as it is not practicable as its contents will be influenced to a great extent by large quantities of other substances present.

The limit test for chlorides is based upon the chemical reaction between soluble chloride ions with a silver nitrate reagent in a nitric acid media. The insoluble silver chloride renders the test solution turbid (depending upon the amount of silver chloride formed and therefore on the amount of chloride present in the substance under test). This turbidity is compared with the standard turbidity produced by the addition of silver nitrate, to the known amount of chloride ion (sodium chloride) solution. If the test solution shows less turbidity than the standard the sample passes the test.

In a limit test for sulphate, the solution of the substance under test is mixed with barium sulphate reagent in a hydrochloric acid medium and the turbidity so produced is compared with the standard in similar manner with a known quantity of sulphate ion (using potassium sulphate). The substance passes the limit test if it produces a turbidity that is less than the standard.

In performing these tests, it is essential to follow the directions indicated by the pharmacopoeia.

**Preparation of the Solution for Tests :**

A specified amount of the substance is dissolved in distilled water, and the volume made to 50 ml in a Nessler's cylinder. Depending upon the nature of the substance, some modifications are carried out for the preparation of the solution. e.g., alkaline substances like carbonates, hydroxides, etc., are dissolved in sufficient quantity of acid so that effervescence ceases, and free acid is present. For insoluble substances like kaolin, a water extract is prepared, filtered and then the filtrate used. Salts of organic acids like sodium benzoate, sodium salicylate, etc., liberate free water-insoluble organic acid, during acidification which is filtered off and the filtrate is used for the test. Coloured substances like crystal violet, malachite green etc., are carbonized and the ash so produced is extracted in water. Reducing substances like nitrate, hypophosphate, etc. are oxidising agents, and the solution is prepared and used. Substances like potassium permanganate are reduced by boiling with alcohol, and the filtrate is used.

## Limit Test for Chloride :

Dissolve the specified quantity of substance in water or prepare a solution as directed in the pharmacopoeia and transfer to a Nessler's cylinder A (Fig. 3.1). Add 1 ml of dilute nitric acid, except when nitric acid is used in the preparation of the solution. Dilute it to 50 ml with water and add 1 ml of silver nitrate solution, stir immediately with a glass rod and set aside for 5 minutes. Simultaneously, for standard opalescence, place 1 ml of 0.05845% w/v solution of sodium chloride in Nessler's cylinder B and add 10 ml of dilute nitric acid, make up the volume to 50 ml with water, add 1 ml of silver nitrate solution, stir with glass rod and set aside for 5 minutes. The opalescence produced by the sample (in cylinder A) should not be greater than standard opalescence.

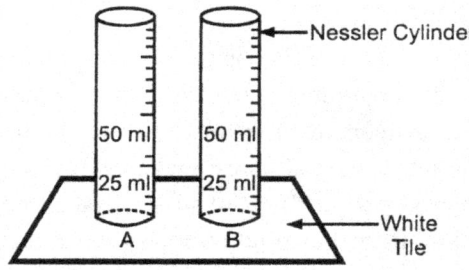

**Fig. 3.1 : Nessler's cylinder**

## Limit Test for Sulphate :

A solution of specified quantity of substance is made in water or prepared as directed in the pharmacopoeia in Nessler's cylinder and add 2 ml dilute hydrochloric acid except when hydrochloric acid is used in the preparation of solution. Dilute it to 45 ml with water, add 5 ml of barium sulphate reagent, stir immediately with the glass rod and set aside for 5 minutes. To produce standard turbidity place 1 ml of 0.1089% w/v solution of potassium sulphate and 2 ml of dilute hydrochloric acid in another Nessler's cylinder, dilute to 45 ml with water, add 5 ml of barium sulphate reagent, stir immediately and set aside for 5 minutes. The turbidity produced by the sample solution is not greater than the standard turbidity.

British Pharmacopoeia makes use of a barium sulphate regent, which contains barium chloride, alcohol and small amount of potassium sulphate. Alcohol prevents supersaturation, and potassium sulphate increases the sensitivity of the test by giving the ionic concentration in the reagent which just exceeds the solubility product of barium sulphate.

## Limit Test for Iron :

This test is based upon the reaction of iron in an ammonical solution, with thioglycollic acid which forms a pink to deep reddish-purple coloured complex of iron-thiogycollate. The colour produced from a specified amount of substance from the test, is compared by viewing vertically, with a standard (Ferric ammonium sulphate). If the colour from test solution is less dark than the standard, then the sample passes the test.

The $Fe(SCH_2COO)_2$ formed with the ferrous form of iron, is quite stable for long period in the absence of air. The colour, however, is destroyed by oxidizing agents and strong alkalies. The original state of iron is unimportant, as thioglycollic acid reduces $Fe^{3+}$ to $Fe^{2+}$. This test is very sensitive. Interference of other metal cations is eliminated, by making use of 20% citric acid, which forms a complex with other metal cations.

**Method :**

Prepare a solution by dissolving a specified amount of substance in 40 ml water or take 10 ml of solution as directed in monograph in Nessler's cylinder. Add 2 ml of 20% w/v solution of iron free citric acid and 0.1 ml of thioglycollic acid, mix and make alkaline with iron free ammonia solution and dilute it to 50 ml with water. Allow to stand for 5 minutes. For standard, simultaneously dilute 2 ml of standard iron solution with 40 ml of water, add same quantity of reagent as in the sample. Any colour produced by the sample is not more intense than the standard.

Earlier, ammonium thiocyanate reagent was used for the limit test of iron. Since thioglycollic acid is a more sensitive reagent for iron, it has replaced ammonium thiocyanate in the test.

**Limit Test for Heavy Metals :**

Besides the limit test for lead, the Indian pharmacopoeia and U.S.P., include limit tests for heavy metals present in many compounds. Lead and other heavy metals are generally found as impurities in pharmaceutical substances. Two separate tests are therefore prescribed, by these pharmacopoeias.

The limit test for heavy metals is based upon the reaction of the metal ion with hydrogen sulphide, under the prescribed conditions of the test resulting in the formation of metal sulphides. These remain distributed in a colloidal state and produce a brownish colouration. The test solution is compared with a standard prepared using a lead solution (as the heavy metal). The metallic impurities in substances are expressed as parts of lead per million parts of the substance. The usual limit as per I.P. is 20 ppm.

**Under Heavy Metals :**

The Indian Pharmacopoeia adopts three methods for the limit tests for heavy metals. The 'Method A' is used for the substance which yields a clear colourless solution under specified conditions. 'Method B' is used for those substances which do not yield clear colourless solution under the test conditions specified for method A. 'Method C' is used for substances that yield clear colourless solution in sodium hydroxide medium. The reagents like acetic acid, ammonia, hydrochloric acid, nitric acid, potassium cyanide and sulphuric acid should be lead free and are designated as 'Sp. reagents'.

**Method A :**

Standard solution is prepared by taking 2 ml of standard lead solution and dilute to 25 ml with water. Adjust the pH between 3 to 4 by using either dilute acetic acid or dilute ammonia solution. Make up the volume to 35 ml with water.

Test solution is prepared as directed in the individual monograph. Take 25 ml and adjust the pH of the solution between 3 to 4 by using dilute acetic acid or dilute ammonia, and adjust the volume to 35 ml with water.

To each of the cylinders containing standard and test solution, add 10 ml of freshly prepared hydrogen sulphide solution, mix, dilute to 50 ml with water and allow it to stand for 5 minutes. The colour when viewed downwards over white surface should not be darker for test than standard solution.

**Method B :**

The standard solution is prepared as directed under method A. Test solution is prepared by weighing a specified quantity of substance as per monograph in crucible. Moisten the substance with sulphuric acid, ignite on a low flame till completely charred. Add few drops of nitric acid and heat to 500°C. Allow to cool, add 4 ml of hydrochloric acid and evaporate to dryness. Moisten the residue with 10 ml hydrochloric acid and digest for two minutes. Neutralize with ammonia solution and make just acidic with acetic acid. Adjust the pH between 3 and 4, filter if necessary. Adjust the volume of filtrate to 35 ml in Nessler's cylinder, add 10 ml of hydrogen sulphide solution, dilute to 50 ml with water and compare the colour with the standard solution.

**Method C :**

The standard solution is prepared by using 2 ml of standard lead solution, adding 5 ml dilute sodium hydroxide solution and making the volume to 50 ml with water. For the test solution take either 25 ml solution prepared as directed in the monograph or take specified quantity of substance, dissolve in 20 ml water, add 5 ml of dilute sodium hydroxide solution and make up the volume to 50 ml.

To each of the above solution in Nessler's cylinder add 5 drops of sodium sulphide solution, mix and set aside for 5 minutes. The colour produced by test solution should not be darker than the standard solution.

**Limit Test for Heavy Metals in Volatile Oils :**

In 25 ml glass stoppered test tubes, 10 ml of the oil is mixed with an equal volume of water containing a drop of hydrochloric acid. Hydrogen sulphide is passed through the mixture until it is saturated. No darkening in colour should be produced either in the oil, or in the water layer, for the sample to pass the test.

**Limit Test for Lead :**

The limit test for lead as per I.P. and U.S.P., is based upon the reaction between lead and diphenylthiocarbazone (dithizone). Dithizone in chloroform, extracts lead from alkaline aqueous solutions as a lead-dithizone complex (red in colour).

$$2\,S=C\begin{array}{c}NH.NH.C_6H_5\\N=N.C_6H_5\end{array} + Pb \longrightarrow S=C\begin{array}{c}\overset{C_6H_5}{\underset{H}{N}}-N\\N=N\\\underset{C_6H_5}{|}\end{array}\overset{C_6H_5}{\underset{C_6H_5}{\underset{|}{Pb}}}\begin{array}{c}N=N\\N=N\\H\end{array}C=S$$

The original dithizone has a green colour in chloroform thus the lead-dithizone shows a violet colour. The intensity of the colour of complex, depends upon the amount of lead in the solution. The colour of the lead-dithizone complex in chloroform, is compared with a standard volume of lead solution, treated in the same manner.

In this method, the lead present as an impurity in the substance, is separated by extracting an alkaline solution with a dithizone extraction solution. The interference and influence of other metal ions etc., is eliminated by adjusting the optimum pH for the extraction, by using ammonium citrate, potassium cyanide, hydroxylamine hydrochloride reagents, etc.

**Method :**

A known quantity of the sample solution is taken in separating funnel. 6 ml of ammonium citrate, and 2 ml of hydroxylamine hydrochloride is added, followed by 2 drops of phenol red, and the solution is made alkaline by adding an ammonia solution. Add 2 ml of potassium cyanide solution and extract immediately with 5 ml portions of dithizone solution (till green). The combined dithizone extracts are shaken for 30 seconds, with 30 ml of 1% nitric acid, and the chloroform layer discarded. To the acid solution 5 ml standard dithizone solution is added along with 4 ml of ammonium cyanide and shaken for 30 seconds. A known quantity of the standard solution of lead (equivalent to the amount of lead permitted in the sample) is treated separately. The colour (violet) of the chloroform layer of sample, should not be darker than the standard for the sample to pass the test.

In the preparation of a sample solution, an appropriate preliminary treatment is given, so as to get lead in the solution, without any interfering substance or ion. All reagents employed under the test (except for standard lead solution), should be free from lead, and are designated as 'Pb T' reagents in pharmacopoeias.

**Limit Test for Lead as Per B. P. :**

B. P. adopts another method for the limit test for lead which is based on the formation of a brownish colouration produced by the colloidal lead sulphide upon addition of sodium sulphide to the solution under test. If the lead content is more, then a brownish black precipitate of lead sulphide is obtained. The colour produced in the test solution is matched against the standard that is made from a known amount of lead in a Nessler's cylinder. In order to carry out this test two solutions, a primary and an auxiliary, are prepared from the sample.

**Method**

Two solutions of the substance under test are prepared, one with hot water and another with acetic acid. One is the primary solution containing a definite but greater amount of substance and placed in a 50 ml Nessler's cylinder. The other is the auxiliary solution, containing a known amount of the test substance in another 50 ml Nessler's cylinder. To this auxiliary solution, a definite amount of a dilute solution of lead nitrate is added. Ammonia and potassium cyanide solutions are added to both solutions in the Nessler's cylinders. Small amounts of burnt sugar solution is added to both solutions, to correct any difference of colour, and the volume is made upto 50 ml. If the solutions appear turbid, then they are filtered and the volume made upto 50 ml. Both solutions are treated with sodium sulphide solution and a colour developed. If the colour in the auxiliary solution is darker than that in the primary, then the substance contains lead within limits.

The object of using primarprimaryuxiliary solutions of substances is to have a comparison made under identical conditions. Interference by any unknown entity present in the solution is eliminated by this technique.

**Limit Test for Arsenic :**

Arsenic is an undesirable and harmful impurity in medicinal products, and all Pharmacopoeias prescribe a limit test for it. There are many qualitative and quantitative tests for arsenic. The Pharmacopoeial method is based on the Gutzeit test. In this test, arsenic is converted into arsine gas, ($AsH_3$) which when passed over a mercuric chloride test paper, produces a yellow stain. The intensity of the stain is proportional to the amount of arsenic present. A standard stain produced from a definite amount of arsenic, is used for comparison.

The chemical reactions involved in the method are given below :

When the sample is dissolved in acid, the arsenic present in the sample is converted to arsenic acid. The arsenic acid is reduced, by reducing agents (like potassium iodide, stannated acid, etc.) to arsenious acid.

$H_3AsO_4 \rightarrow H_3AsO_3$. The nascent hydrogen produced during the reaction, further reduces arsenious acid to arsine (gas), which reacts with mercuric chloride paper, producing a yellow stain.

$$H_3AsO_3 + 3H_2 \rightleftharpoons AsH_3 + 3H_2O$$
$$\text{Arsine (gas)}$$

To carry out the test, a specified apparatus (as described in pharmacopoeias) is used. In order to convert arsenic into arsine gas, various reducing agents like zinc-hydrochloric acid, stannous chloride, and potassium iodide are employed. The rate of evolution of gas is maintained by using a particular size of zinc, and controlling the concentration of acids and other salts of the reaction medium, besides temperature. Any impurity coming along with Arsene (as $H_2S$) is trapped by placing a lead acetate soaked cotton plug in the apparatus. All the reagents employed for the test should be arsenic free, and are designated as 'AsT' in pharmacopoeias.

**Apparatus :**

An apparatus as shown in Fig. 3.2 as per the specification of I.P. is used for the limit test for arsenic.

A wide mouth bottle of 120 ml capacity fitted with rubber bung carrying a glass tube 200 mm long and 6.5 mm internal diameter with a hole of 2 mm at one end is used in the test. The other end of the glass tube is cut smooth and carries rubber bungs (25 × 25 mm). Mercuric chloride paper is sandwiched between the rubber bungs. The rubber bungs are held in place by means of a clip.

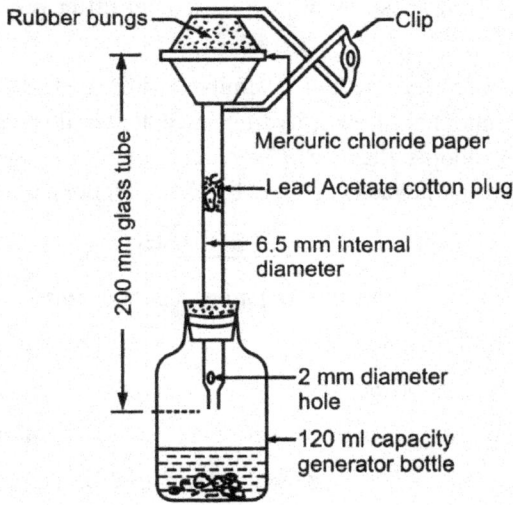

Fig. 3.2 : Apparatus used for arsenic limit test

**General Test :**

A solution of the substance as specified in the monograph is placed in the generator bottle. Potassium iodide 1 g and 10 g of zinc AsT are added. Mercuric chloride test paper is placed in the rubber slit and the stopper is placed in the position immediately. It is set aside for 40 minutes and the stain produced on the paper is compared against standard stain. The standard stain is produced simultaneously by taking 50 ml of water, 10 ml stannated hydrochloric acid and dilute arsenic solution varying from 0.02 ml to 1.0 ml (1 ml = 0.01 mg of arsenic). If the sample shows a stain of lesser intensity than that of the standard then it passes the test. For example if 1 g of a substance under test is compared with 0.01 ml of dilute arsenic solution on matching will contain 1 ppm arsenic in the sample.

The stain produced on paper fades on keeping, and therefore comparison should be made immediately. Stained papers can be preserved by dipping in hot melted paraffin, and keeping away from light. In order to get reproducibility of the results, it is essential to follow the directions given in Pharmacopoeia.

Modification of the general method of testing is carried out for certain substances. This is to have arsenic in the final solution in a readily reducible form. The interference of other substances, ions etc., is eliminated by preliminary treatment. For example, carbonates, hydroxides, and oxides give effervescence, so brominated hydrochloric acid is used. Nitrates are heated with sulphuric acid, to expel nitric acid. Certain organic compounds are insoluble in acid and water, and cause frothing. Hence, organic matter is removed by igniting with calcium hydroxide. Solutions of organic acids like citric, tartaric etc., are prepared in stannated hydrochloric acid. Iron, bismuth and antimony salts are taken in 20% HCl and distilled. Dyes and related compounds are decomposed with sulphuric acid (after preliminary treatment with nitric acid) and then used.

The British Pharmacopoeial method is similar to I. P. method. The apparatus and design is slightly different. The amounts of zinc, hydrochloric acid and other reagents employed are also different. Further, B.P. adopts the use of mercuric bromide test paper. The Gutzeit test for arsenic, is very sensitive and hence is adopted by pharmacopoeias of various countries.

## EXERCISE

1. *Discuss the sources of impurities in pharmaceutical substances.*
2. *Enumerate the effect of impurities on the properties of pharmaceutical substances.*
3. *Discuss the factors to be considered while fixing the limit of impurities.*
4. *Describe the limit test for iron and give the reactions involved.*
5. *Write reactions involved in limit test for 'lead' and 'arsenic'.*
6. *How will you carryout limit test for chloride and sulphate on samples which do not require pretreatment ?*
7. *Draw a well labelled diagram for Gutzeit test apparatus for arsenic limit test.*
8. *Give reasons for :*
   *(a) The solution is made alkaline with ammonia in limit test for iron.*
   *(b) In the limit test for chloride or sulphate on potassium permanganate, alcohol is added to the aqueous solution of sample.*
   *(c) Stannated hydrochloric acid is used in limit test for arsenic.*
9. *Describe the limit test for heavy metal on a sample of Kaolin and Eucalyptus oil.*
10. *Explain the principle and procedure of limit test for lead as per B. P.*

# 4

# WATER

Water is the most widely required solvent for any industry. Pharmaceutical industry also requires water of different types. Water is present in the nature in all its three physical states i.e. solid, liquid and gas.

Water occupies about three quarter of the surface of the earth and mostly it is available and obtained from lakes, rivers dams and wells. The rain water gets carried into streams, rivers and ultimately into sea. Water in the form of solid occurs as snow and ice on very high mountain tops and polar region.

Though water occupies three quarter of the surface of the earth, the potable water is only available on lands under the surface of earth and from rivers, dams etc. The term 'Potable Water' means water fit for human consumption. Water from wells and ponds is free from odour, colour and taste and contains less impurities. It is generally safe for drinking purpose. The water supplied through taps by towns and corporations is purified by chemical treatment and made free from micro-organisms and toxic substances.

**Physical Properties of Water :**

Water in the liquid form is clear, colourless liquid without odour or taste. When cooled it freezes at 0°C to form ice which floats on water. When heated to 100°C it is converted into steam.

Water has high boiling point (100°C) and freezing point when compared with $H_2S$, $NH_3$ etc. It is accounted due to the hydrogen bonding which results in an association of water molecules. The oxygen atom, being relatively more electronegative carries a partial negative charge ($\delta^-$) and the two hydrogen atoms a partial positive charge ($\delta^+$). The net result is molecular association. This feature, further gives rise to charge separation accounting to dipole moment. Water possess a permanent dipole moment.

The permanent electric dipole further accounts for the high dielectric constant for water. When compared with some inorganic and organic solvents water shows high dielectric constant value (81). This fact also accounts for high ionizing power for water. All these characters explain the characteristic of polarity of water molecule. Water being a polar solvent, it has ability to dissolve a variety of substances. It dissolves into it gases, number of inorganic salts and many organic polar compounds.

**Chemical Properties of Water :**

Some of the important chemical properties of water which need mention are as under :

1. **Thermal Stability :** Under ordinary conditions water is chemically stable. Decomposition of water into its constituent gases $H_2$ and $O_2$ requires high energy. Similarly, when $H_2$ and $O_2$ combine to form water about 58,000 calories are evolved per mole of water formed.

2. **Ionic Dissociation :** The dissociation of water into ions $2H_2O \rightleftharpoons H_3O + OH^-$ is significantly less. In a sense it is considered as non-electrolyte and non-ionic in character, for pure water, $Kw = 1.0 \times 10^{-14}$ at 25°C. This dissociation constant varies directly with temperature.

3. **Solvent Property :** The solvent property of water is of great importance in pharmaceutical industry. Water acts as solvent for wide range of substances. This has already been reasoned due to its high dielectric constant and polarity.

4. **Hydration :** When substance is added to water, the electrostatic interactions enable it to form hydrate with the constituent units of solute and the resulting hydrate facilitates further dissolution of solute into it. It follows the saying "like dissolves like". Furthermore, because of its strong permanent dipole, water acts as ligand in formation of complexes. Almost all cations form one or more complexes depending upon the coordination number of cation. The number of water molecules in the complexes are 4. 2, 0, 10 etc. e.g. in copper complex, 4 water molecules are involved.

$$\begin{bmatrix} H_2O & & OH_2 \\ & Cu & \\ H_2O & & OH_2 \end{bmatrix}^{++}$$

5. **Amphoteric Character :** The amphoteric nature of water makes it more useful as solvent in acid-base reactions. Since, water can accept proton (as in $HCl + H_2O \longrightarrow H_3O^+ + Cl^-$) forming hydronium ion $H_3O^+$ it acts as base and as it gives proton it also acts as an acid. This property is of great help in various chemical acid-base reactions.

6. **Redox Property :** This is of minor importance as compared to acid-base property. Water acts as an oxidizing agent in reactions in which any element able to displace one or both of its proton as hydrogen gas, e.g.

$$2Na + 2H_2O \longrightarrow 2NaOH + H_2\uparrow$$

[This reaction occurs at room temperature for active metals] water is capable of acting as a reducing agent in some cases like with fluorine e.g.

$$2H_2O + 2F_2 = 2H_2F_2 + O_2 \uparrow$$

7. **Catalytic Property :** Water acts as catalyst in some well-known reactions. In some chemical reactions presence of water retards reaction. Amount of water plays important role in such reactions.

Water is associated with some chemical salts in hydrated form or as water of crystallization. When there is a spontaneous loss of water from a salt hydrate at room temperature (without heating), the phenomenon of efflorescence occurs. e.g. Sodium carbonate decahydrate effloresces when placed in dry air as :

$$Na_2CO_3 \cdot 10H_2O \longrightarrow Na_2CO_3 + 10H_2O \text{ (water vapour)}$$

when an anhydrous substance absorbs water and becomes soluble in it, the phenomenon is called deliquescence. Deliquescent substances are known as hygroscopic. The calcium chloride, magnesium chloride deliquesce because they absorb water and form solution readily. Deliquescent and efflorescent substances require special conditions of storage.

When water of crystallization from a solid hydrate is removed under controlled conditions of temperature, the process is called as exsication. Different crystalline hydrates lose water of crystallization at different temperatures. e.g. $CuSO_4.5H_2O$ loses 2 water molecule when heated at 30°C, two more on heating at 100°C and for removing last water molecule heating upto 250°C is required.

Substances sometimes absorb water to a varying extent. The removal of such water from substance is carried out mechanically. The process of removing mechanically held water is known as desiccation. In a laboratory 'desiccator' is used to remove the admixed water. Various drying agents (known as desiccants) e.g., silica gel, concentrated sulphuric acid, calcium chloride, phosphorus pentaoxide etc. are employed in desiccator for removal of water.

**Hardness of Water :** Water from natural source of different types contain number of dissolved substances. Depending upon the nature and amount of chemical salts present in the water, the 'hardness' is given to the water. Water containing a large quantity of salts of calcium, magnesium (and sometimes iron) in the form of bicarbonate, carbonate and sulphate is called as hard water. Water which do not produce lather when shaken with a soap solution is called hard water. The 'hardness' of water may be of permanent or temporary type. This depends upon the nature of salts in water. The hardness of water is removable on boiling, then the hardness is called temporary hardness, e.g. hardness due to bicarbonates of calcium or magnesium. These bicarbonates on heating are converted into water insoluble carbonates which can be removed. Thus,

$$Ca(HCO_3)_2 \longrightarrow CaCO_3 \downarrow + H_2O + CO_2 \uparrow$$

The hardness due to the presence of sulphates of calcium or magnesium is known as permanent hardness. The permanent hardness can be removed only by chemical methods.

The degree of hardness of water is expressed in terms of equivalents of calcium carbonate. One degree of hardness is produced by one part of calcium carbonate or its equivalent in parts per million (ppm) of water. The degree of hardness of water is determined by titrating a sample of water with standard soap solution. The strength of soap solution is calculated by titrating it against a standard solution of calcium chloride.

**Methods of Softening of Hard Water :**

Temporary hardness of water is easily removed by boiling. If water contains calcium bicarbonate on boiling, it is converted into insoluble calcium carbonate. If water contains magnesium bicarbonate, then on boiling it is converted into insoluble magnesium hydroxide.

$$Mg(HCO_3)_2 \longrightarrow Mg(OH)_2 + 2CO_2 \uparrow$$

On filtering the precipitate water becomes free from hardness.

In industry, hardness of water is removed by adopting the following processes :

**(a)** Chemical precipitation of calcium, magnesium and other heavy metals, by adopting either cold lime process or by hot lime-soda process. In this technique calcium hydroxide, slaked lime (CaO), sodium carbonate is added to water. By double decomposition insoluble precipitates of $Mg(OH)_2$, $CaCO_3$ are formed which are allowed to settle in tanks and then removed.

$$MgCl_2 + Ca(OH)_2 \longrightarrow Mg(OH)_2 \downarrow + CaCl_2$$

$$CaSO_4 + Na_2CO_3 \longrightarrow CaCO_3 \downarrow + Na_2SO_4$$

$$CaCl_2 + Na_2CO_3 \longrightarrow CaCO_3 \downarrow + 2NaCl$$

In hot soda-lime process the coagulation of precipitate is fast because of higher temperature. Sodium metaaluminate is often used to remove suspended particles by flocculation.

**(b) Using Zeolites :** Zeolite or permutit is a class of aluminium silicate ($Na_2 Al_2 Si_2 O_3 \times H_2O$) types of materials. When water containing calcium or magnesium ions is passed through column containing zeolites, these ions are retained by zeolites and sodium ion is exchanged. In the process softening of water occurs. However, water softened by zeolite is alkaline in pH. The zeolites have now been replaced by more effective ion-exchange resins.

**(c) Ion-Exchange Resin Method :** For demineralization of water, ion-exchange resin method is used. Now-a-days, synthetic organic ion-exchange resins are available containing acidic groups (like $SO_3H^-$, COOH, phenolic – OH) acting as cation exchangers and having basic groups ($NH_2$, OH, $Cl^-$ etc.) as anion exchangers. The cation exchange resins and anion exchange resins are filled in tubes or columns or beds and water is passed through them. By the exchange phenomenon the cations like calcium, magnesium present in the water are exchanged with the $H^+$ or $Na^+$ ion present on cation exchange resin.

The reaction which occurs can be represented as

$$2H\ Res + Ca(HCO_3)_2 \longrightarrow Ca(Resin)_2 + H_2O + 2CO_2 \uparrow$$

$$2H\ Res + MgCl_2 \longrightarrow Mg(Resin)_2 + 2HCl$$

In the exchange resin, as shown above, acidic water is produced, since it is not desirable for the practical purpose, the water is now passed through anion exchanger column. The ion present on resin (anion) if containing $NH_2$, $OH$ react with ions in water as under :

$$Res\ NH_2 + HCl \longrightarrow Res\ NH_3 \cdot Cl \text{ (absorption of total acid)}$$

$$2Res^+OH^- + H_2CO_3 \longrightarrow Res_2CO_3 + 2H_2O$$

The exchanger resins have limited capacity for exchanging ions. For example, in cation exchanger having $H^+$ ion, the resin can be regenerated by passing hydrochloric acid through the column. The various ions like $Ca^{++}$, $Mg^{++}$ $Na^+$ held on resin can be replaced by hydrogen ions. The regeneration reaction is shown as :

$$(Res^-)_2\ Ca^{2+} + 2HCl \longrightarrow 2(Res^-)H^+ + CaCl_2$$

Similarly, in anion exchange resin, the regeneration is carried out by passing a solution of sodium carbonate or sodium hydroxide (depending upon the type of resin) through the anion exchanger.

$$2Res\ N \cdot H_2\ HCl + Na_2CO_3 \longrightarrow 2\ Res\ NH_2 + 2NaCl + CO_2$$

$$R_3NHCl + NaOH \longrightarrow R_3N + NaCl + H_2O$$

Exhausted resin Regenerated resin

The conductivity measurement of water is carried out to determine whether the water is free from dissolved ions and to determine the capacity of resin. Ion-exchanger equipment for demineralization of water have dials for indicating conductivity of water. When the conductivity is high, regeneration of resin is necessary.

**Natural Water and Potable Water :**

Natural water or the rain water is considered as purest form of water. It only contains some dissolved gases before it falls down onto the soil. When water accumulates on the ground, part of it goes into the soil and into the lower strata from which it is brought out or it flows in a form of stream, rivulets or river or gets collected in lakes. During this period a large number of salts, ions, gases get dissolved into it. Besides, the soil particles, plant and animal debris, various kinds of organisms, the industrial waste and sewage gets carried into it. All these ultimately introduce impurities, suspended solids as well as dissolved substances.

For rendering water fit for drinking purposes as well as for industrial use, some treatment is necessary. Depending upon the source of water, the kinds, type and amount of impurities vary.

For soil particles, plants and animal debris, suspended particles treatment of settling and filtration is carried out.

The filtered water is carried to tanks for exposure to atmosphere. Because of exposure to sunlight and air, water is saturated with oxygen, nitrogen and carbon dioxide gas and deodourification occurs because of sunlight.

The dissolved solids are treated depending upon their nature. For organic impurities different treatment is given to decompose them into harmless products. For inorganic substances, precipitation, water softening etc. are carried out.

In order to make water safe for drinking purposes aeration/chlorination/fluoridation etc. is carried out. Different countries have set distinct standards for water purification before it is rendered fit for human consumption or for industrial uses.

**Purified Water :**

According to Pharmacopoeia, purified water is the water prepared from suitable potable water by distillation or by using ion-exchange resins.

Distilled water is purified water and it is prepared by distillation method in a suitable distillation apparatus. By this technique dissolved solids and non-volatile matter or impurities get removed. For obtaining distilled water of high purity, special technique involving treatment special stills, condensers and specialized chemical treatment is required. The demineralization method depends upon the use of ion-exchange resins. Two different resins (cation and anion exchangers) are required for complete removal of salts. The resins are arranged in alternate beds or in mixed beds and water is passed through the bed at room temperature. The outcoming water is almost free of ions. The purity of water is measured by conductivity. Meters reading directly in ppm are fitted to ion-exchange units.

The demineralised water, though considerably pure is not sterile as it is not subjected to heating.

According to I.P. 1985, the purified water should have pH between 4.5 – 7; it should comply to the tests for carbondioxide, ammonia, nitrate, nitrite, chloride, sulphate, calcium, heavy metals oxidisable matter and should have total solids not exceeding 0.001%.

It should be stored in tightly closed containers. When distilled water is prescribed, purified water should be supplied.

## Water for Injection :

It is a water prepared by distilling potable water from neutral glass or metal still fitted with a device for preventing the entrainment of droplets. The first portion of the distillate is rejected as it may contain volatile impurities which are carried over. The remaining distillate is then collected in suitable containers and sterilised in an autoclave or by filtration without adding bacteriostatic agents.

The water should comply with all the requirements for purified water and should also comply with the test for pyrogens. It should be stored in tightly closed containers. The water for injection is used as a solvent in preparation of parenteral solutions which are to be sterilised after preparation. No sterility test is therefore applied to the sample. However, if the parenteral solution is to be prepared under aseptic conditions and not sterilized in the final container, every care should be taken to protect the water from bacterial contamination. Every care of aseptic technique is followed in its preparation by distillation method.

## Sterile Water for Injection :

It is a sterile water for injection and suitably packed, it should not contain any antimicrobial agent or other added substances.

It should comply all the tests described under purified water and water for injection as per I.P. 1985. It should further comply to the test for sterility also. It should be supplied in single dose container.

## Selection of Suitable Water for Use :

Since different types of waters are available for use, judicious choice should be made in its selection. Economics is to be considered most critically, potable water is cheapest, demineralized next cheapest, then distilled water and sterile water, for injection, in that order. Naturally, for other uses, potable water can be used while for parenteral use sterilized water needs to be employed.

Limits of total solids, pH and bacterial purity should be taken into account in selection of water for the purpose. The pH of water should be considered when dissolving pH sensitive substances, especially when chlorinated water is used which has acidic pH. If the dissolved solids are high, possibility of precipitations involving certain cations and anions is more. Considering bacterial purity of water other than parenteral use, potable water and purified water have same limits when required for parenteral use, passing for the sterility and pyrogen tests is mandatory. Similarly, when water is used for preparation of solutions to be used for delicate tissues and organs it should comply to the test for sterility.

The pharamacopoeia, reference books give the standards for different types of waters. These standards need to be observed to comply with good manufacturing practices.

# EXERCISE

1. Enumerate chemical properties of water giving suitable examples.

2. Define the terms 'Hard Water' and 'Soft Water'. Explain permanent hardness and temporary hardness of water.

3. Discuss the methods of softening of hard water.

4. What are ion exchange resins ? How are they used in obtaining soft water?

5. What is purified water and water for injection ? What tests are carried out on water for injection as per the Indian Pharmacopoeia ?

# 5

# SOLUBILITY OF PHARMACEUTICALS

The knowledge of solubility and solubility behaviour is very essential and important to pharmacists. This is not only important in its analytical field but equally useful in all aspects, for manufacture of pharmaceutics. Preparation of various pharmaceutical forms need good knowledge of solubility of drugs. This is especially so because many medicines are combinations of various drugs of different chemical characters. The possibility of precipitation, complexation, chemical reactions and incompatibilities need to be recognised. Thus, the knowledge of chemistry of drugs and of solvents with respect to solubility behaviour is very essential.

The process of dissolution of a solute in a solvent to effect a solution, involves mutual separation of particles from their initial bonds. These particles are ions in case of electrolytes and molecules in case of non-electrolytes. A strong bond existing between ions, in case of electrolytes, needs to be broken by the solvent molecules in a process of solubilization, solute must be able to separate the neighbouring molecules of solvent sufficiently to provide a space for itself in solvent structure. Similarly, solvent molecules must be able to separate solute particles from one another by breaking their internal bonds. The important factor in this process is the field strength of particles involved.

Solvents with high ionic or polar character tend to dissolve most substances of polar (or ionic) in nature. On the other hand, solvents with low dielectric constant or polarity are less effective in solubilization process.

When an electrolyte like NaCl (common salt) is dissolved in water, not only the sodium and chloride ions enter the water from its solid state but some of the sodium and chloride ions already in liquid water will return to solid phase. The number of ions returning to solid will be proportional to the number of ions present in the liquid phase. The process of dissolution continues till the equilibrium stage is reached when the number of ions dissolving become equal to the number of ions coming to the solid state.

At this stage no more sodium chloride dissolves in water and a 'saturation' of water with sodium chloride is said to occur. The same phenomenon will hold true for the dissolution of molecules in case of non-electrolytes in a given solvent.

The term 'solubility' is referred as the concentration of a dissolved solute at an equilibrium at saturation point. Number of substances have a definite solubility in water or other solvents at a given temperature. When the concentration of any solute in a liquid exceeds the solubility, these results either in precipitation of the solute or a stage of supersaturation. In supersaturation more amount of solute is held in liquid phase without being precipitated out.

## Method of Expression of Solubility Behaviour :

It is a common practice to express solubility in terminology like soluble, very soluble, sparingly soluble, insoluble, etc. It is essential to know their meaning for scientific expression. The solubilities are indicated by pharmacopoeias, as the amount of solvent required for a fixed amount of solute. The descriptive phases of solubilities and their ratio of solute/solvent, intended to apply at ambient temperature are given in table 5.1.

**Table 5.1 : Solubility Ratio of Solute/Solvent**

| Descriptive term | Approximate quantities or solvent by volume for one part of soluble by weight |
|---|---|
| Very soluble | less than 1 part |
| Freely soluble | from 1 to 10 parts |
| Soluble | from 10 to 30 parts |
| Sparingly soluble | from 30 to 100 parts |
| Slightly soluble | from 100 to 1000 parts |
| Insoluble | more than 10,000 parts |

## Normal Solution :

When a solution contains 1 g equivalent weight of a substance per litre, it is called normal solution (1N). Solutions are usually prepared in different strengths such as 1N, 0.5N, 0.2N, 0.1N, etc. For the preparation of normal solutions the equivalent weight of the substance should be known.

The equivalent weight of a given solute will depend upon the type of reaction in which it is taking part. In case of acids it is that weight which contains 1 g of replaceable hydrogen (1.008 g). For monobasic acids (like HCl, $HNO_3$ etc.) the equivalent weight is identical to its molecular weight. For dibasic acids (like $H_2SO_4$, oxalic acid etc.) the equivalent weight is 1/2 of the molecular weight. The equivalent weight of a base is that weight which contains one replaceable hydroxyl group i.e. 17.008 g of hydroxyl ion. In certain reactions some compounds possess different equivalent weights.

In red-ox reactions, the equivalent weight of an oxidant or reductant is the molecular weight divided by the number of electrons which 1 mole of substance gains or loses in the reaction. For example, the equivalent weight of $KMnO_4$ is 1/5th its molecular weight.

## Molar Solution :

A solution containing one mole (molecular weight in g) per thousand ml (one litre) of solution is called as molar solution (1 M). Solutions containing very small amounts of solute are expressed in millimolar (mM) concentrations and are defined as the number of millimoles/ml of solution (1 mM = $1 \times 10^{-3}$ M).

**Molal Solution :**

A solution containing one mole of solute per thousand g of solvent is called as molal solution. This mode of expression is less common and is used in reactions or equations to express thermodynamic properties of solutions.

**Per cent Solution :**

It is customary to express the concentrations of solutions in terms of percentage. In per cent w/w, it expresses the number of g of a solute in 100 g of solvent. In case of per cent w/v, the concentration is the number of g of a solute in 100 ml solvent, while in per cent v/v, the expression refers to number of ml or a volume of constituent in 100 ml of solution.

Since, the term solubility indicates a numerical value, it is essential that the mode of reporting is to be specified. It should also be borne in mind that the solubility value is valid for the saturated solutions at the specified temperature. Any change in temperature and also pressure (for the gaseous substances) will change the solubility.

Furthermore, when one is considering solubilization of two or more solutes in the same solvent, the extent of solubility of each solute will be decreased. This aspect needs to be recognised for dissolving substances while preparing multicomponent solution.

**Factors Affecting Solubility :**

The solubility of a solute in a given solvent will be affected by following factors :

**(a) Influence of Temperature and Pressure :** It is well-known that solubility of a salt or solute molecule is temperature dependent. Generally, solubility increases with increase in temperature. A plot of solubility curves (concentration of solute dissolved vs temperature) gives an idea of effect of temperature on solubility. For some solutes the increase in solubility is linear with temperature while for others it is not. Similarly, pressure also affects the solubility in case of gaseous substances. The solubility increases with increase in pressure. When the pressure is reduced (released) the dissolved gas (solute) escapes out from the solution, similar to crystallization of solid (solute) from solution.

**(b) Influence of Other Salts/Solutes :** The solubility of a given solute in a solvent is affected by the presence of other dissolved substances. This effect is more pronounced when foreign substances are present in very high concentrations. If the foreign (other) substance has a common ion, the solubility of solute under study decreases due to common ion effect. Invariably this results in precipitation. This phenomenon is not only shown by electrolyte salts but also by non-electrolyte molecules.

The effect produced by addition of other salts (foreign) or molecule is due to the change brought out in the dielectric constant of solvent. Solubility is also changed by field interactions arising out of ion-pairs. The neutral electrostatic attraction between solute and solvent hold the solute in dissolved state. Disturbance in this is caused by the presence of another solute, which thus changes solubility of both solutes.

## Solubility Product Principle :

The solubility data is used for calculating solubility product (Ksp) of a salt in case of electrolytes. This value is useful as a valuable tool in predicting whether there will be precipitation or not on the tool of certain ions to the solution.

For insoluble salts, however insoluble it may be, it always has some solubility in solvent water. An equilibrium is established between the suspended salt ($X^a Y^b$) in excess of water at its saturation point. Assuming the complete dissociation of salt, the equilibrium can be represented as,

$$X^a Y^b \rightleftharpoons X^a Y^b$$
$$\text{solid} \quad \text{solution}$$

and according to law of mass action,

$$\frac{[X^a][Y]^b}{[X^a Y^b]} = K$$

Since, the solid phase is in excess, the concentration of the dissolved phase can also be considered a constant.

$$K[X^a Y^b] = [X]^a [Y]^b$$

The product of $[X]^a[Y]^b$ = Ksp known as solubility product constant.

According to the solubility product principle the product of concentrations of $[X]^a$ and $[Y]^b$ ions in a saturated solution of $X^a Y^b$ remains constant at a given temperature. If the concentration of $[X]^a$ ion is increased, the concentration of $[Y]^b$ ion will decrease to have the solubility product Ksp constant. Thus, in a saturated solution of $[X^a Y^b]$ addition of any one ion brings precipitation.

Addition of a foreign electrolyte which brings precipitation of a slightly soluble salt is termed as 'salt-effect'. This phenomenon is frequently used as a separational technique in pharmaceutical analysis.

## Colligative Properties of Solutions :

The solutions of electrolytes and non-electrolytes possess colligative properties which are different from the physical and chemical properties of their solutes. These properties are dependent on the number of particles present in the solutions. The greater the number of particles in a solution, greater is the extent of a given colligative property.

Some important colligative properties associated with a solution are (1) the lowering of vapour pressure, (2) the depression of freezing point, (3) the elevation of boiling point, (4) the osmotic pressure and (5) tonicity. The first three properties are inter-related. These are easy to be demonstrated and are of chemical interest. The osmotic pressure phenomena and tonicity are of medicinal importance. This colligative property is also related to the other three properties.

**1. Vapour-pressure Lowering :** It is well-known that the vapour-pressure of a solution is lower than that of pure solvent. This property follows Raoult's law, which states that "the partial pressure of a component of solution is directly proportional to its mole content in the solution". The law is mathematically represented as :

$$P_1 = X_1 P_1^0 = P_1^0 \left(\frac{n_1}{n_1 + n_2}\right)$$

where, $P_1$ refers to the actual vapour-pressure of solvent, $P_1^0$ as vapour-pressure of component 1 is pure state (solvent), $X_1$ as the mole fraction of solvent (component 1) in solution and $n_1$ and $n_2$ are the number of moles of component 1(solvent) and component 2 (solute). Mathematically, we can derive an expression for the lowering of vapour-pressure in terms of mole fraction as $\Delta P = P_1^0 - P_1$ where, $\Delta P$ represents the lowering of vapour-pressure of solvent because of dissolution of solute into it. In dilute solutions the extent of lowering of vapour-pressure is directly related to the concentration of solute in a solution.

**2. Depression of the Freezing Point :** It is known since long that freezing point of a solution is lower than that of pure solvent. A quantitative relationship between the extent of lowering of freezing point and the concentration was established by Charles Blagden. Accordingly, the lowering of freezing point of a solvent is proportional to the amount of solute dissolved in it. Thus, it is now known that the depression of the freezing point of a solvent is proportional to the molecular concentration of the solute present in it. Equimolecular solutions have the same freezing point.

The depression of freezing point is shown by both electrolytes and non-electrolytes. Electrolytes depress the freezing point more than non-electrolytes. This is due to greater ionization. In dilute solution the quantitative relationship holds true. The extent of freezing point lowering is expressed in term of 'Kf' known as molal freezing point depression constant. The equation for Kf is given by

$$Kf = \frac{RT_0 M_1}{1000 \, \Delta Hf}$$

where R = gas constant, $T_0$ is absolute freezing point of pure solvent, $M_1$ is the molecular weight of pure solvent and $\Delta Hf$ is the heat of fusion of pure solvent. The change in freezing point is shown by

$$\Delta Tf = mKf$$

where m is the molality of solution and Kf is the molal freezing point constant.

Different solvents have a fixed depressant value (given in table 5.2). From the constant for a particular solvent the molecular weight of a substance can be calculated. If $M_2$ is the molecular weight of a solute, $W_1$ is the weight of solvent, $W_2$ is the weight of solute, T is the observed lowering of the freezing point and Kf is the freezing point constant for the solvent then,

$$M_2 = \frac{1000 \times Kf \times W_2}{\Delta T \times W_1}$$

This is the easiest method of molecular weight determination for nonelectrolyte solutes.

**3. Elevation of Boiling Point :** When solute is present in a solution, it increases the boiling point of pure solvent. The extent of elevation is related to the amount present in a solution. A molal boiling point elevation constant Kb is shown by equation

$$K_b = \frac{RT_0 M_1}{1000 \, \Delta HV}$$

This equation is similar to the freezing point depression constant, except that $T_0$ is the absolute boiling temperature of pure solvent and $\Delta HV$ is the heat of vapourisation. The change in boiling point is obtained by multiplying '$K_b$' by the molality of solution as

$$\Delta T_b = K_b m$$

where 'm' is the molality of the solution and '$K_b$' is the molal boiling point constant. For different solvents the value of $K_b$ is calculated and recorded. Some are given in table 5.2.

**Table 5.2 : Molal Properties of Solvents**

| Solvents | Freezing point in °C | Boiling point in °C | $K_b$ | $K_f$ |
|---|---|---|---|---|
| Benzene | 5.5 | 81.2 | 2.5 | 5.12 |
| Ethanol | −112 | 78.3 | 1.22 | − |
| Water | 0.0 | 100.0 | 0.512 | 1.86 |

**4. Osmotic Pressure :** This property is of importance to pharmacist. Number of drugs show their mechanism of action by affecting osmotic pressure e.g. saline cathartics, diuretics (osmotic) etc. Osmotic pressure is also important in maintenance of cell function as it acts at biological membrane.

If two solutions of different concentrations are separated by a membrane (permeable to solvent/ions), the solvent tends to flow through the membrane from low concentration to high concentration until concentration on both sides of the membrane is equal. The process of passage of solvent through membrane is known as osmosis. Osmotic pressure ($\pi$) is the pressure gradient which exists across the membrane, due to concentration changes.

According to J.H. Van't Hoff equation

$$\pi = mRT$$

where m is difference of molal concentration of two solutions, R is gas constant and T as absolute temperature.

It is thus seen that osmotic pressure is dependent upon the number of particles (i.e. ions, molecules) in a given volume of solution.

Osmotic pressure is important in biological system for regulation of body fluids for maintenance of isotonic conditions.

For maintaining cell functions, solutions of various tonicity are required and used in pharmacy. Isotonic solutions have osmotic pressure equal to the osmotic pressure of intra-cellular fluid ($\pi$ soln = $\pi$ cell). In hypertonic solutions ($\pi$ soln > $\pi$ cell). The solutions exert more osmotic pressure than the osmotic pressure of intra-cellular fluid, while in hypotonic solutions, ($\pi$ soln < $\pi$ cell). The pressure of solution is less than that of intra-cellular fluid. Isotonic solutions are used for ophthalmic, nasal, lacrymal fluid preparations. In electrolyte therapy isotonic solution (0.9% w/v of sodium chloride) is commonly used.

## EXERCISE

1. *Explain the terms and give examples :*

    *(a) Normal solution,*

    *(b) Molar solution,*

    *(c) Molal solution and*

    *(d) Per cent solution.*

2. *(a) Discuss the factors affecting solubility.*

    *(b) Explain the importance of solubility product principle in pharmacy.*

3. *Enumerate colligative properties of solution and explain in detail the depression of freezing point for molecular weight determination.*

4. *What is osmotic pressure and explain its importance in biological system ?*

■■■

# 6

# ACIDS, BASES AND BUFFERS

The concept of acid and base has undergone a considerable change. The substance called as acid usually has a sour taste. Its aqueous solution turns litmus paper red and has pH less than 7. Similarly, a base has a bitter burning taste and its aqueous solution turns litmus paper blue. It has pH more than 7. Acids and bases vary in their strength.

**Arrhenius Theory :**

The concept of acid and base was first presented by Arrhenius. According to Arrhenius theory any acid or base on dissolution in water dissociates forming ions and establishes equilibrium between ionised and unionised molecule. Arrhenius defined an acid as a substance which when dissolved in water gives hydrogen ions e.g.

$$HCl \rightleftharpoons H^+ + Cl^-$$

$$CH_3COOH \rightleftharpoons H^+ + CH_3COO^-$$

Base is defined as a substance which when dissolved in water yields hydroxyl ions e.g.

$$NaOH \rightleftharpoons Na^+ + OH^-$$

$$NH_4OH \rightleftharpoons NH_4^+ + OH^-$$

Acids and bases undergo a reaction known as neutralisation. The neutralisation reaction results in forming water ($H_2O$) and a salt e.g.

$$HCl + NaOH \longrightarrow H_2O + NaCl$$

The Arrhenius acid base theory though most simple and convenient to explain the reactions in aqueous solutions, has a number of limitations. The limitations of Arrhenius theory are :

(a) The definitions of acid and base are only in terms of aqueous solutions and not in terms of substance.

(b) The theory does not explain acidic and basic properties of substances in non-aqueous solvents.

(c) The neutralisation of acid and base in absence of solvent is not explained.

(d) The basic substances which do not contain hydroxide ion is not explained by the theory.

**Bronsted and Lowry Theory :**

Bronsted in Copenhegan and Lowry in London independently in 1923 proposed simultaneously new definitions for acids and bases. Accordingly acid is a substance that can donate a proton and base is a substance that can accept a proton i.e. acid is a proton donor and base is a proton acceptor.

As per Bronsted-Lowry theory an acid is

$$\text{Acid} = H^+ + \text{base (conjugate)}$$

e.g. $HCl \rightleftharpoons H^+ + Cl^-$ (conjugate)

$CH_3COOH \rightleftharpoons H^+ + CH_3COO^-$ (conjugate)

Thus, acid could be a electrically neutral molecule,

$$HCl \rightleftharpoons H^+ + Cl^-$$

or negative ion,

$$HSO_4^- \rightleftharpoons H^+ + SO_4^-$$

or positive cation like

$$C_5H_5\overset{+}{N}H \rightleftharpoons H^+ + C_5H_5N$$

Similarly, a base could be a electrically neutral like $NH_3$ or a negative ion e.g. $OH^-$, $Cl^-$, $CH_3COO^-$ etc. just as with oxidation-reduction reactions where the free electron cannot exist in solution, free protons do not exist in solution. There must be a proton acceptor (base) for acid to give off its proton.

When gaseous HCl is passed in water, its ionisation takes place as follows :

$$HCl + H_2O \rightleftharpoons H_3O^+ + Cl^-$$
$$\text{acid} \quad \text{base} \quad \text{acid} \quad \text{base}$$

In this reaction HCl donates a proton to $H_2O$ and formation of $H_3O^+ + Cl^-$ takes place. It is a reversible reaction and hence $Cl^-$ accepts a proton and forms HCl. Thus in

$$HCl \rightleftharpoons H^+ + Cl^-$$

where HCl is an acid and $Cl^-$ is a base. Such a pair of acid and base which differs only by a proton is known as conjugate acid-base pair. Here, HCl is a Bronsted acid and $Cl^-$ is a conjugate base of acid HCl.

In the above example, there is a formation of hydronium ion $H_3O^+$ due to acceptance of proton by $H_2O$. This $H_3O^+$ ion loses a proton and forms $H_2O$ i.e. $H_3O^+ \rightleftharpoons H^+ + H_2O$. In this reaction $H_3O^+$ and $H_2O$ is a conjugate acid-base pair. Conjugate acid-base pair is represented in general as,

$$\text{Acid} \rightleftharpoons \text{Proton} + \text{Base}.$$

According to Bronsted-Lowry concept the reaction of an acid with base produces another acid and base. A general form of this reaction is

$$\text{Acid}_1 + \text{Base}_2 \rightleftharpoons \text{Acid}_2 + \text{Base}_1$$
$$H_2SO_4 + H_2O \rightleftharpoons H_3O^+ + HSO_4^-$$
$$CH_3COOH + H_2O \rightleftharpoons H_3O^+ + CH_3COO^-$$
$$NH_4^+ + H_2O \rightleftharpoons H_3O^+ + NH_3$$

Water has a dual character since it can accept a proton or donate. This is illustrated by the following chemical reactions of water :

$$H_2O + HCl \rightleftharpoons H_3O^+ + Cl^- \qquad \ldots(1)$$

$$H_2O + NH_3 \rightleftharpoons NH_4^+ + OH^- \qquad \ldots(2)$$

In the first reaction $H_2O$ accepts a proton from HCl resulting in the formation of hydronium ion $H_3O^+$ and thus $H_2O$ is a base. Whereas in the second reaction $H_2O$ donates a proton to $NH_3$ a base and forms hydroxide ion ($OH^-$), and it acts as an acid. Any substance which can donate as well as accept a proton it is called amphoteric or amphiprotic. A number of other substances, solvents etc. also show amphoteric character.

**Lewis Theory of Acids and Bases :**

Though Bronsted-Lowry theory is widely accepted it failed to take into consideration many other acids which do not have proton or which can transfer proton. To overcome this G.N. Lewis in 1923 proposed a definition of acid and base in terms of electronic structure. According to Lewis theory an acid is a molecule or ion that can accept a lone pair of electrons; and base is a molecule or ion that has a lone pair of electrons which is donated. Thus, an acid may not have a proton to donate. A substance can be called acid provided it accepts electron pair. e.g. in a reaction.

$$H^+ + :NH_3 \longrightarrow NH_4^+$$

$H^+$ accepts a pair of electrons from $NH_3$. Thus, according to Lewis concept $H^+$ is an acid, known as Lewis acid and $NH_3$ is a base or known as Lewis base. Similarly, in a reaction between metal ion copper $Cu^{++}$ and ammonia.

$$Cu^{++} + 4(:NH_3) \longrightarrow Cu(NH_3)_4^{++}$$

Copper ion accepts electrons from ammonia, forming cupra-ammonium ion. In this reaction copper ion $Cu^{++}$ acts as lewis acid and $NH_3$ is lewis base. In a reaction between $Ag^+$ and $CN^-$, the $Ag^+$ acts as Lewis acid and $CN^-$ as Lewis base.

According to this concept acid-base reaction involves the formation of a coordinate covalent bond. A reaction between ammonia and boron trifluoride is given below :

$$BF_3 + :NH_3 \longrightarrow F_3B:NH_3$$

Boron trifluoride is a electron deficient compound and it accepts a lone pair of electrons from ammonia forming covalent bond. The $BF_3$ is a Lewis acid and $NH_3$ a Lewis base. Lewis bases are similar to Bronsted-Lowry bases. Several examples of Lewis acid and bases are given below :

Acid : $H^+$, $NH_4^+$, : $Na^+$, $K^+$, $Cu^{++}$, $Al^{+++}$, $-\overset{|}{\underset{|}{C}}{}^+$ (Carbonium ions etc.)

Bases : $NH_3$, $H_2O$, $OH^-$, $Cl^-$, $CN^-$, $S^{--}$.

**Strong and Weak Acids and Bases :**

It is commonly known that certain substances or electrolytes are strong, moderate or weak acids or bases. The nature of their being strong or weak depends upon their nature, degree or extent of its ionization and the solvent. Hydrochloric acid in water is a strong acid while acetic acid in water is a weak acid. However, acetic acid if dissolved in ammonia shows strong acidic character. When an acid is dissolved in water, it will dissociate or ionise and the amount of ionization is dependent on the strength of acid. A strong electrolyte is completely dissociated, while a 'weak' electrolyte is partially dissociated. Thus, the degree of ionization is of great use to differentiate between strong acids and weak acids or strong bases and weak bases.

Aqueous solutions of HCl, $H_2SO_4$, $HNO_3$, etc. show pronounced acidic characters even at moderate dilution indicating that they are completely dissociated, their degree of ionization is higher and they supply more number of $H^+$ ions. These acids are called as strong acids. Acids like $H_2CO_3$, HCOOH, $CH_3COOH$ etc. ionise to a small extent in aqueous solutions even at high dilutions and supply small number of $H^+$ ions and hence are called as weak acids. Similarly, bases like NaOH or KOH ionise to a greater extent in aqueous solutions and supply large number of $OH^-$ ions. These are called strong bases. Some bases like $NH_4OH$, $Ca(OH)_2$ ionise to a small extent in their aqueous solutions weak at high dilutions, supply small number of $OH^-$ ions and are called weak bases. Examples of some commonly used strong acids, weak acids and strong and weak bases are given in Table 6.1.

**Table 6.1 : Strong/Weak Acids and Bases**

| Acids | | Bases | |
|---|---|---|---|
| **Strong** | **Weak** | **Strong** | **Weak** |
| HCl | $CH_3COOH$ | NaOH | $NH_4OH$ |
| $H_2SO_4$ | HCN | KOH | $NaHCO_3$ |
| $NHO_3$ | $C_6H_5COOH$ | CaO | $C_6H_5NH_2$ |
| $HClO_4$ | HCOOH | $Na_2CO_3$ | $CH_3NH_2$ |
| $HClO_3$ | $H_2CO_3$ | – | – |
| HBr | $C_6H_5OH$ | – | – |
| HI | – | – | – |

**The Hydrogen Ion Concentration, pH and pOH :**

Pure water has equal concentration of $[H^+]$ and $[OH^-]$ ions and each is $1 \times 10^{-7}$ g/ion/litre. Water is regarded as a neutral. The solution becomes acidic if $[H^+] > 1 \times 10^{-7}$ g/ion/litre and alkaline if $[OH^-] > 1 \times 10^{-7}$ g/ion/litre. The product of $[H^+]$ and $[OH^-]$ remains constant in aqueous solutions because when $[H^+]$ increases $[OH^-]$ decreases. Thus, if either $[H^+]$ or $[OH^-]$ in solution is known, the other can be calculated because $[H^+][OH^-] = 10^{-14}$.

From the above discussion we know about the solution, whether it is acidic or basic. In order to know the exact strength it is necessary to have some scale by which the strengths could be measured. Sorenson in 1909 devised a scale known as pH scale. By this, very small concentrations of hydrogen ion in a given solution can be measured in units. The pH scale is thus a measure of acidity.

**Definition of pH :** pH is defined as the negative logarithm to the base 10 of hydrogen ion concentration. This is written as

$$pH = -\log_{10}[H^+]$$

Thus, as $H^+$ is present as hydronium ion. $pH = -\log_{10}[H_3O^+]$. In the definition of pH 'p' is derived from German word Potenz (Power) and H for hydrogen.

Thus,
$$pH = -\log[H^+]$$
$$= -\log[H_3O^+]$$
$$= -\log \frac{1}{[H_3O^+]}$$

**Definition of pOH :** pOH is defined as the negative logarithm to base 10 of hydroxide ion concentration.

$$pOH = -\log_{10}[OH^-]$$
$$= -\log[OH^-]$$

For every aqueous solutions

$$[H^+][OH^-] = K_w \ldots$$

or $\quad K_w = 1 \times 10^{-14}$

Thus, $\log[H^+] - \log[OH^-] = \log 1 \times 10^{-14} = -14$

If we multiply by negative sign,

$$-\log[H^+] - \log[OH^-] = -(-14)$$

As $\quad pH = -\log[H^+]$
and $\quad pOH = -\log[OH^-]$
Thus, $\quad pH + pOH = 14$
In pure water, $[H^+] = 1 \times 10^{-7}$ mole/litre.

$\therefore \quad pH = -\log[H^+]$
$\quad = -\log(1 \times 10^{-7})$
$\quad = -(-7)$
$\quad = 7$

For pure water pH is 7. Now when $pH + pOH = 14$
and when $\quad pH = 7$
then $\quad pOH = 7$

It is thus seen that if the pH of an aqueous solution is less than 7 it is acidic and when it is more than 7, it is basic.

Acidity and alkalinity or basicity is measured by pH scale. The accurate representation of very small concentration of hydrogen ions in conventional way is very inconvenient. It is therefore expressed in terms of pH unit. Thus, pH scale is a measure of acidity.

**pH Scale :** It is clear from the above that pH indicates acidic or basic nature of a given solution. Let us again consider the $[H^+]$ in a given aqueous solution.

1. If solution contains $[H^+] = 1$ mole/litre

   $pH = -\log 1 = 0$

2. If solution contains $[H^+] = 0.1$ mole/litre

   $pH = -\log 0.1 = -(-1.000)$
   $= 1$

3. If $[H^+]$ in solution is 0.01 mole/litre

   $pH = -\log 0.01$
   $= -(-2)$
   $= 2$

It is thus clear as $[H^+]$ decreases the pH value increases.

Similar to hydrogen ion concentration we can calculate pH for the solution having hydroxide ions.

4. If solution has $[OH^-] = 1$ mole/litre

   $pOH = -\log[OH^-]$
   $= -\log 1$
   $= 0$

   Since, $pH + pOH = 14$
   $pH = 14 - 0$
   $pH = 14$

5. If a solution contains $[OH^-] = 0.1$ mole/litre

   $pOH = -\log(0.1)$
   $= -(1)$
   $pOH = 1$
   as $pH + pOH = 14$
   $pH = 14 - 1$
   $= 13$

Thus, as $[OH^-]$ decreases pH also decreases. For pure water $pH = pOH = 7$, and hence water is neutral, neither acidic nor basic.

**Buffer Solutions :**

The solutions that resist the changes in pH values are called buffer solutions. A buffer solution consists of a mixture of weak acid and its salt or of a weak base and its salt. To such solution when small amount of acid or alkali is added no significant change in the pH results.

Buffer solutions are prepared either by mixing a weak acid with its salt or a weak base with its salt.

**Types of Buffer Solutions :** These are mainly of following two types :

(a) **Acidic Buffer Solution :** The solution containing a mixture of weak acid (e.g. acetic acid) and its salt (e.g. sodium acetate) is known as acidic buffer.

(b) **Basic Buffer Solution :** The solution containing a mixture of weak base (e.g. ammonia) and its salt (e.g. ammonium chloride) is a basic buffer.

**Properties of Buffer Solution :**

1. The pH of buffer solution is constant.
2. The pH of solution does not change on dilution.
3. The pH does not change even after addition of small quantities of acids or bases.
4. As the pH of solution remains constant, it is useful in a number of chemical reactions.

**Buffer Action :**

Let us consider an acidic buffer containing acetic acid and sodium acetate. Acetic acid is a weak electrolyte and sodium acetate a strong electrolyte and hence the dissociation of acetic acid is suppressed due to common ion ($CH_3COO^-$). The result is, the solution contains less $H^+$ ions and more $Na^+$ and $CH_3COO^-$ ions. When a small quantity of an acid is added, $H^+$ ions from it combine with $CH_3COO^-$ and forms undissociated $CH_3COOH$ eq. (i) The net result is pH does not change. When small quantity of base is added, the $OH^-$ ions are neutralized by acetic acid and pH does not alter eq. (ii)

$$H^+ + CH_3COO^- \rightleftharpoons CH_3COOH \qquad \ldots(i)$$

$$OH^- + CH_3COOH \rightleftharpoons H_2O + CH_3COO^- \qquad \ldots(ii)$$

Similarly, in basic buffer containing $NH_4OH$ and $NH_4Cl$ addition of small quantity of base $OH^-$ combines with $NH_4^+$ ions and pH does not alter eq. (iii)

$$OH^- + NH_4^+ \rightleftharpoons NH_4OH \text{ (undissociated)} \qquad \ldots(iii)$$

If a small quantity of acid is added, $NH_4OH$ neutralises it and pH does not change eq. (iv)

$$H^+ + NH_4OH \rightleftharpoons NH_4^+ + H_2O \qquad \ldots(iv)$$

The pH of acidic buffer can be calculated by Henderson-Hasselbalch equation viz,

$$pH = pKa + \log \frac{[salt]}{[acid]}$$

**Buffer Capacity :**

Buffer solutions resist changes in pH upon the addition of strong acids or strong bases. The buffering action is measured in terms of buffer capacity.

Buffer capacity is defined as the moles of strong acid or strong base required to change the pH of one litre of buffer solution by one unit. The larger the buffer capacity, the better is the buffer, since it can accommodate more acid or base without significant changes in pH. As a solution with 0.01 N of acetic acid and sodium acetate has the same pH as that of solution with

0.1 N of these constituents, the later solution can consume ten times as much strong acid or strong base for the same change in pH. Thus, higher, the buffer capacity more effective it is in controlling changes in pH.

**Physiological Buffers :**

The pH of blood of a healthy person remains constant around 7.3 – 7.4. This is because of intricate mechanism of controlling pH by buffering. Normally acidic metabolites are produced in greater quantities than basic metabolites. Carbondioxide, proteins and amino acids contribute to acidic metabolite formation. This is counterbalanced by bicarbonate ions. The combined buffering capacity of blood (to neutralise acid) is designated as 'alkali reserve'. When alkali reserve is depleted metabolic acidosis (acidic pH of blood) develops.

**Pharmaceutical Buffer Solutions :**

Buffer solutions of different types are required for different purposes. Standard buffer solutions are solutions of standard pH. They are used for reference purposes in pH measurements and for carrying out specific tests which require adjustments or maintenance of a specified pH. The special buffer solutions are also required for specific microbiological and antibiotic assays. These are prepared using the reagents specified in pharmacopoeias or standard books. There are many well-known combinations of chemicals to give standard pH solutions. Some well-known names are : Feldman's borate buffer (acid and alkaline), Sorenson's modified phosphate buffer, etc.

**Standard Buffer Solutions :**

Standard buffer solutions for various pH range between 1.2 to 10 can be prepared by appropriate combinations of 0.2 N HCl or 0.2 N NaOH or/and 0.2 M solutions of potassium hydrogen phthalate, potassium dihydrogen phosphate, boric acid-potassium chloride as described in pharmacopoeias.

For the preparation of Hydrochloric acid buffer (pH 1.2 to 2.2) 50 ml of 0.2 M potassium chloride is taken in 200 ml volumetric flask and specified volume of 0.2N hydrochloric acid is added and volume made to the mark.

For Acid phthalate buffer (pH 2.2 to 4) – to 50 ml potassium hydrogen phthalate, specified volume of hydrochloric acid is added followed by water to make 200 ml.

Neutralised phthalate buffer (pH 4.2 - 5.8) - 50 ml of potassium hydrogen phthalate is taken in flask and to it specified volume of sodium hydroxide (0.2 N) is added and volume made to 200 ml.

For phosphate buffer (pH 5.8 - 8) – to 50 ml of potassium dihydrogen phosphate solution in 200 ml flask, the specified volume of 0.2 N sodium hydroxide is added followed by water to make the volume upto the mark.

For Alkaline-borate buffer (pH 8 – 10) – 50 ml of boric acid-potassium chloride is taken, to it specified volume of sodium hydroxide is added and the volume made upto 200 ml with water. Other buffer solutions are prepared according to the need as per pharmacopoeias.

## Some Official Acids and Bases :

### Boric Acid ($H_3BO_3$) :

This compound is covered under antimicrobial agents.

Boric acid is a weak acid (pKa = 9.19) and forms sodium salt (Borate). Both are used in pharmaceutical industry. Boric acid solutions are used as an eye and mouthwash. Boric acid solutions are also used externally in irrigation of organs. It acts as mild antiseptic. Boric acid is employed as buffer in epinephrine bitartrate opthalmic solutions. It is also used as dusting powder.

### Hydrochloric Acid :

### HCl                                                                                                           Mol. Wt. 36

Hydrochloric acid is a preparation of hydrogen chloride in water and contains not less than 35% w/w and not more than 38% w/w of HCl.

**Preparation :** It is prepared by the action of sulphuric acid on sodium chloride (common salt). Concentrated sulphuric acid and sodium chloride are heated in the cast iron pans of the salt cake furnace and the hydrochloric acid gas is passed in a tower which is sprayed with water. The dilute hydrochloric acid which is collected at the bottom, is again circulated to the tower to absorb more hydrogen chloride gas till saturated. The acid so produced is then purified. The $NaHSO_4$ formed in the process is mixed with some more quantity of sodium chloride and heated strongly to obtain more hydrogen chloride gas.

$$NaCl + H_2SO_4 \longrightarrow NaHSO_4 + HCl$$

$$NaHSO_4 + NaCl \longrightarrow Na_2SO_4 + HCl$$

**Properties :** It occurs as a colourless, fuming liquid with pungent odour. It is miscible with water, alcohol and has a specific gravity of 1.18. It is a strong acid and attacks metals forming their hydrochlorides with the evolution of hydrogen gas.

**Action and Uses :** Hydrochloric acid as such cannot be used as medicine. The dilute hydrochloric acid is used as acidifying agent (refer the acidifying agents). Hydrochloric acid is extensively used as a solvent in numerous industries. it is also used as a catalyst in manufacture of basic pharmaceuticals. Various strengths of hydrochloric acid are used as reagent.

**Assay :** Hydrochloric acid being strong acid it is titrated by alkalimetric method using sodium hydroxide as titrant and methyl orange as indicator.

**Storage :** It is stored in glass-stoppered containers at a temoerature not exceeding 30°C.

**Dilute Hydrochloric Acid :**

It is prepared from hydrochloric acid and contains 10% w/w of HCl. This is discussed under acidifying agents.

**Phosphoric Acid :**

$H_3PO_4$                                                                                                           Mol. Wt. 98

It contains not less than 85% and not more than 90% w/w of $H_3PO_4$. It is called as orthophosphoric acid.

**Preparation :** Commercially orthophosphoric is prepared by (i) the 'wet process' or (ii) by pyrolytic or thermal method.

In the wet process boneash [$Ca_3(PO_4)_2$] is treated with sulphuric acid and filtered to remove calcium sulphate and other insoluble material. The filtrate contains dilute phosphoric acid which is concentrated by simple evaporation to about 50% $H_3PO_4$. The crude acid so obtained is further purified.

The thermal process consists of melting phosphate rock with coke and silica at high temperature in electric furnace. The elemental phosphorus is burned to produce $P_2O_5$ and it is dissolved in water to form phosphoric acid.

$$Ca_3(PO_4)_2 + 3SiO_2 + 8C \longrightarrow 3CaSiO_2 + 8CO + 2P$$

$$4P + 5O_2 \text{ (air)} \longrightarrow 2P_2O_5$$

$$P_2O_5 + 3H_2O \longrightarrow 2H_3PO_4$$

**Properties :** Phosphoric acid is a colourless, syrupy liquid, odourless, miscible with water and alcohol. It loses water when it is heated and is finally converted to a metaphosphoric acid, which on cooling forms a transparent mass. It is incompatible with alkali and with cations it forms insoluble phosphates.

**Action and Uses :** Phosphoric acid is not used directly as a medicinal agent. It is used as a pharmaceutical aid in the preparation of dilute phosphoric acid. Industrially it is used in beverages as an acidulant.

**Assay :** It is assayed by alkalimetry method. An accurately weighed quantity of sample is mixed with solution of sodium chloride and titrated with standard sodium hydroxide using phenolphthalein as an indicator. Titration is carried out in presence of sodium chloride to obtain a more accurate end point.

**Storage :** It is stored in air-tight glass containers.

## Hypophosphorus Acid ($H_3PO_2$) :

It is discussed under antioxidants. It is mainly used as antioxidant in pharmaceutical preparations. Hypophosphates are a source of phosphorus and are considered as brain tonics. A dilute (10%) solution is used as a reagent.

## Ammonia Solution Strong :

**Syn. :** Liquor ammonia fortis.

It contains 25% w/w of $NH_3$.

**Preparation :** It is prepared by passing ammonia gas into cooled water until the water is saturated with ammonia.

**Properties :** It is a clear colourless liquid having a strong pungent odour with characteristic taste. It is miscible with water in all proportions. The aqueous solution is strongly alkaline in nature. Some chemical reactions are given below.

1. When ammonia gas is passed over the heated oxides of metals, nitrogen gas is evolved.

    $3CuO + 2NH_3 \longrightarrow 3Cu + 3H_2O + N_2 \uparrow$

2. Ammonia reduces potassium permanganate to $MnO_2$.

    $2NH_3 + 2KMnO_4 \longrightarrow 2KOH + 2MnO_2 + 2H_2O + N_2 \uparrow$

3. Ammonia is a base and reacts with acids to form salts.

    $NH_3 + HCl \longrightarrow NH_4Cl$

4. Ammonia solution readily forms complex ions with cations like Ag, Cu, Au, Zn, Co, Cd, Cr and Mn. The most common is the soluble complex with silver as silver ammonium ion.

**Action and Uses :** It is a strong base and hence is not used as such. Dilute solution of ammonia (10%) is a common reagent and a base. Its salts are used as an antacid, counter irritant and stimulant (respiratory). It is used in various strengths as a common laboratory reagent.

**Assay :** It is assayed by acidimetric method. A known quantity is added to an excess of standard acid which is back titrated with standard sodium hydroxide. Methylred is used as indicator.

**Storage :** It is stored in a well-closed container in a cool place. It is usually kept in amber coloured bottles with a rubber stopper.

**Ammonia Solution Dilute :**

It contains approximately 10% w/w of $NH_3$ and is prepared by diluting a strong ammonia solution with purified water.

It is used as a laboratory reagent, and is known as 'ammonia water'.

**Calcium Hydroxide $Ca(CH)_2$ slaked lime :** This compound is covered under calcium compounds. Medicinally calcium hydroxide is used as a source of calcium as an electrolyte. It being a base it is employed in manufacture of soaps by saponifying fatty acids.

**Potassium Hydroxide :**

**KOH**                                                      **Mol. Wt. 56.1**

It is known as caustic potash.

It contains not less than 85% of total alkali calculated as KOH and contains not more than 4% of $K_2CO_3$.

**Preparation :** It is manufactured by the electrolysis of potassium chloride solution. The caustic liquor so obtained is evaporated and the resulting fused KOH is either allowed to solidify, then broken up or cast into sticks or pellets.

**Properties :** Potassium hydroxide is produced in different forms as dry, hard, brittle pellets, sticks or flakes. It is very deliquescent and is strongly caustic and alkaline. Great care should be taken during handling as it is caustic and destroys tissues. It is freely soluble in water, sparingly in alcohol and glycerine.

**Action and Uses :** It is a most widely used alkaline reagent, it is used in saponification reaction to form potassium soap with fatty acids. It is commonly used as a laboratory reagent.

**Assay :** It is assayed by modified Winkler method which is generally regarded as the most satisfactory for determination of alkali hydroxide and carbonate when present together.

A weighed quantity of substance is dissolved in water and to it barium chloride solution is added to precipitate the soluble carbonate as barium carbonate.

$$K_2CO_3 + BaCl_2 \longrightarrow BaCO_3 \downarrow + 2\,KCl$$

The hydroxide remaining in solution is then titrated with standard acid (1 N HCl) using phenolphthalein as an indicator. Then bromophenol blue is added to the titrated solution and titration continued with same acid. The amount of acid consumed in second titration represents the amount of potassium carbonate present in KOH.

$$BaCO_3 + 2HCl \longrightarrow BaCl_2 + H_2O + CO_2\uparrow$$

**Storage :** It is kept in well closed containers as it absorbs moisture and carbondioxide. As it is highly destructive to tissues, it should not be handled with bare hands.

**Sodium Carbonate :**

$Na_2 CO_3.H_2O$                Mol. Wt. 124

$Na_2CO_3$ **(anhydrous)**                106

It contains not less than 98% (anhydrous) and not more than 99.5% $Na_2 CO_3 \cdot H_2O$ when dried at 105°C for four hours. It is commonly known as soda ash.

**Preparation :** It is prepared by solvay-animonia soda process. Bicarbonate obtained in the process is heated to convert it into carbonate and liberated $CO_2$ is recycled to the tower.

$$2NaHCO_3 \longrightarrow Na_2CO_3 + H_2O + CO_2\uparrow$$

**Properties :** It is a white crystalline powder or amorphous powder with alkaline taste. Monohydrate form gets converted into anhydrous at 105°C. It crystallises as monohydrate, heptahydrate or decahydrate. It is soluble in water and glycerine but is insoluble in alcohol. It is a very strong base as 1 M solution has pH 11.6.

**Uses :** Sodium carbonate is used a pharmaceutical aid. It is mainly used as a reagent. It is used in washing clothes and is commonly known as washing soda.

**Assay :** It is assayed by titrating with standard acid (1 N HCl) using bromophenol blue as indicator.

**Sodium Hydroxide :**

**NaOH**                Mol. Wt. 40

It is known as caustic soda.

It contains not less than 95% of total alkali, calculated as NaOH.

**Preparation :** It is prepared by sodalime process. In this method sodium carbonate ($Na_2CO_3$) is heated with milk of lime $Ca(OH)_2$ in large tanks.

$$Na_2CO_3 + Ca(OH)_2 \longrightarrow CaCO_3 + 2NaOH$$

The product is removed to prevent reversal of the reaction. The mother liquor is removed, filtered and evaporated. The mass is moulded into flakes, pellets or sticks.

**Properties :** It occurs as white mass and is odourless. Sodium hydroxide is a very deliquescent salt. It absorbs carbondioxide and gets partially converted into sodium carbonate. It is soluble in water and freely soluble in alcohol and glycerine with the evolution of heat. It is a very strong base and is very caustic. Great care should be taken during handling, as it rapidly destroys tissues.

**Uses :** It is a strong alkali and hence cannot be used therapeutically. It is used as a common laboratory reagent. In industry, it used in preparation of soaps.

**Assay :** It is assayed by using two indicators. A weighed quantity of sample is dissolved in recently boiled and cooled water and it is titrated with standard (1 N) sulphuric acid using phenolphthalein as indicator. Volume required is recorded. Then methyl orange indicator is added and titration continued till persistant pink (red) colour is obtained. The total volume of acid required gives total alkali as NaOH while the volume required in methyl orange titration gives sodium carbonate content.

**Storage :** It is stored in tightly closed containers as it absorbs moisture and carbon-dioxide.

## EXERCISE

1. Explain the Bronsted acid-base theory. What is a conjugate acid ? What is conjugate base ?
2. What do you understand by Physiological buffers ? Describe the mechanisms of maintaining pH of blood.
3. Calculate the pH of a solution prepared by mixing 5 ml of 0.1 M $NH_3$ with 10 ml of 0.02 M HCl.
4. Calculate the pH of a solution which contains $2 \times 10^{-3}$ mole of sodium acetate and $3.3 \times 10^{-4}$ mole of acetic acid in 1 liter of solution (Given pKa = 4.74).
5. Explain the term Lewis acid and Lewis base with suitable examples.
6. What is buffer solution . What is buffer capacity ? Explain the mechanism of buffer action and importance of buffer solutions in pharmacy.
7. Give method of preparation, important properties and uses of phosphoric acid.
8. Describe chemical properties, uses and assay of strong ammonia solution or sodium carbonate.
9. Describe the principle and procedure of assay for sodium hydroxide (I.P.) or potassium hydroxide.

■■■

# 7
# ANTIOXIDANTS

Antioxidants are the agents which inhibit oxidation and are commonly used to prevent rancidity of oils and fats or deterioration of other materials through oxidative processes. Antioxidants are also described as compounds which can act and function chemically as reducing agents. A number of organic class of compounds like ascorbyl palmitate, butylated hydroxy anisole, butylated hydroxy toluene are commonly used in food and pharmaceuticals as well in cosmetic industry.

Besides the antioxidants, preservatives are added to the pharmaceutical dosage forms to prevent microbial growth and spoilage of the preparation. Some preservatives do act by antioxidation mechanism but others act by different mechanisms.

The inorganic type of antioxidants basically act as reducing agents. They are used in pharmaceutical preparations containing easily oxidizable substances to protect them in their original form. The antioxidant usually prevent the oxidation of active compound and in place gets oxidised itself.

**Mechanism of Action :**

The mechanism of action of inorganic type of antioxidants is the same as it is involved in red-ox chemical reaction.

In a red-ox reaction there is a transfer of electrons from one compound to the other. Since, oxidation is the loss of electrons from chemical species and reduction is the gain of electrons the overall reaction can be shown as

$$\text{Oxidation} + e^- \rightleftharpoons \text{Reduction}$$

when a substance acts as antioxidant (it being a reducing agent) it gets oxidised itself and prevents the oxidation of the active pharmaceutical species.

The efficacy of chemical substance to undergo oxidation reduction can be determined by electrode system. The electrical potential developed in cell can be measured by voltmeter and the measurement of electrode potential is made by the Nernst equation :

$$E_{red} = E^o_{red} = -\frac{0.0591}{n} \log \frac{[\text{Oxidation}]}{[\text{Reduction}]}$$

$E_{red}$ = Observed/formal reduction, electrode potential

$E^o_{red}$ = Standard reduction electrode potential

where $E_{cell}$ is the potential of cell in volts, $E^o_{cell}$ is the standard potential, 0.0591 is the numerical combination of gas constant, absolute temperature, Faraday constant; n being the number of electrons involved and [Ox]/[Red] is the ratio of concentration of oxidant and reductant respectively. The value of $E^o_{cell}$ is found out from the table of standard electrode potentials. The values of standard electrode potentials of half reactions are recorded in books either in American sign convention i.e. oxidation showing positive sign or in European convention as reactions as reductions in negative signs. Hydrogen is taken as a arbitrary zero point for arranging electromotive series of metals. All metals above hydrogen in such series of presentation evolve hydrogen upon reaction with acid while no hydrogen is given out by metals below the hydrogen.

This classification of activity reflects about the nature and strength of substance acting as antioxidant. A strong antioxidant will protect the material when used in small amount and for longer period.

**Other Antioxidants :**

Besides the inorganic substances, a variety of organic compounds selectively act as antioxidant-cum-preservatives. The essential criteria of such compounds is that it should be non-toxic, palatable, computable, neutral in nature, soluble in normal aqueous solvents, and should give no colour or odour to the product. Accordingly, organic type of antioxidants are classified into

(a) **Quinol group :** e.g. tocopherols, hydrochromans, hydroxy coumarans.

(b) **Pyrogallol group :** e.g. amyl gallate, n-propyl gallate,.

(c) **Amines :** e.g. Cephalins, lecithin.

(b) **Benzoic acid derivatives :** e.g. benzoic acid, esters of p-aminobenzoic acid as methyl and propylparabens etc.

The organic type compounds mainly act as preservatives and are commonly used in foods and pharmaceutical formulations These act as antibacterial, antiseptic, antifungal, bacteriostatic etc. and by different mechanism. The discussion of this organic class is beyond the scope of this book.

**The Selection of Inorganic Antioxidants :**

The most important criteria for selection is the activity. It should have a desired redox reaction which can be measured from standard electrode potential and by Nernst equation.

The other considerations are that it should be (i) non-toxic (ii) should be physiologically and chemically compatible. (iii) should be chemically inert and (iv) it should not pose any solubility problem in either its reduced or oxidised form. Some important antioxidants used in pharmaceutical formulations are discussed below :

## Hypophosphorus Acid :

**$HPH_2O_2(H_3PO_2)$**  Mol. Wt. 132

**Preparation :** Hypophosphorus acid does not occur in nature. It is obtained commercially by decomposing boiling aqueous solution of calcium hypophosphite with oxalic acid.

$$Ca(PH_2O_2)_2 + H_2C_2O_4 \cdot 2H_2O \longrightarrow CaC_2O_4H_2O \downarrow + 2HPH_2O_2 + H_2O$$

The insoluble precipitate of calcium oxalate is filtered and the filtrate concentrated in vacuum. Alternatively it is prepared by reacting, calcium hypophosphite with slight excess of sulphuric acid. The precipitate of calcium sulphate is filtered and filtrate concentrated.

**Properties :** Hypophosphorus acid is a colourless to slightly yellowish tinted and is odourless. It is syrupy in nature but forms crystalline solid at 17.4°C. The hypophosphorus acid contains between 30-32% $HPH_2O_2$ and is freely water soluble.

Hypophosphorus acid has two important chemical properties : (i) acidic properties and (ii) reducing properties.

It acts as monobasic acid as only one hydrogen is ionizable.

$$HPH_2O_2 + H_2O \rightleftharpoons H_3O^+ + PH_2O_2^-$$

The acid can be neutralised with alkali hydroxides or carbonates e.g.

$$2\ HPH_2O_2 + Na_2CO_3 \longrightarrow 2NaPH_2O_2 + H_2O + CO_2 \uparrow$$

More importantly it acts as a powerful reducing agent. It reduces many compounds to form phosphorus acid $H_2PHO_3$ (oxidation state +3) and finally to phosphoric acid ($H_3PO_4$) (having an oxidation state +5). Thus, with iodine it forms iodide ions and it decolourises acidic solution of potassium permanganate

$$HPH_2O_2 + 2I_2 + 2H_2O \longrightarrow 4HI + H_3PO_4$$

**Incompatabilities :** Since hypophosphorus acid is a reducing agent it gets readily oxidised by usual oxidising agents. Mercury, silver, bismuth, lead salts are reduced partly to metallic state exhibiting darkening in colour and partial precipitation.

**Action and Uses :** Hypophosphorus acid or the hypophosphite ion do not have any marked pharmacological actions. It is mainly used as a reducing agent in syrup of ferrous iodide wherein it prevents formation of ferric ions and colouration and in diluted hydriodic acid to form free iodine. It is usually employed in 0.5 to 1% as an antioxidant.

**Assay :** Since hypophosphorus acid is a monobasic acid it can be directly titrated with standard sodium hydroxide solution using methyl orange or methyl red as indicator.

**Sulphur Dioxide :**

$SO_2$                      Mol. Wt. 64

**Preparation :** Sulphur dioxide is a gas and it is obtained on small and large scale by several methods. On a laboratory scale it can be prepared by burning sulphur in presence of air or oxygen.

$$2S + 2O_2 \longrightarrow 2SO_2$$

Alternatively it is formed when sulphites are decomposed with dilute acids.

$$NaHSO_3 + H_2SO_4 \longrightarrow NaHSO_4 + SO_2 \uparrow + H_2O$$

Industrial method involves roasting of metallic sulphides like

$$Cu_2S + 2O_2 \longrightarrow 2CuO + SO_2 \uparrow$$

$$2ZnS + 3O_2 \longrightarrow 2ZnO + 2SO_2 \uparrow \text{ etc.}$$

**Properties :** Sulphur dioxide is a colourless, non-inflammable gas with characteristic pungent odour. The gas is soluble in water and in alcohol. Aqueous solution of gas is acidic ($H_2SO_3$) to litmus. The gas can be liquified which boils at $-10°C$.

Sulphurdioxide is a very good reducing agent and thus acts as an antioxidant. When $SO_2$ gas is passed through iodine solution, sulphuric acid and hydroiodic acid are formed.

$$SO_2 + I_2 + 2H_2O \longrightarrow 2HI + H_2SO_4$$

Similarly, it reduces permanganate solution to colourless manganous salt.

$$2KMnO_4 + 2H_2O + 5SO_2 \longrightarrow K_2SO_4 + 2MnSO_4 + 2H_2SO_4$$

Sulphurdioxide is stable only in acidic pH. At alkaline pH it is converted to bisulphite and sulphite.

**Incompatabilities :** Sulphurdioxide being a reducing agent it is in general incompatible with oxidising agents. Its bleaching action removes colour from the preparation.

**Uses :** It is extensively used in industries for manufacture of sulphuric acid. Sulphurdioxide is used for wool, wood pulp and in sugar industry for arresting fermentation and removing colour. Upto 500 ppm is used in soft drinks and other preparations. It acts as antioxidants in some pharmaceutical preparations like injections. The gas is stored in cylinders.

**Assay :** The assay method is based upon the absorption of $SO_2$ into 0.1 N sodium hydroxide to form sodiumbisulphite. The bisulphite so formed is then titrated against 0.1N iodine solution to a pale blue end point with starch solution as indicator.

## Sodium Metabisulphite :

**Na$_2$S$_2$O$_5$**  Mol. Wt. 190

**Preparation :** Sodium metabisulphite is obtained by passing sulphurdioxide gas through a hot solution of sodium hydroxide. In the process, sodium bisulphite (NaHSO$_3$) is formed which decomposes to give Na$_2$S$_2$O$_5$. From cold solution sodium metabisulphite is crystallised out.

$$NaOH + SO_2 \longrightarrow NaHSO_3$$

$$2NaHSO_3 \longrightarrow Na_2S_2O_5 + H_2O$$

Most commercial sodium bisulphite is actually sodium metabisulphite which when dissolved in water, gets converted to bisulphite. The physical and most chemical properties of bisulphite are similar to sodium metabisulphite.

**Properties :** It occurs as a whitish yellow deliquescent powder having an odour of sulphur dioxide. It is soluble in water and forms NaHSO$_3$. The solution of sodium metabisulphite is acidic and neutralises bases like sodium carbonate.

$$2NaHSO_3 + Na_2CO_3 \longrightarrow 2Na_2SO_3 + H_2O + CO_2 \uparrow$$

Sodium metabisulphite and bisulphite are strong reducing agents. Solutions of permanganate, iodine are decolorised by sodium bisulphite and by metabisulphite.

**Action and Uses :** Sodium metabisulphite and bisulphite act as antioxidant. They are used in pharmaceutical preparations like injections to prevent oxidation of phenols, catechols and related compounds.

Sodium bisulphite is used as a preservative in ascorbic acid injection. Sodium metabisulphite is commonly employed as a stabilizer or in many injections in 0.1% concentration. It is also used in preservation of food materials. Potassium salt is more preferred as food preservative. It is stored in tightly closed containers.

**Assay :** This is based on the oxidation reduction reaction as sodium metabisulphite is a strong reducing agent. It gets oxidised to sulphate by iodine solution. A weighed amount of sample is dissolved in water. To it a known excess of 0.1 N iodine solution and 1 ml HCl is added. The excess of iodine is back titrated with 0.1 N Sodium thiosulphate using starer mucilage as indicator towards the end of titration.

$$Na_2S_2O_5 + H_2O \longrightarrow 2NaHSO_3$$

$$2NaHSO_3 + 2H_2O + 2I_2 \longrightarrow 2NaHSO_4 + 4HI$$

$$2I_2 + 2Na_2S_2O_3 \longrightarrow Na_2S_4O_6 + 2NaI$$

## Sodium Nitrite :

**NaNO$_2$**                                                                                                 **Mol. Wt. 69**

It contains not less than 97% and not more than 101% NaNO$_2$ with reference to the substance dried over silica gel.

**Preparation :** The commercial method of manufacture consists of absorbing nitrogen oxide gas (NO) (obtained during the catalytic oxidation of ammonia) and oxygen into sodium carbonates solution. The solution is concentrated to crystallise out the product.

$$2Na_2CO_3 + 4NO + O_2 \longrightarrow 4NaNO_2 + 2CO_2 \uparrow$$

The other methods include the reduction of sodium nitrate by lead in iron pans at around 450°C or by the action of quick lime followed by sulphurdioxide where in calcium sulphate precipitate formed is filtered off and filtrate allowed to crystallize out sodium nitrite. The recrystallization is done from hot water.

**Properties :** Sodium nitrite occurs in the form of white granular powder or white crystals with a saline taste. When it is exposed to the atmosphere it deliquesces and gets oxidised to sodium nitrate. It is very soluble in water and sparingly soluble in alcohol. The aqueous solution of sodium nitrite is alkaline because nitrous acid is a weak acid and its salts are readily hydrolysed in solution.

Sodium nitrite is easily decomposed by acidification with sulphuric acid through nitric oxide to NO$_2$.

$$2NaNO_2 + H_2SO_4 \rightleftharpoons Na_2SO_4 + 2HNO_2$$

$$2HNO_2 \rightleftharpoons H_2O + 2NO + HNO_3$$

$$2NO + O_2 \text{ (from air)} \longrightarrow 2NO_2 \uparrow$$

Sodium nitrite is a good reducing agent. It is assayed against potassium permanganate because of its reducing property.

Sodium nitrite also acts as an oxidising agent as seen in acidified potassium iodide solution.

$$2HNO_2 + 2KI + H_2SO_4 \longrightarrow I_2 + 2NO \uparrow + 2H_2O + K_2SO_4$$

**Action and Uses :** Pharmacologically nitrite action is relaxation of smooth muscles and vasodilation of coronary blood vessels. Because of this action it is considered to be effective in angina pectoris. However, inorganic nitrites have slow onset of action. The organic nitrite like ethyl nitrite, amyl nitrite, glyceryltrinitrite have better onset of action and hence are used clinically.

Nitrites easily form methemoglobin which is turn reacts with cyanide ion and forms cyanmethemoglobin. For this mechanism sodium nitrite is used in cyanide poisoning. Sodium nitrite is also used as food preservative.

**Assay :** The assay method is based upon oxidation-reduction reaction in which nitrite is oxidised to nitrate by potassium permanganate solution. A solution (1:100) from a weighed quantity of substance is slowly added (10 ml) into 50 ml of 0.1 N potassium permanganate solution acidified with 5 ml of sulphuric acid, immediately on contact with acid nitrous acid is produced which is oxidised to nitric acid. Since $HNO_2$ is volatile while adding the solution of sodium nitrite, the tip of pipette is kept below the level of solution. Then excess of standard 25 ml oxalic acid (0.1N) is added, the mixture heated to 80°C and the excess of oxalic acid is back titrated with standard potassium permanganate solution. The reason of titrating excess of oxalic acid with permanganate instead of titrating excess permanganate with oxalic acid is that it is easier to detect appearance of colour than disappearance of colour in a solution.

$$NaNO_2 + H_2SO_4 \longrightarrow NaHSO_4 + NHO_2$$

$$NHO_2 + O \longrightarrow HNO_3$$

(Form permangnate)

**Sodium Thiosulphate :**

It contains not less than 99% and not more than 101% $Na_2S_2O_3\ 5H_2O$.

**$Na_2S_2O_3 \cdot 5H_2O$**　　　　　　　　　　　　　　　　　　　　　　　　　　　Mol. Wt. 248.2

**Preparation :** It is prepared from soda ash, sulphurdioxide and sulphur. Soda ash is dissolved in hot water into which sulphurdioxide is passed. The resulting solution is treated with further quantity of soda ash which is then heated with sulphur. The solution is then concentrated, allowed to settle and is then crystallised.

$$Na_2CO_3 + H_2O + 2SO_2 \longrightarrow 2NaHSO_3 + CO_2 \uparrow$$

$$2NaHSO_3 + Na_2CO_3 \longrightarrow 2Na_2SO_3 + H_2O + CO_2 \uparrow$$

$$Na_2SO_3 + S \longrightarrow Na_2S_2O_3$$

**Properties :** Sodium thiosulphate occurs as transparent, colourless, monoclinic prisms, or as a crystalline powder. It has a cooling, bitter taste. It effloresces in dry air and deliquesces in moist air. It is soluble in water but insoluble in alcohol. The aqueous solution decomposes on boiling because of reduction to sulphide and oxidation to sulphate.

$$4Na_2S_2O_3 \longrightarrow 2Na_2SO_4 + Na_2S_5$$

It is a good reducing agent. The reaction of solution of sodium thiosulphate against iodine is as follows :

$$2Na_2S_2O_3 + I_2 \longrightarrow 2NaI + Na_2S_4O_6$$
$$\text{Sodium tetrathionate}$$

It reduces ferric salt to ferrous salt in both neutral and acidic medium.

1. $2FeCl_3 + 2Na_2S_2O_3 \longrightarrow 2FeCl_2 + 2NaCl + Na_2S_4O_6$
   (Neutral media)

2. $2FeCl_3 + Na_2S_2O_3 + H_2O \longrightarrow 2FeCl_2 + 2NaCl + H_2SO_4 + S$
   (Acid media)

**Action and Uses :** Sodium thiosulphate was considered useful in parasitic skin diseases, in ringworm and in controlling 'athlete's foot' etc. However, now-a-days, it is not used clinically for skin disorders because of availability of more effective drugs. It is effective in cyanide poisoning as an antidote. When used in large doses it causes cathartic action. It is used extensively in photographic industry as 'hypo'.

**Assay :** Sodiumthiosulphate is assayed directly by titrating an accurately weighed (about 1 g) sample in 25 ml water with 0.1N iodine solution using starch solution as an indicator.

## EXERCISE

1. *What are antioxidants ? Discuss the mechanism of action of inorganic antioxidants.*

2. *(a) What are the criteria for selection of inorganic antioxidants ?*

   *(b) Give method of preparation, properties and uses of hypophosphorous acid.*

3. *List the compounds of sodium which act as antioxidants. Give method of preparation, uses and assay for any two.*

■■■

# 8
# GASTROINTESTINAL AGENTS

Gastrointestinal agents are the drugs which are used to treat gastrointestinal disorders. Various inorganic and organic compounds are used for specific actions. In this book only the inorganic compounds acting as acidifying agents, antacids, protectives-adsorbents and cathartic (saline) are discussed.

## (A) ACIDIFYING AGENTS

Drugs which increase acidity are known as acidifying agents. Some drugs are used to increase metabolic acidosis while some are used to increase the gastric hydrochloric acid. In a normal person, hydrochloric acid is secreted which helps in the digestion of food. Because of secretion of hydrochloric acid the stomach has acidic pH. The stomach pH varies from pH 1 when stomach is empty to pH 6-7 when food is ingested.

The epithelial cells of gastric mucosa secrete endogenous hydrochloric acid and enzymes required for digestion. The hydrochloric acid softens fibrous food, promotes, the formation of proteolytic enzyme pepsin from pepsinogen at acidic pH and kills harmful bacteria in ingested food. The proteolytic activity of pepsin is best at pH below 3-5.

If due to some reasons, there is no secretion of hydrochloric acid in gastric secretion the condition is called as achlorhydria. The symptoms of achlorhydria vary in patients. It includes mild diarrhoea, abdominal pain, sensitivity to spicy foods, loss of appetite etc. The lack of secretion of hydrochloric acid thus causes gastrointestinal disturbances.

Some patients suffering from achlohydria respond to stimulation by histamine. The patients suffering from chronic alcoholism, tuberculosis, hyperthyroidism, elderly persons above 50 years can be treated by histamine phosphate. In contrast some patients suffering from carcinoma of stomach, chronic gastritis, gastrectomy there is a total achlorhydria. In such patients administration of hydrochloric acid or acidifying agents is essential. Furthermore, in pernicious anaemia, the lack of intrinsic factor is related to non-availability of hydrochloric acid.

Thus, in order to counteract the effect of achlorhydria, dilute hydrochloric acid is used.

**Dilute Hydrochloric Acid :**

It contains about 10% w/w of HCl and is prepared by dilution of hydrochloric acid. It is employed in 5 ml dose after diluting with 200 ml of water in order to protect teeth from adverse effects. The diluted solution can be injested using straw.

## (B) ANTACIDS

Antacids are the drugs or preparations which neutralise the excess hydrochloric acid secreted in the body. These drugs give relief from pain due to hyperchlorhydria. The efficacy of antacid is measured in terms of its neutralising capacity.

Under the normal physiological conditions, hydrochloric acid is secreted by epithelial cells of gastric mucosa. The pH of the stomach contents vary from pH 1 to 6-7 depending upon the intake of food etc. Due to inflammation of gastric mucosa as in gastritis, there results hyper-secretion of hydrochloric acid which is known as hyperchlorhydria.

This condition sometimes leads to peptic ulcers. Depending upon the portion where erosion of mucosal layer results, it is known as esophageal ulcer, gastric ulcer, deodenal ulcer etc. Invariably there is an intense and continual pain in ulcerative condition and treatment includes, eating certain types of food, use of antacids, antichlonergic drugs and bed rest.

The hyperchlorhydria is treated with antacids. Antacids have alkaline bases and they neutralise the acid. Since the gastric hydrochloric acid production is a continual process, administration of antacids is also required frequently. The use of strong alkaline bases cannot be considered as antacids as they will have damaging effect on mucosal layer. The antacid action should be gradual without evoking rebound acidity. Further, since antacid therapy is usually of longer duration the drugs should not have any side effects.

Antacid, if is water soluble may produce systemic alkalosis because of absorbable ions disturbing acid-base balance of body fluid. With exception of sodium bicarbonate, other antacids in general are water insoluble.

Since antacids act on gastrointestinal tract they exert their effect after being converted into soluble salts by hydrochloric acid. The cations like calcium, aluminium have constipating while that of magnesium has laxative, effect. For this reason calcium-magnesium or aluminium-magnesium salt combinations are commonly marketed.

As stated earlier, the use of antacids is to give symptomatic relief from pain by neutralising the excess of hydrochloric acid. Antacids thus are useful in treatment of ulcers by reducing pain. However, there is no method of evaluation of antacid by measuring pain reduction.

For evaluation of antacid activity, acid neutralising capacity test is employed. It is an *in vitro* test which is based on adding a known quantity of antacid to given amount of hydrochloric acid and measuring the pH of acid at different time intervals for determining the amount of acid consumed by the sample. Some attempts have been made to evolve *in vivo* test similar to *in vitro* test by removing aliquots of gastric contents at different time intervals and measuring pH of the gastric contents. This has not yet been successful and official.

Antacids besides having acid neutralising activity may bring inactivation of proteases enzyme, or denaturation of it by metal cation or by adsorption of enzyme by antacid itself. However, these tests have neither been proved conclusive nor become official.

**Drug Interactions :**

Since antacids act by altering gastric and urinary pH, they do alter rates of dissolution, absorption, bioavailability and renal elimination of number of drugs. It is advisable to avoid concurrent use of antacids and other drugs intended for systemic absorption.

Antacids have been reported to decrease bioavailability of iron, tetracyclines, isoniazid, ethambutal, benzodiazepines, phenothiazines and some vitamins.

Since antacids act by neutralization mechanism, carbondioxide gas is liberated. The evolution of gas causes discomfort and distortion of stomach. To counteract this antiflatulant, compounds are used with antacid preparations. Some preparations contain simethicone a surface active agent to disperse foam. This effect is helpful in reducing gastro esophageal reflexes. Sometimes alginic acid is used as it is thought to protect against irritating effect of HCl during periods of oesophageal reflux.

The following properties are considered as an ideal for effective antacid :

1. It should be insoluble in water and should have fine particle size.
2. It should not produce systemic alkalosis.
3. It should produce its effect gradually and over a longer period of time.
4. It should not have side effects.
5. It should be stable, readily available and
6. It should not evolve large quantities of gas on reacting with hydrochloric acid.

Though no compound or preparation is found ideal for the above criteria some compounds of aluminium, calcium, magnesium are widely in use. Some important compounds or preparations which are official and very common in use are discussed here.

## ALUMINIUM COMPOUNDS AS ANTACIDS

One of the most widely used class of antacid includes aluminium compounds particularly aluminium hydroxide. It is used in three forms : aluminium hydroxide gel, dried aluminium hydroxide gel and dried aluminium hydroxide tablets, which are official in various pharmacopoeias :

**1. Aluminium Hydroxide Gel (I.P.) :**

It is an aqueous suspension of hydrated aluminium oxide with varying quantities of basic aluminium carbonate and bicarbonate. The preparation contains not less than 3.5% and not more than 4.4% w/w of $Al_2O_3$. The preparation may contain glycerine, sorbitol, saccharine or sucrose as sweetening agents, oil of metha or peppermint oil as flavouring agent and a suitable preservative such as sodium benzoate.

**Preparation :** A hot solution of potash alum is added slowly with constant stirring to a hot solution of sodium carbonate. After complete expulsion of carbondioxide the precipitated aluminium hydroxide is filtered, washed throughly with hot water until free from sulphate ion and the precipitate is suspended in water to the required strength and the gel is homogenized.

$$3Na_2CO_3 + 2KAl(SO_4)_2 + 3H_2O \longrightarrow 3Na_2SO_4 + K_2SO_4 + 2Al(OH)_3\downarrow + 3CO_2\uparrow$$

In the preparation, the alum solution is added to the solution of sodium carbonate and not vice versa because that would give a precipitate containing alkali sulphate which will be difficult to wash. In washing the precipitate of Al(OH)$_3$ hot water but not boiling water is used because the latter tends to decompose the aluminium hydroxide. It is to be noted that in the reaction aluminium hydroxide is formed instead of carbonate. This is because aluminium carbonate is unstable and it immediately hydrolyses to give aluminium hydroxide and carbon-dioxide. The precipitation is carried out in a very dilute solution so as to get very fine particle size which is important for maximum adsorption capacity as it gives larger surface area.

Aluminium hydroxide gel is a white viscous suspension and a small amount of clear liquid may separate on standing.

## 2. Dried Aluminium Hydroxide Gel (I.P., B.P.):

It consists largely of hydrated aluminium hydroxide and varing small amounts of basic aluminium carbonate and bicarbonate. It contains not less than 47% $Al_2O_3$ (I.P.) and not less than 47% and not more than 60% $Al_2O_3$ (B.P.)

**Properties:** Dried aluminium hydroxide gel is a light white amorphous powder containing some aggregates and is odourless and tasteless. It is insoluble in water, and alcohol, but dissolves in dilute mineral acids and alkali hydroxides. Heating of this product results in gradual dehydration and loss of therapeutic value. In humid atmosphere, particularly in rainy season, it absorbs substantial amount of moisture and also during processing, thus preservation poses a problem. It should be kept in an airtight container, in a cool and dry place.

## 3. Aluminium Hydroxide Tablets (I.P., B.P.):

Aluminium hydroxide tablets are prepared by wet granulation technique using dried aluminium hydroxide gel. The usual strength is 500 mg. The tablets are evaluated on the basis of $Al_2O_3$ contents. The $Al_2O_3$ contents should not be less than 45% of the stated amount of dried aluminium hydroxide gel.

## 4. Dried Aluminium Phosphate

### Dried Aluminium Phosphate Gel (B.P):

It consists mainly hydrated aluminium orthophosphate. It contains not less than 80% of aluminium phosphate ($AlPO_4$).

**Preparation:** The above product is usually prepared by interaction between aqueous solution of aluminium salts (aluminium chloride) and alkaliphosphate (sodium phosphate). The soluble salts formed are removed by washing and decantation with water or better by dialysis through suitable membrane. The product is dried under suitable conditions. In this product also the particle size is important in its acid adsorption. The particle size depends upon various factors like concentration of reactants, temperature, pH maintained and the manner of addition etc.

**Properties:** Dried aluminium phosphate gel is a white powder containing some friable aggregates. It is practically insoluble in water and ethanol, soluble in dilute mineral acids and practically insoluble in solutions of the alkali hydroxides.

Aluminium phosphate tablets are official in B.P. and each tablet contains 500 mg of dried aluminium phosphate in a suitable basis with a peppermint flavour. The content of aluminium phosphate is between 0.36 to 0.44 g.

### 5. Aluminium Glycinate (B.P.) :

$H_2NCH_2\ COOAl(OH)_2 \cdot XH_2O$

**Preparation :** It is prepared by the interaction of aqueous solution of glycine with aluminium hydroxide. It is a basic aluminium monoglycinate and is partially hydrated. It contains not less than 34.5% and not more than 38.5% of $Al_2O_3$ and not less than 9.9 % and not more than 10.8% of nitrogen both calculated with reference to sample dried to constant weight at 130°C.

**Properties :** It is a white to almost white powder, odourless, practically insoluble in water and usual organic solvents, dissolves in dilute mineral acids and aqueous solutions of alkali hydroxides.

Aluminium glycinate also known as dihydroxy aluminium amino acetate is official in N.F. and used in the form of gel (magma) and tablets.

**Assay :** Aluminium hydroxide gel, dried aluminium hydroxide gel and aluminium hydroxide tablets are assayed for the content of $Al_2O_3$ by complexometric titration, adopting back titrating technique. A known weight of the sample is dissolved in hydrochloric acid and water mixture by warming. Standard known amount of disodium edetate is added, pH adjusted with sodium hydroxide solution and the excess of disodium edetate is determined by adding hexamine and titrating with standard lead nitrate solution using xylenol orange as indicator.

Aluminium phosphate gel and tablets (B.P.) are assayed in terms of $AlPO_4$ content by complexometric titrations using excess of disodium edetate which is back titrated using standard zinc chloride solution.

Aluminium glycinate is assayed for its $Al_2O_3$ content by edetate method and for nitrogen by Kjeldhal method.

Besides assay, another important standard for all above preparations is its acid consuming capacity as described in various pharmacopoeias.

## ACTION AND USES OF ALUMINIUM SALTS

In general, this category contains slow acting antacids. They have mild astringents and adsorptive properties. Aluminium hydroxide gel preparations are used in the treatment of peptic ulcers and hyperchlorhydria. The tablet forms are to be masticated before swollowing while the liquid preparations are administered with water or milk. In peptic ulcers they are administered every 2-3 hours just after food. Aluminium hydroxide preparations react with hydrochloric acid to form aluminium chloride, which has astringent properties and can cause constipation and occasionally vomiting. These preparations on continuous use may cause phosphate deficiency. The aluminium hydroxide preparations are ideal buffers in the pH 3-5 due to their amphoteric character. Aluminium phosphate offers advantage as it does not cause phosphate deficiency, however, it has approximately half the acid neutralising capacity of aluminium hydroxide gel.

Aluminium glycinate acts more promptly and the preparation is not affected by ageing like other aluminium preparations. Aluminium hydroxide gel preparations usually diminish the absorption of tetracyclines and vitamins.

**Dose Regime :**

1. Aluminium hydroxide gel - 7.5 to 15 ml.
2. Dried aluminium hydroxide gel - 0.5 to 1 g.
3. Aluminium phosphate gel - 15 to 45 ml.
4. Aluminium glycinate - 0.5 g to 2 g four times a day or as directed by physician.

**Storage :**

The antacids containing aluminium should be stored in airtight containers in a cool and dry place. The liquid gel preparation should not be stored in freezer as it may break the gel.

## CALCIUM COMPOUNDS AS ANTACIDS

Under the calcium containing antacid, calcium carbonate is of importance. It produces rapid onset of action and largely act as nonsystematic antacid. It produces effect because of its basic property and not because of amphoteric nature as of aluminium compounds.

**Calcium Carbonate (I.P., B.P.)**

$CaCO_3$  Mol. Wt. 100.09

Calcium carbonate contains not less than 98% and not more than the equivalent of 100.5% of $CaCO_3$, calculated with reference to dried substance. It is one of the most abundant and widely distributed calcium salts. It occurs as chalk, limestone, marble, aragonite and calcities and is chief constituent of shells, corals and pearls.

**Preparation :** It is prepared commercially by the interaction of sodium carbonate and calcium chloride. The resulting precipitate is filtered and washed.

$$Na_2CO_3 + CaCl_2 \longrightarrow CaCO_3 \downarrow + 2NaCl$$

**Properties :** It is a fine white, micro crystalline powder, odourless and tasteless. It is stable in air. It is nearly insoluble in water and alcohol. The water solubility is increased by the presence of $CO_2$ and also by ammonium salts.

$$CaCO_3 + H_2CO_3 \longrightarrow Ca(HCO_3)_2$$
$$CaCO_3 + 2NH_4^+ \longrightarrow Ca^{++} + 2NH_3 + H_2O + CO_2$$

Calcium carbonate neutralises acids. This property is common with all other carbonates, for e.g.

$$CaCO_3 + 2HCl \longrightarrow CaCl_2 + CO_2 + H_2O$$

**Action and Uses :** It acts as non-systemic antacid. It produces a rapid onset of action. The antacid action is due to its basic property and is not of amphoteric nature as of aluminium compounds. It has been obseved that it can produce alkalosis inspite of its water insolubility. It has a tendency to cause constipation, and hence it is usually administered along with magnesium salts.

**Dose :** 1-5 g daily according to need.

**Assay :** It is analysed by complexometric titration technique using disodium edetate as titrant and calcon mixture as indicator.

## MAGNESIUM COMPOUNDS AS ANTACID

There are large number of antacids containing magnesium and are official in various pharmacopoeias. They are as follows :

### 1. Heavy Magnesium Carbonate and Light Magnesium Carbonate :

Their approximate composition is $3 MgCO_3.Mg(OH)_2.5H_2O$. They are hydrated basic magnesium carbonate and contains the equivalent of not less than 40% and not more than 45 % of MgO. They differ in their bulk densities. 15 g of heavy magnesium carbonate occupies a volume of 30 ml, whereas light magnesium carbonate occupies a volume of 125 ml (as per I.P.).

**Preparation :** Heavy magnesium carbonate is prepared by the double decomposition from magnesium sulphate and sodium carbonate. Magnesium sulphate and sodium carbonate are dissolved separately in water and the solution are mixed (1:1 ratio) and concentrated. The residue is boiled with water and the insoluble magnesium carbonate is filtered on cloth, washed till it is free of sulphate ions and dried. In the preparation of light magnesium carbonate the process differs in the concentration of reagents used and the temperature of the reaction.

$$MgSO_4 + Na_2CO_3 \longrightarrow MgCO_3 \downarrow + Na_2SO_4$$

**Properties :** Heavy magnesium carbonate is available as granular powder, whereas light magnesium carbonate is available as very light powder. Both are white, odourless and tasteless. They are insoluble in water and alcohol and are soluble in mineral acids with effervescence. When heated they are converted to MgO losing carbondioxide and water.

### 2. Heavy Magnesium Oxide and Light Magnesium Oxide :

**MgO**                                                                                                                                         **Mol. Wt. 40.3**

Both magnesium oxides contain not less than 98% MgO, calculated with reference to the substance ignited at 900°C. They differ in their densities. 15 g of heavy magnesium oxide occupies a volume about 30 ml while 15 g of light magnesium oxide occupies a volume of about 150 ml.

**Preparation :** The magnesium oxides are prepared by heating the respective magnesium carbonates to white heat in an oven.

**Properties :** Both magnesium oxides are white powders, odourless, slightly alkaline in taste. They are practically insoluble in water and alcohol and soluble in dilute mineral acids. When exposed to air they readily absorb carbondioxide.

### 3. Milk of Magnesia (I.P.) :

It is an aqueous suspension of hydrated magnesium hydroxide. It contains not less than 7% w/w and not more than 8.5% w/w of $Mg(OH)_2$. It may contain one or more suitable preservatives.

**Preparation :** Though the preparation contains magnesium hydroxide, it is not made by suspending magnesium hydroxide but by interacting sodium hydroxide with magnesium sulphate. Light magnesium oxide is mixed into a smooth cream with a solution of sodium hydroxide, diluted with water and the suspension is poured in thin-stream into a solution of magnesium sulphate, stirring continuously. The precipitate is allowed to settle, the upper clear liquid is removed by decantation, the residue is transferred on a calico fitter, washed with water until free from sulphate ions. The precipitate is mixed with sufficient water to produce required volume.

$$MgO + H_2O \longrightarrow Mg(OH)_2$$
$$MgSO_4 + 2NaOH \longrightarrow Mg(OH)_2 + Na_2SO_4$$

If the preparation is made with only magnesium sulphate and sodium hydroxide, then the precipitate of magnesium hydroxide gives a gelatinous translucent suspension. With the use of magnesium oxide the suspension appears white and of creamy consistency. Sometimes 0.1% citric acid is added to minimise the action of glass container on milk of magnesia. Besides, it gives a better taste. Usually, 0.5 ml of volatile oils per 1000 ml is used for flavouring purpose. Furthermore 0.2% methyl paraben or 0.125% sodium benzoate may also be used as preservative. The milk of magnesia is dispensed in blue coloured bottles as it enhances whiteness and makes the appearance of preparation more pleasing.

### 4. Magnesium Hydroxide (B.P.) :

$Mg(OH)_2$                                                                                           Mol. Wt. 58.32

It contains not less than 95.0% and not more than 100.5% of $Mg(OH)_2$.

**Preparation :** The magnesium hydroxide obtained in the preparation of milk of magnesia is evaporated to dryness. It can also be prepared by treating sea water or other natural brines with sufficient calcium hydroxide to precipitate magnesium as magnesium hydroxide, then washing and drying of precipitate.

**Properties :** It is a white fine amorphous powder; practically insoluble in water yielding a solution which is slightly alkaline. It dissolves in dilute mineral acids. It slowly absorbs carbondioxide from atmosphere.

Magnesium hydroxide and its tablets are official in N.F.

### 5. Magnesium Trisilicate :

Magnesium trisilicate is a hydrated magnesium silicate of the approximate composition $2MgO, 3SiO_2$, containing water of crystallization. It contains not less than 29% and not more than 32% MgO and not less than 65% and not more than 68.5%. $SiO_2$, both calculated with reference to the substance ignited at 1000°C.

**Preparation :** It is prepared from sodium silicate and magnesium sulphate. Sodium silicate $Na_2O : SiO_2$ of ratio (2 : 3) is prepared by adding sodium hydroxide to sodium silicate. The magnesium trisilicate is precipitated by slowly running a solution of magnesium sulphate into a solution of sodium silicate. The precipitate is washed, dried and powdered.

**Properties :** It is a fine, white powder free from grittiness, odourless and tasteless. It is insoluble in water and alcohol. When treated with acid, it decomposes. When treated with hydrochloric acid, magnesium chloride and trisilic acid are formed.

## ACTION AND USES OF MAGNESIUM SALTS

All the magnesium containing antacids have very poor solubility in water. They go into solution when the acid consumes a small amount of anion already present. When the pH of the stomach approaches neutrality, the dissolution of magnesium salt decreases and stops when pH of stomach is neutral. Therefore, the anion of antacid rather than the magnesium cation gives its antacid property. Because of the magnesium cation, these antacids have laxative action. They are used in combination with aluminium or calcium antacids which are constipative. The insoluble magnesium salts are excreted as such, but the soluble magnesium cation is excreted through kidney, and if the kidney function is impared then it can be reabsorbed and can lead to magnesium poisoning.

Magnesium carbonate is used as antacid as well as cathartic. Light magnesium carbonate being fine powder, is used as adsorbent in preventing the formation of eutectic mixtures in capsules. Light magnesium carbonate is used to diffuse oils in the preparation of aromatic Water. It gives slight alkalinity to it, and if such waters are used to make solutions of alkaloidal salts like atropine or strychnine, then the akaloids get precipitated slowly.

Magnesium oxide is most commonly used as non-systemic antacid. It also acts as cathartic. Light magnesium oxide is preferred over heavy for administering in liquid form as it is a fine powder and suspends more easily. Magnesium oxide absorbs moisture and gets hydrated slowly. In presence of small quantity of water it sets like cement.

Milk of magnesia is a popular antacid and has laxative action. As it has alkaline reaction, it is used as alkaline mouth wash. However, because of alkalinity, it can cause liberation of alkaloids from their solutions.

Magnesium trisilicate being insoluble in water has advantage over other carbonate and hydroxide type antacids of alkaline earth. It neutralises the excess acidity of stomach, without causing the alkalinization of the system. When magnesium trisilicate is ingested, the silicon dioxide associated forms a colloid and acts as a protective agent for the ulcers, thus preventing further attack of acid on peptic ulcers. Dose regims of magnesium compounds are :

(a) **Magnesium carbonate :** 0.3 to 0.6 g as antacid and 2 to 4 g as laxative.

(b) **Magnesium oxide :** Same as magnesium carbonate.

(c) **Milk of magnesia :** 5 to 10 ml as antacid and 15 to 30 ml as laxative.

(d) **Magnesium trisilicate :** 0.5 to 2 g, as antacid.

The above doses are repeated as per the need of the patient.

**Assay :** Magnesium carbonate (heavy and light) and magnesium oxide (heavy and light) are assayed by dissolving them in acid water mixture and titrating with disodium edetate after adjusting pH with ammonia-ammonium chloride buffer.

Magnesium trisilicate is assayed for magnesium oxide content by complexometric (disodium edetate) method after preliminary treatment with acid, neutralization of acid and buffering with ammonia solution.

Milk of maganesia is assayed by adding excess standard acid followed by back titration with standard alkali using methyl red as indicator.

## SODIUM COMPOUNDS AS ANTACIDS

Sodium bicarbonate is the only compound belonging to this class.

**Sodium Bicarbonate :**

$NaHCO_3$ Mol. Wt. 84.01

It contains 99% to 100.5% of $NaHCO_3$, calculated with reference to dried substance.

**Preparation :** On industrial scale, it is prepared by the solvency process. Brine solution (NaCl) is saturated with ammonia to remove impurities, the solution is filtered and passed through the carbonating tower. In this it is allowed to react with a current of $CO_2$ and the tower is cooled to enhance precipitation (sodium-bicarbonate is less soluble in water below 15°C). The precipitate is filtered out and dried.

$$H_2O + CO_2 \longrightarrow H_2CO_3$$
$$NH_3 + H_2CO_3 \longrightarrow NH_4HCO_3$$
$$NaCl + NH_4HCO_3 \longrightarrow NaHCO_3 + NH_4Cl$$

In the laboratory it is prepared by passing $CO_2$ gas through solution of sodium hydroxide. The solution is concentrated to obtain the product.

$$2NaOH + CO_2 \longrightarrow Na_2CO_3 + H_2O$$
$$Na_2CO_3 + H_2O + CO_2 \longrightarrow 2NaHCO_3$$

The medicinal grade sodium bicarbonate is not obtained by solvency process, but it is prepared from sodium carbonate.

**Properties :** It is a white crystalline powder with a saline taste, soluble in water but insoluble in alcohol. Its aqueous solutions are alkaline in nature. When heated to 100°C it is converted to sequicarbonate ($Na_2CO_3 \cdot NaHCO_3 \cdot H_2O$). It reacts with mineral acid with effervescence.

**Action and Uses :** It is used as antacid to combact systemic acidosis. It gives rapid onset of action of relatively short duration. As it is a soluble type of antacid it may result in alkolysis and may cause sodium retention on continuous use. It is an ingredient of effervescent powder.

**Dose :** 300 mg to 2 g.

**Assay :** It is assayed as base by titrating with standard acid using methyl orange as indicator.

## PREPARATIONS CONTAINING COMBINATION OF ANTACIDS

As it is well-known that no antacid satisfies the requirement of an ideal antacid, number of preparations containing combination of antacids are available in the market. The rational behind such combination is to balance the constipative action of calcium and aluminium containing antacids, with a laxative effect of magnesium containing antacid. Sometimes the combination antacid preparation contains one with rapid onset of action, with an antacid with a longer duration of action. In another type, the antacid is combined with simethicone type of compounds which has antiflatulent action as they are antifoaming agents and causes dispersion of gases. Few such combination are official in B.P.

**Combination Preparations :**
1. **Compound magnesium trisilicate oral powder :** It contains magnesium trisilicate, chalk powder, sodium bicarbonate and heavy magnesium carbonate each 250 g.
2. **Magnesium trisilicate mixture :** It is a suspension containing 5% w/w of each of magnesium trisilicate, light magnesium carbonate and sodium carbonate in a suitable vehicle with a peppermint flavour.
3. **Compound magnesium trisilicate tablets :** Each contains 250 mg of magnesium trisilicate and 120 mg of dried aluminium hydroxide gel. Peppermint oil or menthol is added as flavour.

## (C) PROTECTIVES AND ADSORBENTS

Protectives and adsorbents are the chemical agents used internally in treatment of disturbances of gastrointestinal tract. Disturbance in the normal functioning of gastrointestinal tract, frequently results in dysentry or diarrhoea. Dysentery is a disease marked by frequent elimination of watery fluid with or without mucus or blood and results mainly due to infection of protozoa like amoeba. Specific organic antidysentry drugs are now-a-days used to treat dysentry.

Diarrhoea mainly results due to improper digestion or absorption of food or by bacterial infection. Sometimes bacterial toxins and chemical or poisonous drugs also cause diarrhoea. In diarrhoea, there results frequent discharges of intestinal contents from anus in the form of watery fluid. The loss of fluid is accompanied by loss of electrolytes, which frequently leads to dehydration. This also causes electrolyte imbalance.

Number of chemical agents are used to treat diarrhoea . Their main action is of protective and adsorbent in nature. Substances like bismuth subcarbonate, kaolin, bentonite etc. are insoluble salts and they form a protective coat on the mucosal membrane and offer mechanical protection. Furthermore, they adsorb bacterial toxins which are believed to stimulate flow of electrolytes into the intestine resulting in watery stool. These inorganic compounds thus act as protective-adsorbent antidiarrhoeal with little or no antibacterial action. When diarrhoea results due to bacterial infection, or by virus or by bacterial toxins, specific antibacterial or antiviral agents of chemotherapeutic class are used.

Some useful inorganic compounds which act as protectives and adsorbents and which are commonly in use are discussed herein.

**Bismuth Compounds :**

Amongst the bismuth, compounds bismuth subcarbonate, bismuth sub-nitrate are important antidiarrhoeal agents. The milk of bismuth, which is suspension of bismuth hydroxide and bismuth subcarbonate is also an important astringent-protective preparation.

## Bismuth Subcarbonate :

It has approximate molecular formula $[(BiO_2)_2(CO_3)]_2 \cdot H_2O$. It is a basic carbonate and on ignition yields not less than 90% and not more than 92% of $Bi_2O_3$ with reference to the substance dried at 105°C.

**Preparation :** It is made by adding an acid solution of bismuth salt to a hot solution of sodium carbonate and stirring constantly. The precipitate is washed once with equal volume of water and dried at 60°C.

$$4Bi(NO_3)_3 + 6Na_2CO_3 + H_2O \longrightarrow [(BiO_2)_2CO_3]_2 \cdot H_2O + 12NaNO_3 + 4CO_2\uparrow$$

**Properties :** It is available as white or pale yellowish white tasteless powder. It is stable in air but is affected by light. It is insoluble in alcohol and water but dissolves with effervescence in HCl or $HNO_3$. When ignited, it decomposes into yellow bismuth trioxide.

**Action and Uses :** Bismuth subcarbonate mainly acts as antidiarrhoeal by protective-adsorbent mechanism. Since bismuth subcarbonate is basic and water insoluble it also acts as antacid. The small amount of solubility of bismuth cation exerts a mild astringent and antiseptic action.

**Assay :** About 1 g of accurately weighed substance is ignited in a tared crucible to a constant weight, cooled and the $Bi_2O_3$ so obtained is weighed.

## Bismuth Subnitrate :

It has an approximate formula $[Bi(OH)_2NO_3]_4 \cdot BiO(OH)$ and a basic bismuth nitrate. On ignition at 105°C it gives not less than 79% of $Bi_2O_3$.

**Preparation :** It is prepared by adding a solution of sodium hydroxide to a solution of bismuth nitrate at about 15°C with stirring till the pH is about 5. The stirring is continued for some more time and the precipitate of bismuth subnitrate is collected by filtration washed with cold water and dried at about 50°C.

**Properties :** It occurs as a white, slight hygroscopic powder. It is practically insoluble in water and alcohol but dissolves readily in excess of hydrochloric or nitric acid. As bismuth subnitrate slowly hydrolyses in water and liberates nitric acid, incompatibilities with carbonates, iodides, salts of organic acids, reducing agents are encountered.

**Action and Uses :** Its main action is as an astringent, adsorbent and protectant protection and is commonly used in treatment of diarrhoeas and intestinal inflammation. It is given in 2-5 g dose at 4 hours interval. It is a main constituent of milk of bismuth.

**Assay :** An accurately weighed amount (about 1 g) of sample is ignited in a tared crucible to constant weight and the $Bi_2O_3$ is weighed.

## Bismuth Subgallate :

It is a basic salt of bismuth and contains not less than 52% and not more than 57% of $Bi_2O_3$ with reference to a sample dried to constant weight at 105°C.

**Properties :** It is an amorphous bright yellow powder, odourless and tasteless. It is stable in air but is affected by light. It is practically insoluble in water, alcohol and ether. When treated with mineral acids, it goes into solution with decomposition and with alkali hydroxide it forms a clear yellow solution which rapidly turns red.

**Action and Uses :** It is used as an astringent-antacid and protective like the bismuth salts discussed above.

**Assay :** It is assayed in terms of bismuth trioxide, $Bi_2O_3$ gravimetrically.

**Milk of Bismuth :** It is commonly known as "Bismuth Magma" or "Bismuth Cream".

It is a suspension prepared using bismuth hydroxide and bismuth subcarbonate in water. It contains not less than 5.2 and not more than 5.8% of $Bi_2O_3$.

This preparation is mainly used as astringent and antacid rather than protective-adsorbent. It is given in 4-5 ml dose.

Besides bismuth compounds form a clay like material known as 'Kaolin' which acts as protective-adsorbent.

**Kaolin :** It is a hydrated aluminium silicate with variable composition containing traces of compounds of magnesium, calcium and iron.

It is prepared from natural clay by grinding and making it free from gritty particles by eluctriation. Depending upon the physical size of the particle, it is classified as heavy Kaolin and light Kaolin.

It occurs as a soft white powder, odourless and has a clay like taste. It is insoluble in water, in mineral acids and in solution of alkali hydroxides.

**Action and Uses :** It is used in mixtures intented for treatment in dysentery, diarrhoea and for symptomatic treatment of colitis, cholera etc. It is employed in the treatment of food and alkaloidal poisoning as it adsorbs toxins. It also finds use in dusting powder, cosmetic preparations and is an ingredient of Kaolin poultice. For the internal use it is mainly the light Kaolin which is employed.

## (D) SALINE CATHARTICS

Cathartics are the drugs which brings about defecation. Purgatives act similarly but are generally mild in their nature of action; while laxatives are the mild type of purgatives. They bring about the same effect but vary in nature and by mechanism of action.

In normal habits, peristalsis lead to defecation. The peristaltic waves stimulate bowel and relieve its contents. The peristaltic motion normally occur about three to four times a day. By ignoring the urge to defecate voluntarily or for psychological reasons leads to constipation. Constipation can also be caused by many factors like weakness of intestine, intestinal spasm, injury or use of certain drugs and diet etc. In constipation, fecal matter becomes dry and hard. Use of laxative or purgative (lubricants) gives relief in constipation by elimination of bowel contents.

Cathartics or purgatives generally act by four different mechanisms. They are viz. :

1. **Stimulant :** In this, the drugs or chemicals act by local irritation on intestinal tract and bring stimulation of peristalsis activity. Since they act directly on intestine and stimulate peristalsis they are called as stimulants. Drugs like senna, rhubarb, cascara, podophyllum, castor oil, aloe, bisacodyl, etc. belong to this class.

2. **Bulk purgatives** : Bulk purgatives are the agents which increase bulk of intestinal contents. These are cellulose or non-digestable type of materials which swell considerably when wet and due to increased bulk stimulate peristalsis. Methylcellulose, sodium CMC, gum, sapgol are bulk purgatives.

3. **Lubricants** : Third category are the lubricants. Since in constipation, contents of intestine become hard due to absorption of water by body, there results difficulty in clearing of bowels. Substances like liquid paraffin, glycerine, mineral oils etc. act as lubricants and bring smooth clearance of the fecal material.

4. **Saline cathartics** : Fourth category are known as saline cathartics. The saline cathartics act by increasing the osmotic load of intestine by absorbing large quantity of water and thus stimulate peristalsis. Poorly absorbable cations like calcium, magnesium and anions like phosphate, sulphate tartrate contribute to this effect. The saline cathartics are water soluble mainly inorganic chemicals and they are taken with plenty of water. This helps in restricting excessive loss of body fluid and reduces nausea and vomiting.

The following saline cathartics are commonly used for their mild purgative action. The chemicals are taken in the form of suspension, tablet or in other suitable formulations. Saline laxative and cathartic agents include various magnesium salts, sulphate, and tartrate salts of sodium and potassium. These drugs are poorly absorbed and mainly act by osmosis in intestinal lumen.

**Magnesium Hydroxide :**

This compound is discussed under antacids. Magnesium hydroxide is official in pharmacopoeias and act both as antacid and cathartic, in larger doses (2 to 4 g) this acts as cathartic and is commonly administered as emulsion or suspension.

**Magnesium Sulphate :**

$MgSO_4.7H_2O$                                                                                           Mol. Wt. 246.47

It is commonly known as epsom salt. It contains not less than 99% and not more than equivalent of 100% of $MgSO_4$, calculated with reference to the ignited substance.

**Preparation** : It is obtained by the action of dilute sulphuric acid on magnesium carbonate or magnesium oxide or from native carbonate

$$MgCO_3 + H_2SO_4 \longrightarrow MgSO_4 + H_2O + CO_2 \uparrow$$

The solution after reaction is concentrated and crystals filtered out.

**Properties** : It occurs as colourless crystals, with cool, saline and bitter taste. It effloresces in dry air. It is freely soluble in water, sparingly soluble in alcohol and dissolves slowly in glycerin.

**Action and Uses** : Magnesium sulphate is given orally in dilute solutions. About 5 g (which is 40 mEq of $Mg^{2+}$) produces laxative effect. Because of bitter and nauseating taste it is given in fruit juices. The mechanism of action is that magnesium sulphate is not absorbed from intestinal tract and thus retains sufficient water within the lumen. The hydrostatic presser promotes motor activity or perstalsis of bowel. Usual dose is 10-15 g. It should be used with care in patients with impaired renal function. It is also used as antidote in heavy metal poisoning.

**Assay :** It is analysed by complexometric titration using disodium edetate as titrant and using mordant black 11 mixture as indicator. It is stored in well closed container.

## Sodium Phosphate (Disodium Hydrogen Phosphate) :

**$Na_2HPO_4 \cdot 12H_2O$**                  Mol. Wt. 358.2

It contains not less than 98.5% and not more than 101% of $Na_2HPO_4$ calculated with reference to the substance dried at 130°C.

**Preparation :** It is prepared by adding sodium carbonate to a hot solution of phosphoric acid. The sodium carbonate (in the quantity used) does not affect the third hydrogen of phosphoric acid and forms disodium hydrogen phosphate. The solution is neutralised, concentrated and the crystals separated out.

$$H_3PO_4 + Na_2CO_3 \longrightarrow Na_2HPO_4 + H_2O + CO_2 \uparrow$$

**Properties :** It occurs as colourless crystals with saline taste. It is soluble in water but insoluble in alcohol. On heating above 300°C it is converted into converted into sodium pyrophosphate.

$$2Na_2HPO_4 \xrightarrow[300°C]{\Delta} Na_4P_2O_7 + H_2O$$

## Dried Sodium Phosphate :

It is an anhydrous salt and occurs as white powder. It is freely soluble in water but insoluble in alcohol. It readily absorbs moisture and hence should be stored in tightly closed container.

**Action and Uses :** The ionised phosphate in $\overline{HPO_4}$ produces saline cathartic effect due to poor intestinal permeability. The advantage of sodium phosphate is its relatively pleasant taste. It is given in solutions containing 1-8 g of dibasic sodium phosphate and 4.8 g of monobasic sodium phosphate in 10 ml, usual dose, is 20-30 ml.

**Assay :** It is assayed by dissolving in water and titrating with sodium hydroxide potentiometrically till complete neutralization.

**Storage :** Sodium phosphate is kept in well closed container.

## Sodium Potassium Tartrate :

CHOH COONa
|
CHOH COOK.$4H_2O$                Mol. Wt. 282.2

It is commonly known as Rochelle salt. It contains not less than 99% and not more than 104% $C_4H_4O_6$ NaK.$4H_2O$.

**Preparation :** It is prepared by neutralizing a solution of sodium carbonate with potassium bitartrate. The solution is boiled for sometime and neutralised. The solution is filtered, allowed to crystallise and crystals separated out.

$$2KHC_4H_4O_6 + Na_2CO_3 \longrightarrow 2KNaC_4H_4O_6 + H_2O + CO_2 \uparrow$$

**Properties :** It occurs as white crystals or powder with saline taste. It is water soluble but insoluble in alcohol. The salt effloresces in warm dry air. On heating, carbonates of sodium and potassium are formed.

$$2KNaC_4H_4O_6 + 5O_2 \longrightarrow K_2CO_3 + Na_2CO_3 + 4H_2O + 6CO_2 \uparrow$$

Incompatibility occurs with acids, magnesium sulphate and calcium salts.

**Action and Uses :** It exhibits its action by tartrate ions by similar mechanism as of phosphate ions. It is given in solution form for its saline cathartic action. Usual dose is 10 g. It is an ingredient of compound effervescent powder.

**Assay :** An accurately weighed quantity of substance is carbonized in porcelain dish. The residue is extracted with water and sulphuric acid. The solution is filtered and residue washed with more water. The filtrate and washings are combined and titrated for excess of acid with sodium hydroxide using methyl orange as an indicator.

**Potassium Bitartrate :**

**$KHC_4 H_4O_6$** $\hspace{6cm}$ **Mol. Wt. 188.2**

It is commonly known as 'cream of tartar' or potassium hydrogen tartrate. It contains not less than 99.5% of $C_4H_5O_6K$, calculated with reference to the substance dried to a constant weight at 105°C.

**Preparation :** It is usually obtained from the juice of grapes. After fermentation, the crude tartar is known as Argol, which is composed of potassium acid tartrate and calcium tartrate. Argol is dissolved in hot water, neutralised with sodium carbonate and the resulting solution is passed through beds of soda ash and filtered through charcoal to remove the colouring matter. The filtered solution containing sodium potassium tartrate is decomposed by acetic acid when almost pure potassium acid tartrate settles down as a very fine precipitate. Further purification is done by recrystallization.

$$KNaC_4H_4O_6 + CH_3COOH \longrightarrow KHC_4H_4O_6 + CH_3COONa$$

Sodium potassium tartrate

**Properties :** It is found as colourless or slightly opaque, gritty, white crystalline powder, soluble in water, insoluble in alcohol and chloroform.

**Action and Uses :** The mode of action is similar to sodium potassium tartrate. It is used as saline purgative in 2 g dose. In large doses it may cause renal damage. It is also used as a dusting powder in surgery as it is bacteriostatic, and in baking powder to raise the dough.

**Assay :** An accurately weighed quantity is dissolved in boiling water and titrated while hot with sodium hydroxide using phenolphthalein as an indicator.

It is stored in well closed container.

**Calomel (Mercurous Chloride) :**

**HgCl**                                                                                         Mol. Wt. 236.1

It contains not less than 99.6% of HgCl.

**Preparation :** It is prepared by heating a mixture of mercurous sulphate and sodium chloride and condensing the vapours of mercurous chloride thus produced. Mercurous sulphate is obtained by heating mercury with sulphuric acid until dry mercuric sulphate is obtained. The fine amorphous product of mercurous chloride is washed with water to remove mercuric chloride (poisonous) and then washed with dilute nitric acid to remove metallic mercury. It is again washed with water, heated again and sublimate collected.

$$Hg + 2H_2SO_4 \longrightarrow HgSO_4 + SO_2\uparrow + 2H_2O$$

$$HgSO_4 + Hg \longrightarrow Hg_2SO_4$$

$$Hg_2SO_4 + 2NaCl \longrightarrow Hg_2Cl_2 + Na_2SO_4$$

**Properties :** It is a white, heavy, powder, tasteless and odourless. It is insoluble in water/alcohol and cold dilute acids. It is stable in air but turns slightly grey when exposed to light. When triturated with pressure it becomes yellowish white.

**Action and Uses :** It is a well-known cathartic and acts in a dose of 120 mg. The action is due to release of small amount of mercuric ion in the bowel. Now-a-days, it is not used much as mercury salts are in general poisonous.

**Assay :** It is analysed by forming a complex with iodine. An accurately weighed sample is transferred to iodine flask. Excess iodine solution and potassium iodide solution is added, flask stoppered, kept aside, shaking occasionally. The excess iodine is titrated with sodium thiosulphate solution using starch solution as an indicator.

**Storage :** It is kept in a tightly closed container and protected from light.

## EXERCISE

1. Classify the inorganic compounds acting as gastrointestinal agents, give examples.
2. What is an antacid ? Discuss the preparation and uses of aluminium hydroxide gel as an antacid.
3. State the requirements for an ideal antacid ? How is antacid property evaluated ?

4. List the compounds of calcium and magnesium used as antacid. Give method of preparation and uses of calcium carbonate or magnesium trisilicate.

5. Give the mechanism of action of magnesium containing antacids. Describe the method of preparation and assay of milk of magnesia.

6. Which combinations of antacids are commercially available ? Why is simethicone added in antacid preparation ?

7. List the compounds of bismuth used as protectives. Outline method of preparation, action and uses for bismuth subnitrate.

8. Discuss the mechanisms of action of cathartic / purgatives, giving examples.

9. Give method of preparation, uses and assay of magnesium sulphate or mercurous chloride (calomel).

10. (a) What are protective adsorbents, antacid and purgatives, give two examples in each class ?

    (b) Explain the term achlorhydria. How is this condition treated ?

■■■

# 9

# TOPICAL AGENTS

Topical agents are the compounds that act locally on skin or mucous membrane. Their action is of different types depending upon the nature of compound and its chemical properties. They mainly act by mechanical or physical manner. The compounds have very little distinct pharmacological properties as they are not absorbed in systemic circulation.

The effects of compounds are confined to the site of application when they are applied and produce variety of effects like adsorbent, astringent demulcent, emollient or protective. Some compounds also, exhibit antimicrobial and astringent activity topically. Besides large category of organic compounds which exhibit distinct pharmacological activity, some inorganic compounds do have topical action of overlapping type. In this chapter, the role and usefulness of some important inorganic compounds and their preparations having topical local activity is discussed.

The compounds used topically are broadly categorised according to their main action. These are :

(A) Protectives and adsorbents.

(B) Antimicrobial agents.

(C) Astringents.

(D) Miscellaneous compounds.

## (A) PROTECTIVES AND ADSORBENTS

Protectives are the agents that cover skin or mucous membrane from possible irritants. Certain substances being insoluble type and chemically inert act by forming a coat or a film on the skin. Dusting powders being finely by sub-divided, form an adherent continuous film on intact skin and exhibits protective action.

Some chemically inert substances adsorb dissolved or suspended particles or gases, toxins, etc. and are known as adsorbents. Mainly they are used internally to prevent the irritant and unwanted action on mucous membrane [This category is covered under-gastrointestinal protectives and adsorbents]. There are some inorganic chemicals which processes both protective and adsorbent properties when applied topically.

The protective action shown is known as mechanical protection. The protection is given from the external environment by forming a film or coat or a layer on the skin. Some chemicals in the form of fine particles, or when dissolved or suspended in solvents or vehicles, form a flexible-protective film or a layer. The materials in the form of adhesive tapes, bandages, creams or pastes, etc. are used for external applications. The chemicals used for protective purposes are generally, water insoluble type and are not wetted by moisture. The following inorganic chemicals are mainly used as protectives cum adsorbents.

**Silicone Polymers :**

The silicone polymers are generally known as silicone oils. They are represented by a general formula :

$$CH_3-\underset{\underset{CH_3}{|}}{\overset{\overset{CH_3}{|}}{Si}}-O\left[-\underset{\underset{CH_3}{|}}{\overset{\overset{CH_3}{|}}{Si}}-O\right]_n-\underset{\underset{CH_3}{|}}{\overset{\overset{CH_3}{|}}{Si}}-CH_3$$

with the variation of 'n' the viscosity of oils vary.

The silicone polymers are prepared synthetically by polymerisation.

The oily nature of materials make it useful as water repellent and protective to skin from contact with irritants. The silicone oils thus in general act as protective, it also acts as an antiflatulent and used in varying amounts in antacid preparations.

Dimethicone is on inert silicone, oily in nature, it is stable and has low surface tension. It forms a protective layer on skin like plastic and acts as water protective agent. It is mainly used in ointments, sprays, lotions and creams.

**Simethicone :** It occurs as a light gray, translucent liquid with greasy consistency. It is prepared from dimethylpolysiloxane.

It is used as antiflatulent and is employed in antacid antispasdmodic, sedative and digestant preparations. Taken in 40 – 80 mg dose at bed time.

**Talc :**

Purified Talc, Talcum.

It is a purified magnesium silicate corresponding approximately to the formula $3MgO.4SiO_2.H_2O$. It may contain small amounts of aluminium silicate. In nature it occurs as soapstone in the form of a lump.

**Preparation :** It is prepared by boiling fine powdered talc with dilute hydrochloric acid and allowing the insoluble talc to settle. The supernatant liquid is decanted and washed thoroughly with water until free from acid. Acid treatment removes impurities from talc.

**Properties :** Talc is a very fine white powder, free from grittiness. It is odourless and tasteless. It is unctous to touch and adheres to skin. It is practically insoluble in water and in dilute solutions of acids or alkalis.

**Uses :** The inert and unctous nature of talc makes it useful as lubricant and as a protective and dusting powder. It protects the skin from irritation due to friction. Talc is commonly used in cosmetic preparations for external use. Talc is also used as filtering aid. The particle size of 80/100 mesh is employed for filtration purpose.

## Titanium Dioxide :

$TiO_2$                                                                 Mol. Wt. 79.90

Titanium dioxide is a oxide of titanium (IV). It contains not less than 98% $TiO_2$, calculated with reference to the dried substance.

**Preparation :** It is obtained from natural samples of ilmenite or from rutile. The ore is heated with conc. sulphuric acid when sulphates of iron and titanium are dissolved in water. The precipitate of titanium dioxide is obtained by hydrolysis.

**Properties :** It is a white or almost white fluffy powder, odourless and tasteless. It is practically insoluble in water and in dilute mineral acids. It dissolves slowly in hot sulphuric acid.

**Uses :** Titanium dioxide is a good topical protective. The protective action is due to opacity of the compound. It protects skin from harmful ultraviolet radiation and hence is commonly employed in skin protective creams, pastes, etc. Due to white colour it is used in cosmetic preparations and also in paints.

**Assay :** It is analysed by complexometric sodium edetate back titration method. Sample is dissolved in hot sulphuric acid using ammonium sulphate and a definite volume made. To a known volume, hydrogenperoxide, strong ammonia solution, hexamine buffer and excess disodium EDTA is added and the excess edetate is back titrated with zinc chloride.

**Store :** It is stored in well-closed containers.

## Calamine :

Calamine is a zinc oxide with small amount of ferric oxide (to give faint pink colour) and contains after ignition, not less than 98% and not more than 100.5% zinc oxide.

According to British Pharmacopoeia, calamine is a basic zinc carbonate suitably coloured with iron oxide.

**Preparation :** The zinc oxide required for calamine is manufactured by heating native zinc carbonate. The calamine is then prepared by thoroughly mixing zinc oxide with ferric oxide (upto 1%). It is sieved and fine powder is collected.

**Properties :** It occurs as a pink powder, almost odourless and tasteless. It passes through sieve number 100. It is practically insoluble in water and dissolves in mineral acids with effervescence.

**Action and Uses :** It acts as mild astringent, antiseptic and protectant for skin. It has a soothing effect on itching skin and irritations for which it is employed in various forms like aqueous calamine cream, calamine and coal-tar ointment, calamine lotion, calamine ointment, etc.

**Assay :** An ignited and cooled sample is weighed, dissolved in excess sulphuric acid (1 N) and filtered. The residue is washed with hot water till free from acidity. Filtrate and washings are combined, ammonium chloride is added (to prevent precipitation of ferric hydroxide during titration) and contents titrated with sodium hydroxide (1 N) using methyl orange as indicator. The contents are calculated in terms of zinc oxide.

Preparations of calamine common in use :

## Calamine Lotion :

Composition :

| Calamine | .... | 150 g |
| --- | --- | --- |
| Zinc oxide | .... | 50 g |
| Bentonite | .... | 30 g |
| Sodium citrate | .... | 5 g |
| Liquified phenol | .... | 5 ml |
| Glycerine | .... | 50 ml |
| Rose water | .... | to produce 1000 ml |

**Preparation :** The first three ingredients are triturated with a solution of sodium citrate in about 700 ml rose water; liquified phenol, glycerine and sufficient rose water is added to produce 1000 ml.

## Aqueous Calamine Cream :

Composition :

| Calamine | ... | 40 g |
| --- | --- | --- |
| Zinc oxide | ... | 30 g |
| Liquid paraffin | ... | 200 g |
| Self-emulsifying glycerylmonostearate | ... | 50 g |
| Cetamacrogol emulsifying wax | ... | 50 g |
| Phenoxyethanol | ... | 5 g |
| Purified water | ... | 625 g |

**Preparation :** Self-emulsifying glyceryl monostearate and cetamacrogol emulsifying wax are dissolved in liquid paraffin at 60°C and with stirring phenoxy ethanol in 450 g of purified water at same temperature is added. On cooling, calamine, zinc oxide are triturated in it and remainder of water added to produce cream.

## Calamine Ointment :

Composition :

| Calamine finely powdered | ... | 150 g |
| --- | --- | --- |
| White soft paraffin | ... | 850 g |

**Preparation :** Calamine is triturated in white soft paraffin until smooth consistency is obtained.

## Zinc Oxide :

**ZnO**             Mol. Wt. 81.38

It contains between 99-100.5% of zinc oxide, calculated with reference to the substance ignited to constant weight.

**Preparation :** Commercially zinc oxide is obtained by heating metallic zinc in a current of air at high temperature. The metal turns into oxide, which is collected as a fine white powder.

$$2Zn + O_2 \xrightarrow{\Delta} 2\,ZnO$$

The medicinal grade zinc oxide is obtained from zinc sulphate by double decomposition. Zinc sulphate is added to a boiling solution of sodium carbonate. The precipitated zinc carbonate is collected, washed until free from sulphate, dried and ignited.

$$ZnSO_4 + Na_2CO_3 \longrightarrow ZnCO_3 + Na_2SO_4$$

$$ZnCO_3 \xrightarrow{\Delta} ZnO + CO_2 \uparrow$$

**Properties :** It occurs as a white amorphous, fine powder, odourless, tasteless. It absorbs carbondioxide from air. It is insoluble in water and alcohol but soluble in dilute mineral acids and ammonia showing amphoteric character.

$$ZnO + H_2SO_4 \longrightarrow ZnSO_4 + H_2O$$

$$ZnO + 2NaOH \longrightarrow Na_2ZnO_2 + H_2O$$

**Action and Uses :** Zinc oxide acts as mild antiseptic and as astringent. In the form of ointment or dusting powder it is employed in the treatment of eczema, ringworm, varicose ulcers and psoriasis. It is also used in manufacture of adhesive tapes and bandages.

**Assay :** Zinc oxide is analysed by acidimetric back titration method. Though zinc oxide is base, it is insoluble in water and cannot be titrated directly with acid. It is therefore dissolved in excess of standard acid and the excess acid back titrated. Ammonium chloride is used in the titration to prevent the precipitation of zinc hydroxide. The gelatinous white precipitate of zinc hydroxide interferes in the detection of end point. Methyl orange is used as indicator.

**Storage :** Since zinc oxide absorbs carbondioxide, it is stored in well-closed containers.

## Preparations of Zinc Oxide :

**Zinc oxide compound paste :** The preparation contains 25% of zinc oxide (limit 23.5 - 26.5%).

Composition :

| | | |
|---|---|---|
| Zinc oxide, finely powdered | ... | 250 g |
| Starch fine | ... | 250 g |
| White soft paraffin | ... | 500 g |

Into melted white soft paraffin, zinc oxide and starch are incorporated by trituration or stirring till a smooth consistency is obtained.

### Hydrous Zinc Oxide Ointment :

The preparation contains 15% zinc oxide (limit 14 - 15.5%).

Composition :

| | | |
|---|---|---|
| Zinc oxide, finely sifted | ... | 150 g |
| Hydrous ointment | ... | 850 g |

The weighed amount of zinc oxide is triturated with small portions of hydrous ointment until smooth consistency is obtained.

### Zinc Oxide Ointment :

The ointment contains 15.0% zinc oxide (limit 14 - 15.5%).

Composition :

| | | |
|---|---|---|
| Zinc oxide, finely sifted | ... | 150 g |
| Simple ointment | ... | 850 g |

The zinc oxide is triturated in small portions in simple ointment till smooth appearance.

### Zinc Gelatin :

The preparation contains 15% of zinc oxide (limit 14 - 16%).

Composition :

| | | |
|---|---|---|
| Zinc oxide, finely sifted | ... | 150 g |
| Gelatin | ... | 150 g |
| Glycerine | ... | 350 g |
| Purified water | ... | Sufficient or 350 ml |

The gelatin powder is softened with purified water, heated with glycerine on a waterbath till it gets dissolved. The mixture is weighed (adjusted to 850 g) and zinc oxide is incorporated into it with trituration and it is allowed to set to form a paste.

All the above zinc oxide preparations are used for their protective actions on skin.

### Zinc Stearate :

$CH_3[(CH_2)_{16}COO]_2Zn$

It is a compound of zinc with mixture of solid organic acids obtained from fats. It contains variable proportions of zinc stearate and zinc palmitate and contains not less than 12.5% and not more than 14.5% of zinc oxide.

**Preparation :** It is prepared from zinc sulphate and sodium stearate. The sodium stearate is prepared by adding gradually with constant stirring the melted stearic acid to a hot solution of sodium hydroxide or sodium carbonate in a jacketed hot pan. After the addition, the sodium stearate is allowed to cool and zinc sulphate incorporated into it. The precipitate of zinc stearate is collected, washed with water until free from sulphate and dried.

$$C_{17}H_{35}COOH + NaOH \longrightarrow C_{17}H_{35}COONa + H_2O$$

$$2C_{17}H_{35}COONa + ZnSO_4 \longrightarrow (C_{17}H_{35}COO)_2 Zn + Na_2SO_4$$

**Properties :** It occurs as a white fine powder free from grittiness. It is unctous to touch. It is sparingly soluble in water. Aqueous suspension is neutral to litmus.

**Action and Uses :** It is a mild astringent and possesses antimicrobial properties. It is used in dermatalogy for its protective properties and also as an ingredient in ointments and dusting powders. It has lubricant property and hence mixed with granules for manufacture of tablets.

**Assay :** It is analysed by sodium edetate method. An accurately weighed amount of sample is dissolved in sulphuric acid (0.1 N) by boiling. The solution is filtered and residue washed with water. The combined filtrate and washings are titrated against standard disodium edetate solution using ammonia-ammonium chloride buffer and eriochrome black T as indicator.

## (B) ANTIMICROBIAL AGENTS

Antimicrobial is a broad terminology describing activity against microboes. Specific terminology describes exact mode or mechanism of action.

1. Antiseptics are substances that kill or prevent the growth of microorganisms. This term is specific for preparations intended to be applied to living tissues.
2. Disinfectant is a agent that prevents infection by the destruction of pathogenic microorganisms. It is generally used with reference to the substances applied to inanimate objects.
3. Germicide in a broad sense describes agents which kill microorganisms. More specific terminology like 'bactericide' (against bacteria), 'fungicide' (against fungi), 'virucide' (against virus) etc. denotes exact action.
4. Bacteriostatic is an agent which primarily functions by inhibiting the growth of bacteria. Thus, bacteriostatic drugs or agents do not kill but arrest the growth of bacteria.

Desirable properties of antimicrobial agent used as topical antiinfectives are (i) It should have antiseptic or germicide activity and not bacteriostatic activity. If the microorganisms are not killed, they may resume growth and cause infections. (ii) It should have rapid onset and sustained activity. This will reduce incidence of drug resistance. (iii) It should have good therapeutic index indicating usefulness in the concentration employed. (iv) It should not produce local cellular damage or should not interfere with body defenses. (v) It should show no systemic toxicity from topical applications. (vi) It should have, in general, broad spectrum of activity against bacteria, fungi, protozoa, virus etc. (vii) The topical antimicrobial agent should possess favourable lipid-water distribution coefficient so that its effectiveness is best.

**Mechanism of Action :** Various chemical agents are used as antimicrobial, both for their systemic and topical applications. The mode of action of organic class of compounds including antibiotics is well-documented and is not discussed here. Since quite a few inorganic compounds are still in use as antiseptic-disinfectant especially for topical use their role and mechanism of action needs elaboration.

Most inorganic compounds possess some degree of germicidal action yet few find use in actual medical practice. Compounds acting as effective antimicrobial should atleast have some specific property to exhibit action.

Inorganic compounds generally exhibit antimicrobial action by either of the three mechanisms viz. (i) oxidation (ii) halogenation (iii) protein binding or precipitation.

**Oxidation Mechanism :** Compounds acting by this mechanism belong to class of peroxide peroxyacids, oxygen liberating like permanganate and certain oxo-halogen anions. They act on proteins containing sulphadryl group and oxidises free sulphadyl to disulphide bridge and inactivate its function.

**Halogenation Mechanisms :** Compounds which liberate chlorine or hypochlorite or iodine act by this mechanism. The category of agents act on peptide linkage and alter its potential and property. The destruction of specific function of protein results in death of microorganisms.

**Protein Precipitation :** Many metals in their cationic forms exhibit protein binding or protein precipitation. The nature of interaction with protein occurs through polar group of protein which acts as ligands and metal ion as Lewis acid. The complex formed may be strong chelate leading to inactivation of protein. This action in general is non-specific. Protein precipitants do not distinguish between the protein of microbe and that of host. Germicidal action results when the concentration of ion is such that reaction is restricted largely to the parasite cell. Depending upon the concentration used and the extent of reaction, astringent, irritant, corrosive or even caustic action is observed on the host.

Metallic cations with germicidal action of recognisable nature is seen with silver (I), copper (II), mercury (II) and zinc.

## COMPOUNDS ACTING BY OXIDATION MECHANISM

**Hydrogen Peroxide :**

It is an aqueous solution of hydrogen peroxide containing not less than 5% and not more than 7% w/v of $H_2O_2$, corresponding to about 20 times its volume of available oxygen. It contains not more than 0.025% w/v of a suitable stabilizing agent.

**Preparation :** It is prepared by adding a paste of barium peroxide in ice-cold water to a calculated quantity of ice cold dilute sulphuric acid. The insoluble barium sulphate is filtered off.

$$BaO_2 + H_2SO_4 \longrightarrow BaSO_4\downarrow + H_2O_2$$

It is also manufactured by the electrolysis of ice-cold 50% sulphuric acid followed by distillation under reduced pressure.

**Properties:** Hydrogen peroxide solution is a colourless liquid with slightly acidic taste. The solution decomposes in contact with oxidisable matter, reducing agent, when made alkaline or even on standing.

$$2H_2O_2 \longrightarrow 2H_2O + O_2 \uparrow$$

The solutions are stabilised by the addition of small quantities of acid and by adjusting the pH between 2 to 3. Some stabilizers like acetanilid, quinine sulphate, 8-hydroxyquinoline and other complexing or chelating agents are used in 0.02 to 0.05% concentration range. Polyvalent metal ions catalyse decomposition of hydrogen peroxide and complexing agent prevent it by acting as stabilizer.

Hydrogen peroxide acts as oxidizing or reducing agent depending upon the chemical environment. In oxidation reaction (mostly in acidic medium), it accepts two electrons as :

$$H_2O_2 + 2H^+ + 2e^- \longrightarrow 2H_2O$$

In reduction, it helps in evolution of molecular oxygen. This involves release of two electrons. e.g. in decolourisatiom of permanganate solution.

$$5H_2O_2 + 2KMnO_4 + 3H_2SO_4 \longrightarrow K_2SO_4 + 2MnSO_4 + 8H_2O + 5O_2 \uparrow$$

**Action and Uses :** Hydrogen peroxide solution primarily used for its antiseptic action. It exhibits its antiseptic or germicidal action by oxidizing mechanisms. When $H_2O_2$ comes in contact with enzyme catalyst in abrassed (Cut) tissues, the enzyme brings decomposition of $H_2O_2$ into water and oxygen.

$$2H_2O_2 \xrightarrow{\text{Enzyme Catalyst}} 2H_2O + O_2 \uparrow$$

The liberated oxygen acts as oxidising agent on bacteria. The antiseptic action is associated with mechanical cleansing provided by rapid foaming release of oxygen. This helps in removal of dirt, bacterias from cuts and wounds and acts as cleaning-antiseptic.

Hydrogen peroxide is effective against many pathogenic bacterias including anerobic bacterias. The diluted solution (1:1 with water) is used for gargle, mouth wash or for treatment of infections of throat. It is also used for treatment as earwash and vaginal douche. Hydrogen peroxide solution is an effective antidote for phosphorus and cyanide poisoning.

**Assay :** The solution is assayed by oxidation-reaction by permanganate method. Sample of $H_2O_2$ is suitably diluted and to aliquot of dilute sample, sulphuric acid (5N) is added and the contents titrated with potassium permanganate solution till faint pink colour is obtained.

$$2KMnO_4 + 3H_2SO_4 + 5H_2O_2 \longrightarrow K_2SO_4 + 2MnSO_4 + 8H_2O + 5O_2 \uparrow$$

**Storage :** It is stored in containers protected from light, in bottles closed with glass stoppers or plastic caps provided with a vent for the escape of oxygen. It is kept in cool place. The label of container should indicate whether it contains stabilizing agent or not.

## Sodium Perborate :

**NaBO$_3$·4H$_2$O**  Mol. Wt. 153.9

It contains not less than 96% and not more than 103% NaBO$_3$.4H$_2$O.

**Preparation :** It is obtained (i) by adding sodium hydroxide and double the theoretical quantity of hydrogen peroxide to a saturated solution of borax or (ii) by adding sodium peroxide to a solution of boric acid and passing carbondioxide gas into it.

$$Na_2B_4O_7 + 2NaOH + 4H_2O_2 \longrightarrow 4NaBO_3 + 5H_2O \quad \ldots(i)$$

In this reaction the temperature is kept very low (ice). Finally, the mother liquor is saturated with sodium chloride to salt out sodium perborate.

$$2H_3BO_3 + 2Na_2O_2 + CO_2 \longrightarrow 2NaBO_3 + Na_2CO_3 + 3H_2O \quad \ldots(ii)$$

**Properties :** It occurs as white granules or powder odourless with saline taste. It is stable in cool and dry place. It is soluble in water and aqueous solution on acidification liberates H$_2$O$_2$ which decolorise potassium permanganate solution.

$$NaBO_3 + 4H_2O \rightleftharpoons NaBO_2 + H_2O_2 + 3H_2O$$

**Uses :** It is used as an oxidant and local antiinfective. The action is due to liberation of H$_2$O$_2$ and oxygen. It is used in 2% as mouth wash and for treatment of oral infections. It is also used in 10-20% concentrations in dentifrices and dusting powder. It also acts as nonchlorine type bleaching agent.

**Assay :** A known quantity is dissolved in water, solution acidified with sulphuric acid and titrated with potassium permanganate solution.

**Storage :** It is stored in tight containers in a cool place.

## Potassium Permanganate :

**KMnO$_4$**  Mol. Wt. 158.03

**Preparation :** Potassium permanganate is commercially prepared by mixing solution of KOH and powdered manganese oxide, with oxidising agents like potassium chlorate. The mixture is boiled, evaporated and the residue is heated in iron pans until it has acquired a pasty consistency.

$$6KOH + 3MnO_2 + 6KClO_3 \longrightarrow 3K_2MnO_9 + 6KCl + 3H_2O$$

The potassium manganate (green) so formed is boiled with large quantity of water and current of chlorine, CO$_2$ and ozonised air is passed into the liquid until it is converted into permanganate. The MnO$_2$ formed is removed continuously in order to prevent its breaking down the permanganate.

$$6K_2MnO_4 + 3Cl_2 \longrightarrow 6KMnO_4 + 6KCl$$

The solution of KMnO$_4$ is drawn off from any precipitate of MnO$_2$ concentrated and crystallized. The crystals are centrifuged and dried.

**Properties :** Potassium permanganate occurs in the form of dark purple coloured monoclinic prisms, almost opaque with a blue metallic luster. It is odourless. An aqueous solution has sweetish astringent taste. It is water soluble and more soluble in boiling water. When heated, it decrepitates and decomposes at a high temperature (240°C).

$$2KMnO_4 \xrightarrow{\Delta} K_2MnO_4 + MnO_2 + O_2 \uparrow$$

Potassium permanganate is a powerful oxidising agent. In acidic solution potassium permanganate is reduced from $Mn^{+7}$ to manganous ion in $Mn^{+2}$ with evolution of oxygen.

$$2KMnO_4 + 3H_2SO_4 \longrightarrow K_2SO_4 + 2MnSO_4 + 3H_2O + 5[O] \uparrow$$

In neutral or alkaline media also oxygen is liberated. It brings bleaching action.

Potassium permanganate oxidise alcohol to aldehyde, sulphide to free sulphur, ferrous salt to ferric state, nitrites to nitrates and iodide to free iodine under acidic conditions.

**Action and Uses :** Potassium permanganate solutions are used for antiseptic and antibacterial action. It is antiinfective due to its oxidising properties.

The antibacterial action is dependent on its oxidation of proteins of bacterias or tissues. It leaves a stain on skin or tissues. Since it acts by destructive-oxidation process on all organic matter, its use is restricted for external purpose only. Solutions in 1 : 5000 – 1 : 15,000 concentrations are used in cleaning wounds and ulcers and for skin infections caused by bacteria and fungi.

Potassium permanganate acts as antidote in barbiturates, chloral hydrate and alkaloidal poisoning. A solution of 1 : 5000 of permanganate when used as gastric wash, oxidises poison and prevents their absorption. It is also used by vets as antiseptic and in alkaloidal poisoning.

**Assay :** The assay is based upon the oxidation-reduction reaction.

A known weight of sample (0.8 g) is dissolved in water and volume made to 250 ml. To 25 ml of 0.1N oxalic acid is added 5 ml sulphuric acid, contents warmed to 70°C and titrated with the prepared solution of potassium permanganate maintaining the temperature at 70°C throughout the titration.

$$5(COOH)_2 + 2KMnO_4 + 4H_2SO_4 \xrightarrow{Warm} 2KSO_4 + 2MnSO_4 + 10CO_2 + 8H_2O$$

**Storage :** It is kept in tightly closed container. It should be handled with care since explosion may occur when it comes in contact with readily oxidisable substances.

## COMPOUNDS ACTING BY HALOGEN MECHANISM

**Chlorinated lime :**

**Ca(OCl) Cl·H$_2$O**

It is commonly known as bleaching powder. It contains about 30% w/w of available chlorine.

**Preparation :** Chlorinated lime is a product obtained by the action of chlorine on calcium hydroxide. Thoroughly slaked lime is spread on shelves in a suitable container and chlorine gas is introduced at the top of the chamber and passed through the contents of the shelves. This is usually done at 25°C thus minimising the formation of calcium chloride. When absorption of chlorine is completed, powdered lime is blown into the chamber to absorb the excess of chlorine.

$$Ca(OH)_2 + Cl_2 \longrightarrow Ca(OCl)Cl + H_2O$$

The process is rather complex. The first products are basic chlorides, $CaCl_2$, $Ca(OH)_2 \cdot H_2O$ and basic hypochlorite $Ca(OCl)_2 \cdot 2Ca(OH)_2$ etc. The latter is then changed by the further action of chlorine into calcium hypochlorite. The commercial sample also contains small portions of calcium chloride.

**Properties :** It is a dull white powder with characteristic odour. On exposure to air it absorbs moisture and decomposes by liberating chlorine. It is sparingly water soluble and insoluble in alcohol.

When bleaching powder is added to water, hypochlorite goes into the solution and bleaching and oxidising properties are shown.

**Action and Uses :** It is mainly used for its disinfecting and bleaching properties. It is commonly employed in chlorination of water and in treatment of swimming tank. The action is due to liberated chlorine.

**Assay :** The assay is based upon the oxidation-reduction reaction. Chlorinated lime liberates chlorine slowly when it is added to water. However, on trituration and shaking with water, the available chlorine in the sample, is released readily. An aqueous suspension of the sample is treated with acetic acid in presence of potassium iodide in iodine flask. The acetic acid liberates chlorine from the sample which displaces an equivalent amount of iodine from the potassium iodide. The liberated iodine is titrated with standard (0.1 N) sodium thiosulphate using starch solution as indicator towards the end of titration.

$$Ca(OCl)Cl + 2CH_3COOH \longrightarrow (CH_3COO)_2Ca + HOCl + HCl$$

$$HOCl + HCl \rightleftharpoons Cl_2 + H_2O$$

$$2KI + Cl_2 \longrightarrow 2KCl + I_2$$

$$I_2 + 2Na_2S_2O_3 \longrightarrow Na_2S_4O_6 + 2NaI$$

**Storage :** It should be stored in well-closed container and kept in a cool place. It is affected by moisture and heat.

**Sodium Hypochlorite Solution :**

Sodium hypochlorite as a substance in solid form is extremely unstable. For practical purpose sodium hypochlorite in solution form (containing 4 - 6% of NaOCl) is used.

**Preparation :** Sodium hypochlorite solution is generally manufactured by passing appropriate quantity of chlorine gas into a cold solution of sodium hydroxide or sodium carbonate.

$$2NaOH + Cl_2 \longrightarrow NaOCl + NaCl + H_2O$$
$$\text{Sodium hypochlorite}$$

The solution is kept cool during the passage of chlorine gas, otherwise chlorate instead of hypochlorite is formed.

**Description :** The solution is a pale-greenish liquid with a smell of chlorine. The solution is affected by light. It turns red litmus blue and then bleaches it.

**Dilute Sodium Hypochlorite Solution :**

It is prepared from sodium hypochlorite solution. The solution contains about 0.45-0.5% of NaOCl. Official solution (B.P.) states to contain 1% available chlorine. It may contain suitable stabilizing agents and sodium chloride.

Sodium hypochlorite solution is diluted five times by using purified water. The pH of solution is adjusted with 5% sodium bicarbonate solution such that it does not give colour with phenolphthalein indicator. The solution is almost colourless or has slight yellow colour with faint odour of chlorine. The label should state (i) the date of expiry and (ii) the container under which it should be stored.

**Action and Uses :** The solution of sodium hypochlorite is too strong to be used on tissues because of its caustic (alkalinity) and oxidising actions. The dilute solution is primarily used for disinfectant and antibacterial action. The action is partly due to liberation of chlorine (on contact with acid) and due to oxidising action produced, by liberation of oxygen.

$$4NaOCl + 4HCl \longrightarrow 4NaCl + 4HOCl$$
$$4HOCl \longrightarrow 2Cl_2 \uparrow + O_2 \uparrow + 2H_2O$$

The diluted solution moreover, reduces caustic action of high alkalinity of solution and increases effectiveness of hypochlorite

$$HCO_3^- + OH^- \rightleftharpoons CO_3^{-2} + H_2O$$

The equilibrium is shifted to right side by providing excess of bicarbonate ions. Sodium hypochlorite solution is primarily used as disinfectant (for instruments, utensils etc.), deodorant and bleaching in laundry wash. The diluted solution is used as germicidal by continuous irrigation. It not only exerts a germicidal action but also dissolves necrotic tissue. It has a disadvantage that it dissolves blood clot, delays clotting and thus leads to haemorrhage. The diluted solution is used as foot bath (prevent fungal infection) and also as deodorant.

**Assay :** Hypochlorites are often evaluated in terms of 'available chlorine'. The method is similar to chlorinated lime.

A weighed amount of sample is treated with acetic acid and potassium iodide. The iodine liberated is titrated with standard sodium thiosulphate solution using starch as an indicator.

**Storage :** The sodium hypochlorite being unstable, the solution is stored in tight, light-resistant containers and kept in a cool place. The diluted solution (1 : 3) is commonly used for antibacterial action.

## Iodine and Iodine Preparations :

**Iodine :** This is discussed separately under the chapter 'Official Compounds of Iodine'. The important iodine preparations acting as antimicrobial by halogenation mechanisms are given below :

### Aqueous Iodine Solution :

It is known as Lugol's solution. It contains 5% w/v of iodine and 10% w/v of potassium iodide in water.

Composition :

| | | |
|---|---|---|
| Iodine | ... | 50 g |
| Potassium iodide | ... | 100 g |
| Purified water sufficient to produce | ... | 1000 ml |

**Preparation :** Potassium iodide and iodine are dissolved in 100 ml of water with trituration and shaking. The volume is made up to 1000 ml.

**Description :** It is a transparent, brown liquid with the smell of iodine.

### Weak Iodine Solution :

It is commonly known as "tincture of iodine". The solution contains 2% w/v of iodine and 2.5% w/v of potassium iodide in 50% alcohol.

Composition :

| | | |
|---|---|---|
| Iodine | ... | 20 g |
| Potassium iodide | ... | 25 g |
| Alcolol (50%) | ... | 1000 ml |

**Preparation :** Potassium iodide and iodine are dissolved in sufficient 50% alcohol by shaking and volume is made up to 1000 ml.

**Description :** It is a transparent, brown liquid with strong smell of iodine and alcohol.

### Strong Iodine Solution :

It contains 10% w/v of iodine and 6% w/v of potassium iodide in alcohol-water mixture.

Composition :

| | | |
|---|---|---|
| Iodine | ... | 100 g |
| Potassium iodide | ... | 60 g |
| Purified water Alcohol (90%) sufficient to produce | ... | 1000 ml |

**Preparation :** Potassium iodide and iodine are dissolved by trituration in purified water and sufficient alcohol (90%) is added to produce 1000 ml.

**Description :** It is a transparent liquid having reddish brown colour with the odour of iodine and alcohol. It is affected by light.

The other iodine containing preparations for antibacterial action are :

Iodine ointment (containing about 6.5-7.5% iodine in yellow-waxpetrolatum base), phenolated iodine solution (containing 15 ml of strong iodine solution, 6 ml liquified phenol in glycerine-water-1000 ml). These preparations are not much in use now-a-days.

**Action and Uses :** The aqueous iodine solution and weak iodine (tincture) solutions are well-known antiseptic for topical applications. They are used for disinfection of skin prior to surgery. The dilute solutions are used for application to wounds, abrasions and cuts. Tile official solution and tincture are effective against bacterial and fungal infectious of skin. The alcohol in tincture preparation causes irritation, to open tissues than aqueous solution. Aqueous solutions of 0.5 to 2% iodine with iodide are suitable for wounds and abrasions and 0.1% is suitable for irrigations. Iodine tincture is also used to disinfect drinking water 2 to 4 drops of tincture to a quart of water acts as amoebicidal and bactericidal. Iodine preparations should be used with caution in patients showing hypersensitivity to iodine.

**Assay :** In the aqueous iodine solution, iodine is titrated against standard sodium thiosulphate and potassium iodide is titrated in acid medium against potassium iodate using chloroform for detection of end point (Andrew's method).

Weak iodine solution is assayed for iodine content (against sodium thiosulphate solution), potassium iodide using potassium iodate (in presence of HCl and potassium cyanide) and for alcohol content.

The strong iodine solution is analysed for its alcohol content by pharmacopoeial method.

**Storage :** The iodine preparations are stored in well-closed containers of glass or plastic having wax liner bungs.

**Povidone-Iodine Solution :**

Povidone-iodine solution is an aqueous solution of povidone-iodine a complex produced by the interaction between iodine and povidone (polyvinyl pyrrolidine). The complex contains about 10% w/v of available iodine.

**Description :** The complex is a yellowish brown, amorphous powder and has characteristic odour. It is soluble in water and alcohol. The solution is transparent in nature and has reddish-brown colour and faint smell of iodine. The aqueous solution has acidic pH.

**Action and Uses :** In 10% povidone-iodine, the free iodine content is only 0.001%. When this is diluted to 0.1% the free iodine content increases and becomes more powerful bactericidal. Thus, povidoneiodine should be diluted before use.

Disinfection of skin, mouth or wounds by using povidone-iodine solution is very common. It is also effective in the management of burns and cuts. Povidone iodine is available in wide variety of preparations for applications to the skin and mucous membrane and for use as disinfectant.

Important advantage of this preparation over usual iodine preparations being its water solubility, non-irritation, less toxicity and non-staining nature. It can be easily removed from skin and clothes by washing.

**Assay :** It is analysed for the available iodine content. For the povidone-iodine complex, a known weight of sample is dissolved in water (Using stirrer for complete solution) and it is titrated against standard sodium thiosulphate using starch as indicator. A blank is also performed.

**For Solution :** A known volume of sample is titrated against standard sodium thiosulphate solution (0.02 N).

**Storage :** It is kept in a closed container.

Aqueous solutions (0.1-1% of available iodine), aerosol (0.5%), surgical scrub (0.75-1%) and vaginal gel (0.1%) are commonly used preparations of povidone-iodine.

## COMPOUNDS ACTING BY PROTEIN PRECIPITATION

Compounds discussed under here act mainly by their ability to inactivate protein by precipitation or complexation. They have weak to strong action depending upon the inorganic ion (cation) playing role. It is well-known that inorganic acids also have germicidal action. Dilute hydrochloric acid, dilute nitric acid were known germicidal for external use. Though these are not used now-a-days, boric acid and borax do have mild bacteriostic action.

Some medicinally useful inorganic compounds acting by protein precipitation mechanism are given below :

**Boric Acid :**

$H_3O_3$ $\qquad$ Mol. Wt. 61.83

It contains not less than 99.5% and not more than 100.5% $H_3BO_3$, calculated with reference to the substance dried over sulphuric acid for five hours.

Boric acid occurs abundantly in nature in various forms like $Na_2B_4O_7 \cdot 4H_2O$ (resonate), $Na_2B_4O_7 \cdot 10 H_2O$ (borax), $CaB_4O_7 \cdot 4H_2O$ (boracalcite) and $Ca_2B_6O_{11} 5H_2O$ (colemanite).

**Preparation :** It is prepared by adding dilute sulphuric acid to a boiling solution of borax in water on a laboratory scale.

$$Na_2B_4O_7 + H_2SO_4 + 5H_2O \longrightarrow Na_2SO_4 + 4H_3BO_3$$

High grado boric acid for medicinal use is prepared by treating borax with hydrochloric acid. Since HCl is volatile, residual traces of HCl do not remain on the crystals, when dried in air.

**Commercial Manufacture :** It is obtained by decomposition of certain naturally occurring borates, like colemanite, resonite, etc. For example, colemanite is reduced to a powder, mixed with boiling water and the suspension is then treated with sulphurdioxide gas to liberate boric acid.

$$Ca_2B_6O_{11} \cdot 5H_2O + 2SO_2 + 4H_2O \longrightarrow 2CaSO_3 + 6H_3BO_3$$

The solution is cooled and boric acid is crystallised out.

**Properties :** Boric acid is a solid available mostly in three forms (i) colourless, odourless pearly scales, (ii) six sided triclinic crystals and (ii) white odourless powder which is unctous to touch. It is stable in air and has a density of 1.46. It is sparingly soluble in water, more in boiling water and alcohol. It dissolves readily in glycerine.

Boric acid is weak acid and has pKa = 9.19 for the ionization of its first proton. Heating orthoboric acid to certain temperatures, produces various dehydration products.

Heating at 100°C $\quad\quad H_3BO_3 \longrightarrow HBO_2 + H_2O$
$\quad\quad\quad\quad\quad\quad\quad\quad\quad\quad\quad\quad\quad\quad\quad$ (metaboric acid)

Heating at 160°C $\quad\quad 4HBO_2 \longrightarrow H_2B_4O_7 + H_2O$
$\quad\quad\quad\quad\quad\quad\quad\quad\quad\quad\quad\quad\quad\quad\quad$ (tetraboric acid)

Further heating $\quad\quad\quad H_2B_4O_7 \longrightarrow 2B_2O_3 + H_2O$
$\quad\quad\quad\quad\quad\quad\quad\quad\quad\quad\quad\quad\quad\quad\quad$ (borontrioxide)

Boric acid, when dissolved in glycerine, behaves as a strong acid. The glyceroboric acid is monoprotic acid.

$$2\begin{array}{c}CH_2OH\\|\\CHOH\\|\\CH_2OH\end{array} + H_3BO_3 \longrightarrow \left[\begin{array}{c}H_2-C-OH \quad HO-C-H_2\\|\quad\quad\quad\quad\quad\quad\quad|\\H-C-O\diagdown\quad\diagup O-C-H\\\quad\quad\quad B\\H_2-C-O\diagup\quad\diagdown O-C-H_2\end{array}\right]^- + H_3O^+ + 2H_2O$$

**Action and Uses :** Boric acid is used in preparation of buffer solution. It is also used to maintain acidic pH of medium in various topical medications. It finds use in opthalmic solutions. Boric acid and borate have no germicidal action. It has feeble bacteriostatic action. It is used in solutions, ointments, cream and as dusting powder. Boric acid being non-irritating and less toxic (when applied to intact skin) it is used in ointment for emolliant and antiseptic action. However, when it is ingested (accidentally) or absorbed through broken skin produces toxicity. Boric acid solutions are used mainly as eye and mouth wash (in 2 to 5%) for local antiinfective action. Since boric acid has smooth unctous touch it is employed as a ingredient in dusting powder.

**Assay :** Boric acid in aqueous solution is a weak acid and hence it cannot be titrated accurately with standard alkali. However, when it is dissolved in glycerine-water mixture it acts like a strong monobasic acid and can be titrated with standard alkali using phenolpthalein as an indicator. Instead of glycerine other polyhydroxy compounds like mannitol can be used to enhance its acidity.

**Storage :** It is stored in well-closed container.

Boric acid ointment (10% Boric acid), boric acid solution (5%) and boroglycerin glycerite 3% are some commonly used preparations of boric acid.

## Borax :

### $Na_2B_4O_7 \cdot 10H_2O$ 
Mol. Wt. 378

It is known as sodium borate. It contains not less than 99% and not more than the equivalent of 103% of $Na_2B_4O_7.10H_2O$.

### Preparation :

1. The mineral colemanite is mixed with sodium sulphate and heated to redness but not to fusion in a rotary furnace. After the mass has cooled, borax is dissolved in water and allowed to crystallise, after removing insoluble calcium sulphate.

   $$2Ca_2B_6O_{11} + 3Na_2SO_2 \longrightarrow 3CaSO_4 \downarrow + CaO + 2Na_3B_6O_8$$

2. The mineral borocalcite is also converted into borax by this method.

   $$CaB_4O_7 \cdot 4H_2O + Na_2SO_4 \longrightarrow Na_2B_4O_7 + CaSO_4 \downarrow + 4H_2O$$

**Properties :** Borax occurs as colourless, odourless crystals or as a white crystalline powder that has sweetish, alkaline taste. It effloresces in warm dry air. It is soluble in water, more in boiling water and in glycerine. It is insoluble in alcohol.

On heating it loses part of its water of hydration and swells to a white porous powder. When heated to red hot, on cooling forms a transparent mass known as borax bead. An aqueous solution of sodium borate is distinctly alkaline to litmus. Alkali borates are water soluble. Borates of other metals undergo hydrolysis and forms insoluble hydroxides or oxides.

**Action and Uses :** Similar to boric acid, borax is used in external application preparations. It is a feeble germicide or fair bacteriostatic. Borax is used in preparations of eye wash (1-2%) and as mouth wash and gargles. Borax has been used as food preservative. It is used in cosmetic preparations as emulsifier and also in lotions.

## Silver Compounds and Preparations :

From the various silver compounds silver nitrate and its preparations are mainly of medicinal interest. Solutions of soluble silver salts are in general germicidal, astringent, irritant and corrosive depending upon the concentration used.

Silver ion precipitates proteins as well as chloride ion of tissue fluids. The germicidal property of silver ions is due to precipitation of proteins. The precipitating action also localises the irritating effect of silver ion within specified area of treatment.

Silver ions being photosensitive, causes discoloration of skin. Silver compounds show several types of incompatabilities. Because of light sensitivity, silver compounds and preparations are stored in darkcoloured bottles.

## Silver Nitrate :

### $AgNO_3$
Mol. Wt. 170

It contains between 99.5 - 100 5% w/w of $AgNO_3$.

**Preparation**: It is prepared by the action of diluted nitric acid on pure silver. 3 parts of silver are added to a solution of 25% nitric acid (about 10 parts) and it is warmed. Then it is heated to expell the nitrous fumes, filtered and evaporated until it is dry. The mass is then fused so that any copper nitrate present is converted into insoluble oxide. The product so obtained is dissolved in hot water, filtered and kept aside in dark place for crystallization. The crystals are collected on sintered glass crucible or any suitable device and dried at about 50°C in dark.

$$3\,Ag + 4\,HNO_3 \longrightarrow 3AgNO_3 + NO\uparrow + 2H_2O$$

$$2Cu(NO_3)_2 \xrightarrow{\Delta} 2CuO + 4NO_2\uparrow + O_2$$

The purification of silver nitrate is costly, thus it is preferred to use pure silver and nitric acid (free from halogen, sulphur).

**Properties**: Silver nitrate occurs as colourless crystalline compound, odourless, bitter to taste and metallic in lusture. When it is exposed to light or organic matter it turns grey or greyish black. It is highly soluble in water, more soluble in boiling water and also in alcohol.

When it is heated, it melts at 212°C to yellowish liquid and when heated further to red heat, it decomposes into metallic silver with evolution of $NO_2$ and $O_2$.

$$2AgNO_3 \longrightarrow 2Ag + 2NO_2\uparrow + O_2\uparrow$$

Solution of silver nitrate gives white-yellow-white precipitate with hydrochloric acid and other halogen containing salts. This is the most common incompatability of silver nitrate. The silver halide precipitate is insoluble in dilute acids but dissolves in ammonia.

With ammonium hydroxide, silver nitrate forms silver-ammonium complex. To this solution of complex, if a reducing agent like formaldehyde or glucose is added, the silver ions are reduced to metallic silver and silver mirror is formed. The incompatabilities result with reducing agents, tartrate, sugars and tannins. In neutral and alkaline conditions precipitation results with halides, borax, hydroxide, phosphate, sulphate, chromates, etc.

The protein precipitation action of silver ion and of other metal, ions is not selective as it precipitates both bacterial and human proteins. The range of activity from antibacterial to corrosive depends on the concentration employed.

**Action and Uses**: Silver nitrate is used as antibacterial in concentration from 0.01 to 0.5%. In higher concentration (1% and above) it has astringent, irritant properties on tissues. In low concentrations; (0.0025 – 0.005%) it acts as bacteriostatic. This is due to oligodynamic action of silver ion. The antibacterial action is due to protein precipitation of bacterial cells. The polar groups present in protein like – SH, – $NH_2$, – COOH are reacted with silver ions.

Silver nitrate ophthalmic solution in 1% strength is used as eye wash, in 0.5% aqueous strength is used in treating burn injuries and in wet dressings. Silver nitrate solutions are effective against coccal (gonococcal, staphylococcal etc.) infections.

**Assay :** Argentometric method is used. An accurately weighed amount of substance is dissolved in water, acidified with dilute nitric acid and it is titrated with standard ammonium thiocyanate solution using ferric ammonium sulphate as an indicator (until brick-red colour is obtained).

**Storage :** Since silver nitrate is light sensitive, it is stored in amber-coloured bottles in a cool and dark place.

### Mild Silver Protein :

It is a preparation wherein silver is rendered colloidal by the presence of proteins or in combination with it. It contains not less than 19% and not more than 23% of silver.

**Preparation :** It is prepared by using silver salts with an excess of denatured protein (serum albumin, casein or alkaline gelatin). The product is dried in vacuum and stored in amber coloured bottles.

**Properties :** It is dark brown-blackish shining scales or granules, odourless and is hygroscopic. It is soluble in water but insoluble in alcohol, ether and chloroform.

**Action and Uses :** Aqueous solutions in concentration range of 1-2% are used as antibacterial. In treatment of rhinits, tonsilities it is used in 0.5-10%; in conjunctintis in 2-10%; in urethritis in 0.25-1%; in cervico vaginitis in 2-10%. Only freshly prepared solutions should be used. The mild silver protein though has less free silver ions it is an effective antibacterial and shows less irritation or astringent effect.

**Assay :** An accurately weighed sample is first heated gently and then ignited to destroy carbonaceous matter. The residue is dissolved in nitric acid, diluted with water and titrated with ammonium thiocyanate using ferric ammonium sulphate as indicator.

**Storage :** It is stored in tightly closed amber-coloured glass containers, in dry and dark place. Disodium-edetate in 10 mg/ml concentration is used as stabilizer for aqueous solutions.

### Strong Silver Protein :

It is a compound of silver and protein, partially hydrolysed peptone and albumose and contains not less than 7.5% and not more than 8.5% of silver.

**Preparation :** It is prepared by the action of soluble silver salts on proteins. One of the method makes use of precipitation of peptone solution with silver nitrate or moist silver oxide and dissolving the silver-peptone in excess of peptone and drying in vacuum.

**Properties :** It is available as brown odourless hygroscopic powder. It slowly dissolves in water forming dark brown solution and is insoluble in alcohol and chloroform.

**Action and Uses :** Similar to mild silver protein, this also acts as antibacterial. It contains high amount of free silver ions and hence is irritating to the mucous membrane. It is employed in 0.25 - 0.5% as aqueous suspension for creating burns and for irrigation of urethra bladder and in treatment of gonorrhoea.

**Assay :** The method is same as described under mild-silver protein.

**Storage :** It is also photosensitive and hence stored in amber-coloured bottles.

The indiscriminate use of silver preparation in variety of treatments has led to cases of 'argyria'. In this condition, the skin becomes pigmented. Use of silver preparations, which were very popular earlier have diminished because of availability of better drugs.

**Mercury Compounds :**

Mercury compounds find number of applications in pharmaceutical and medicinal field. Mercury, mercurous (I) and mercuric (II) compounds are strong oxidizing agents, and even mild reducing agents cause, decomposition. Mercury (II) forms complex readily with a wide range of ligands.

From medicinal point of view, in general, mercury compounds are light-sensitive, toxic, irritant, bacteriostatic and have non-specific protein precipitation action. Organomercuric compounds are less irritating, germicidal diuretic, antifungal, disinfectant, antisyphilitic etc. Some important compounds mainly useful for topical applications are discussed here.

**Mercury :**

**Hg** At. Wt. 201

It contains not less than 99.5% Hg. It occurs naturally as a sulphide called cinnabar. It is also found in small globules diseminated through rocks and as a amalgam of silver or of gold. It is obtained by roasting cinnabar in a current of air.

$$HgS + O_2 \longrightarrow Hg + SO_2$$

**Properties :** It is a shining silvery white, heavy liquid, easily divisible into globules and extremely mobile. It is practically insoluble in water, alcohol and hydrochloric acid but completely soluble in nitric acid and boiling sulphuric acid. It boils at 356°C. Mercury expands rapidly and uniformly when heated and thus used in thermometers.

**Action and Uses :** Formerly, mercury was used for preparation of mild mercurial ointment to be used as local parasiticide and in treatment of syphilis. This use is less popular and almost extinct because of availability of better drugs. A preparation known as mercury with chalk acts as purgative because of irritant action of mercury ion. Mercury in general being toxic, is not used medicinally. There are number of other pharmaceutical uses of mercury like preparation of mercury compounds, amalgams, etc.

**Assay :** An accurately weighed quantity is dissolved in equal volume of nitric acid-water by heating to form mercuric nitrate. It is then titrated with ammonium thiocyanate using ferric ammonium sulphate as indicator.

**Storage :** As it is volatile, it is stored in tightly closed container in a cool place.

## Yellow Mercuric Oxide :

**HgO**  Mol. Wt. 217

It contains not less than 99% of HgO, calculated with reference to the substance dried at 105°C for one hour.

**Preparation :** It is prepared by pouring a concentrated solution of mercuric chloride into a dilute solution of sodium hydroxide with constant agitation. This is then allowed to stand at room temperature for about an hour. Then the supernatant liquid is decanted off and the precipitate is washed many times with water until the washings are free from alkali. The yellow precipitate is drained and dried on an absorbent paper at 30°C. All the above operations are carried out in dark so as to get bright orange-yellow product.

$$HgCl_2 + 2NaOH \longrightarrow Hg(OH)_2 + 2NaCl$$
$$Hg(OH)_2 \longrightarrow HgO + H_2O$$

**Properties :** It is a orange-yellow, heavy amorphous powder, odourless and stable in air but gets discoloured on exposure to light. It is practically insoluble in water and alcohol but readily soluble in dilute hydrochloric acid and dilute nitric acid.

With oleic acid it forms mercury oleate, a compound of medicinal use. On heating to red hot it decomposes into oxygen and vapour of metallic mercury

$$2HgO \longrightarrow O_2\uparrow + 2Hg$$

**Action and Uses :** It has mild antiseptic action. It is mainly used in 1% strength for ophthalmic use to treat inflammation and conjunctivitis. The antiseptic action is probably because of slow release of mercuric ion which has protein precipitating action.

**Assay :** It is assayed by titrimetric thiocyanate method. An accurately weighed quantity is dissolved in nitric acid and water. It is diluted and the solution is titrated with ammonium thiocyanate solution using ferric ammonium sulphate as an indicator.

**Storage :** It is preserved in tightly closed containers protected from light.

## Mercuric Oxide Eye Ointment :

The preparation contains between 0.9 to 1.1% of HgO in simple ointment. While preparation of ointment, contact with metallic utensils is avoided. This precaution is necessary to avoid release of free mercury ion which has damaging effect on eye.

**Uses :** Ointment is used to allay inflammation and as antiseptic in conjunctivitis.

## Ammoniated Mercury :

**$NH_2$(Hg) Cl**  Mol. Wt. 252.07

It contains not less than 98% w/w $NH_2HgCl$.

**Preparation :** It is generally prepared by adding mercuric chloride solution (5%) to a mixture of dilute ammonia (4 parts) and water (20 parts) with constant stirring. The precipitate is collected, washed with cold water and dried below 30°C.

$$HgCl_2 + 2NH_3 \longrightarrow Hg\begin{smallmatrix}NH_2\\Cl\end{smallmatrix} + NH_4Cl$$

**Properties :** It is a white amorphous powder and is odourless, stable in air but darkens on exposure to light. It is practically insoluble in water, alcohol and ether.

**Action and Uses :** It acts as mild antiseptic because of slow release of mercuric ions. It is used topically in treatment of various skin infections caused by fungi, lice and other infestations. It is commonly employed in 5% strength as ointment and also as a dusting powder.

**Assay :** Ammoniated mercury sample is treated with potassium iodide solution with stirring. Any mercuric iodide formed in the reaction is converted to potassium mercury iodide ($K_2HgI_4$) by KI. The liberated alkali (ammonia and potassium hydroxide) is titrated with hydrochloric acid using methyl orange as indicator.

$$NH_2HgCl + 2KI + H_2O \longrightarrow HgI_2 + NH_3 + KOH + KCl$$

$$HgI_2 + 2KI \longrightarrow K_2HgI_4$$

The assay procedure adopted by USP is different. The mercury from ammoniated mercury is separated as zinc amalgam from a hot acetic acid solution. The amalgam is dissolved in dilute nitric acid by heating, thus mercury is converted into mercuric nitrate. The solution is diluted, treated with dilute potassium permanganate drop by drop to oxidise any mercurous into mercuric ions. Any slight excess of permanganate is reduced by careful addition of oxalic acid. The resulting solution is titrated with ammonium thiocyanate using ferric ammonium sulphate as indicator.

**Preparations :** Ammoniated mercury ointment. It contains 2.25–2.75% of $NH_2HgCl$. It is prepared by triturating ammoniated mercuric (25 g) into simple ointment (975 g).

The preparation is used for external application similar to ammoniated mercury.

Mercury, mercury compounds and their preparations discussed above have been deleted from Indian Pharmocopoeia (1985) and British Pharmocopoeia (1988). Some of the compounds are used as reagents and their specifications are given in appendices of Pharmacopoeias.

## (C) ASTRINGENTS

In general term, astringents are the compounds that bring about protein precipitation. This action may be on mucosal membrane when taken internally or on skin for topical use. The internal use of astringents as antidiarrhoeal is discussed earlier. The astringents for topical applications are covered herein.

Astringents when applied topically cause precipitation of protein of surface cell by coagulation. The action depends upon the extent of penetration of agent and the type of chemical action resulting with protein. In general, astringent compounds do show (i) styptic action i.e. stopping of bleeding by coagulation of blood and constriction of small capillaries, (ii) anti-inflammatory action by decreasing supply of food to the tissues, (iii) antiperspirant action by decreasing secretion of perspiration by reducing pore size of skin and (iv) antimicrobial by protein precipitation mechanism.

Useful compounds for external use having antimicrobial astringent action are given below :

## Alum :

**KAl (SO$_4$)$_2$·12H$_2$O**

Alum is potassium aluminium sulphate. It is a double salt and contains an amount of aluminium now less than 99.5% of KAl (SO$_4$)$_2$·12H$_2$O.

**Preparation :** It is prepared by adding a concentrated solution of potassium sulphate to a hot solution of an equimolecular proportion of aluminium sulphate. When the solution is cooled, characteristics octahedral crystals are separated.

$$K_2SO_4 + Al_2(SO_4)_3 + 12H_2O \longrightarrow 2KAl(SO_4)_2 \cdot 12H_2O$$

**Properties :** It occurs as colourless, transparent or granular crystals with a sweet astringent taste. When heated slowly it melts in its water of crystallization. At 200°C, it loses its water of crystallization and becomes anhydrous. It is soluble in water but insoluble in alcohol.

**Action and Uses :** It is used externally for its astringent properties. It has protein precipitation property and hence is used in the preparation of toxoids. Astringent solution of alum containing 0.5 to 5% is useful antiseptic and commonly used for local styptic action.

**Assay :** Formerly, alum used to be analysed by gravimetric method. A known weight is dissolved in water to which ammonia and ammonium chloride is added. It is heated to boiling, filtered and precipitate washed with ammonium nitrate solution until free from chloride. The precipitate of Al$_2$O$_3$ is dried to constant weight at 120°C and weighed.

According to B.P., aluminium of alum is estimated by complexometric titration using disodium edetate as titrant.

## Aluminium Chloride :

**AlCl$_3$·6H$_2$O**                                                                    Mol. Wt. 241.43

Aluminium chloride when dried over sulphuric acid for four hours, contain not less than 95% of AlCl$_3$·6H$_2$O.

**Preparation :** Aluminium chloride is made by heating metallic aluminium in a current of chlorine and then dissolving th product in water and crystallised.

$$2Al + 3Cl_2 \longrightarrow 2AlCl_3$$

Alternatively, aluminium hydroxide is dissolved in hydrochloric acid, upon concentrating the liquid and allowing it to cool, crystals of aluminium chloride separate out.

$$Al(OH)_3 + 3HCl + 3H_2O \longrightarrow AlCl_3 \cdot 6H_2O$$

**Properties :** It occurs as white-deliquescent, crystalline powder. It has sweet astringent taste and faint odour. It is very soluble in water and freely soluble in alcohol. In non-polar solvents it exists as a dimmer, Al$_2$Cl$_6$. It hydrolyses in water and liberates hydrochloric acid. Thus, aqueous solution is acidic to litmus. The hydrochloric acid formed is an irritant to tissues and hence buffering is necessary.

**Uses :** The aqueous solution of the compound in 10-25% strength is used as mild-antiseptic and astringent. Because of tissue irritation and staining of clothes, the compound is not used now-a-days.

## Aluminium Sulphate

$Al_2(SO_4)_3 \cdot XH_2O$                                                                                    **Mol. Wt. 360 (anhydrous)**

It should contain not less than 51.0% and not more then 59.0% of $Al_2(SO_4)_3$. It contains varying amount of water of crystallization.

**Preparation :** It is prepared by the interaction of freshly precipitated aluminium hydroxide with equivalent quantity of sulphuric acid. After the reaction is over, the resultant solution is concentrated and allowed to crystallise. The crystals are filtered and dried.

**Properties :** Aluminium sulphate occurs as white crystalline powder or shining plates. It is almost odourless and has sweet astringent taste. It is very soluble in water, insoluble in alcohol. The crystalline salt dehydrates on heating at 250°C. Aqueous solution (1 : 20) is acidic and has pH 2.9.

**Uses :** It is used in 5.25% solutions topically. A 10% solution is used for disinfection of dental cavities. As an antiperspirant, it is used 10-15% in creams. It is used as liquid deodorant in solution.

**Assay :** It is based upon the complexometric back titration method. A known weight is dissolved in 1 N hydrochloric acid, excess disodium edetate is added, solution neutralised to methyl orange, heated and titrated with standard lead nitrate solution using xylenol orange as indicator.

## Aluminium Subacetate Solution :

The U.S.P. XVIII states that 100 ml contains not less than 2.3 and not more than 2.6 g of aluminium oxide and not less than 5.4 and not more tan 6.1 g of acetic acid. This preparation is no longer official.

**Preparation :** The solution is prepared by adding dry precipitated calcium carbonate to a solution of aluminium sulphate. Aluminium hydroxide and calcium sulphate both are precipitated. To the mixture acetic acid is added. This reacts with aluminium hydroxide and aluminium subacetate is formed. It is filtered, precipitate washed with more water and volume is made. Boric acid 0.9% is sometimes added as stabilizer.

$$Al_2(SO_4)_3 + 3CaCO_3 + 3H_2O \longrightarrow 2Al(OH)_3 + 3CaSO_4 + 3CO_2\uparrow$$

$$2Al(OH)_3 + 4CH_3COOH \longrightarrow 2Al(CH_3COO)_2OH + 4H_2O\uparrow$$

**Properties :** The solution has faint yellow colour and acetic acid odour. It is acidic in nature.

**Uses :** The solution is diluted 20 to 40 times with water and then used as astringent wash or it is applied to wet dressing. Formerly it was used as mouth wash or gargle for deodorant purpose.

### Zinc Chloride :

**ZnCl₂**  Mol. Wt. 136.29

It contains not less than 95% and not more than 100.5% $ZnCl_2$.

**Preparation :** It is obtained by reacting metallic or granular zinc with hydrochloric acid. The solution is evaporated to dryness.

$$Zn + 2\ HCl \longrightarrow ZnCl_2 + H_2 \uparrow$$

Alternately, it is obtained by treating zinc oxide or carbonate with appropriate amount of hydrochloric acid.

**Properties :** It is a white crystalline powder or granules, odourless and is deliquescent. It is very soluble in water, freely soluble in alcohol and glycerine. The compound is reasonably soluble in polar organic solvents. Aqueous solution is distinctly Acidic (pH 4.0). This is due to its hydrolysis to form hydrochloric acid and basic zinc chloride similar to aluminium salts.

$$ZnCl_2 + H_2O \rightleftharpoons Zn(OH)Cl + H^+ + Cl^-$$

**Uses :** Zinc chloride is a powerful astringent and mild antiseptic. It is also used in mouth wash and deodorant preparations. The antiseptic action is considered to be due to its interaction of the metal with certain microbial enzymes. The protein precipitation action also contributes to this effect.

The other uses of zinc chloride include protein precipitation, in various insulin preparations also as desensitizer of dentin (in dental preparations). It is also used in fire proofing wood.

**Assay :** It is assayed by complexometric titration method using disodium edetate as titrant. An accurately weighed amount is dissolved in water and a definite volume made. To a known volume of solution, ammonia-ammonium chloride solution as buffer, eriochrome black T as indicator is added and the solution is titrated with standard disodium edetate.

**Storage :** As zinc chloride is deliquescent and absorbs carbondioxide, hence it is stored in closed container.

### Zinc Sulphate :

**ZnSO₄.7H₂O**  Mol. Wt. 287.6

It contains between 99 – 108% of $ZnSO_4.7H_2O$.

**Preparation :** Industrially, it is prepared by heating zinc blend (zinc sulphide) in the presence of air under specified conditions. The heated mass is dissolved in hot water, filtered and the solution concentrated for crystallization.

$$ZnS + 2O_2 \longrightarrow ZnSO_4$$

It is also prepared by digesting metallic zinc granules in dilute sulphuric acid. The solution is filtered and treated with chlorine to oxidise any ferrous impurity into ferric sulphate which is then precipitated by hydroxide and removed. The filtrate is concentrated and left for crystallization.

$$Zn + H_2SO_4 \longrightarrow ZnSO_4 + H_2 \uparrow$$

**Properties :** It occurs as colourless, transparent crystals or needles or powder is odourless and has an astringent taste. It effloresces in dry air. It is very soluble in water and glycerine but is insoluble in alcohol. Aqueous solution is acidic to litmus (pH 5.0). With ammonium and potassium sulphate it forms double salt ($ZnSO_4$, $K_2SO_4.6H_2O$). When it is strongly heated it decomposes.

**Action and Uses :** Zinc ions exhibit mild germicidal, astringent and styptic action depending upon the concentration of salt used. This is due to slow release of zinc ions from its salt or solution. The insoluble zinc compounds act as protective and are used in topical applications.

Zinc sulphate solutions in 0.1–1% is used as ophthalmic astringent, in 0.25–1.5% for topical application as astringent. Solution of zinc sulphate is also employed in protein precipitation. Zinc sulphate is also used internally as an emetic.

Other zinc salts having astringent properties are zinc iodide, zinc permanganate and zinc phenol sulphonate. The insoluble zinc compounds are mainly used as protectives and are used in bandages, adhesive tapes, etc. These are discussed separately.

## (D) MISCELLANEOUS COMPOUNDS

**Sulphur and Sulphur Compounds :**

Sulphur occurs in nature in free and in various forms like sulphide and sulphate. In the free elemental form it exists in several allotropic forms including solid and liquid states. The important minerals for the source of sulphur are pyrite ($FeS_2$), zinc blend (ZnS), galena (PbS), gypsum ($CaSO_4.2H_2O$), barytes ($BaSO_4$) etc.

Sulphur and sulphur compounds find extensive use in pharmaceutical and medicinal field. Though elemental sulphur has little use internally (it acts as cathartic), topically it is used as antibacterial. It also acts as fungicide, parasiticide and in the treatment of various skin diseases. The antibacterial or germicide action of elemental sulphur is very weak. It acts either by its oxidation reduction products like sulphurdioxide, sulphides, pentathionic acid etc.

Sulphur when burned forms sulphurdioxide which is used for fumigation or insecticide purpose. Sulphur is also used as scabicide. Sulphides of various elements have depilatory property. In alkaline solution, sulphide reduces the disulphide linkage in amino acid cystine in hair. This results in softening of hair and thus acts as depilatory.

Some medicinally useful sulphur forms and compounds for topical use are described herein.

**Sublimed Sulphur :**

It is known as "Flowers of Sulphur".

**Preparation :** It is obtained by sublimation process in which sulphur vapours produced by heating any form of sulphur are condensed. In refinery, the molten sulphur is placed in iron retorts which communicate with the stone chambers. When sulphur vapours enter the stone chamber, they ignite and convert into $SO_2$. The subsequent vapour pass through relatively cold gas and condenses on the walls and floors of the chambers in fine crystalline form. This is known as flower of sulphur.

**Properties :** It is a fine crystalline (rhombic) yellow powder with faint odour. It is practically insoluble in water, alcohol and is soluble in carbondisulphide. Microscopical appearance show opaqe rounded, amorphous particles or aggregates of semicrystalline mass.

**Uses :** It is an ingredient of sulphur ointment and is used as scabicide.

**Precipitated Sulphur :**

It is a solid allotropic form of sulphur.

**Preparation :** It is prepared by heating together sublimed sulphur and milk of lime for about an hour. During this process calcium pentasulphide and thiosulphate are formed.

$$3Ca(OH)_2 + 12S \longrightarrow 2CaS_5 + CaS_2O_3 + 3H_2O$$

The mixture is filtered and dilute hydrochloric acid is added. It is kept stirring until liquid is just alkaline to litmus. The precipitated sulphur is filtered, washed with water until washings are neutral to litmus and does not give test for calcium with ammonium oxalate solution. The product is rapidly dried.

$$CaS_5 + 2HCl \longrightarrow CaCl_2 + H_2S + 4S\downarrow$$

**Properties :** It occurs as a pale greyish, yellowish or pale yellow soft-powder, free from grittiness. It has no odour or taste. It is almost insoluble in water and alcohol (90%) but dissolves in carbondisulphide. When heated, it burns with blue flame. Microscopical appearance, show that it consists of amorphous particles without crystals.

**Uses :** Sulphur is primarily used in ointment form as scabicides. When sulphur ointment (10%) is applied on skin, it kills the parasites. Sulphur is also used in treatment of seborrhea, acne, pimples and psoriasis. It also acts as kerotolytic agent.

Chemically sulphur is very reactive element. When heated it burns with a blue flame and produces sulphurdioxide.

$$S + O_2 \longrightarrow SO_2$$

It combines with most metals and non-metals to form sulphides,

$$2Cu + S \longrightarrow Cu_2S$$
$$C + 2S \longrightarrow CS_2$$

Sulphur dissolves readily in alkali-hydroxides, carbonate, sulphide etc. and yields polysulphide, thiosulphate, etc.

$$6\,KOH + 8S \longrightarrow 2K_2S_3 + K_2S_2O_3 + 3H_2O$$
$$3Ca(OH)_2 + 12S \longrightarrow 2CaS_5 + CaS_2O_3 + 3H_2O$$
$$Na_2S + S \longrightarrow Na_2S_2$$
$$Na_2S + 4S \longrightarrow Na_2S_5$$

## Sulphur Ointment :

It contains 9.5 - 10.5% of sublimed sulphur.

Composition

| | | |
|---|---|---|
| Sublimed sulphur finely sieved | ... | 100g |
| Simple ointment with white soft paraffin | ... | 900g |

Sublimed sulphur is triturated with small quantities of simple ointment until a smooth cream is obtained.

It is used as scabicide.

## Selenium Sulphide :

$SeS_2$                                            Mol. Wt. 143.09

It contains between 52 - 55% of selenium.

**Preparation :** Selenium disulphide is generally prepared by passing hydrogen sulphide gas into selenious acid or by adding selenious acid to a saturated solution of hydrogen sulphide. The precipitate is collected and dried.

$$H_2SeO_3 + 2H_2S \longrightarrow SeS_2\downarrow + 3H_2O$$

**Properties :** It occurs as bright orange powder with faint sulphide odour. It is practically insoluble in water, alcohol and organic solvents.

**Uses :** It is mainly used topically as antidandruff. Selenium sulphide is used in shampoos in 1 to 2.5% as antiseborrhic. The usual treatment uses 5-10 ml of 2.5% suspension to be applied on scalp. After application to scalp, it is allowed to remain in contact for five minute and then it is washed off. Longer exposure produces irritation. While using, care is taken not to let it get into the eyes or mouth, as the compound is highly toxic.

## EXERCISE

1. *What are topical agents ? Classify them with suitable examples.*
2. *Describe the action of protective adsorbents. Write a brief account of silicone polymers as protectives.*
3. *Give method of preparation, properties and assay of titanium dioxide and calamine.*
4. *List important preparations of calamine and zinc oxide and mention their uses.*
5. *Discuss the various mechanism of action of inorganic antimicrobial agents.*
6. *Give method of preparation and assay of :*
   *(a) Hydrogen peroxide,*
   *(b) Potassium permanganate and*
   *(c) Chlorinated lime.*
7. *(a) List official preparations of iodine.*
   *(b) Describe the action, uses and assay of povidone iodine solution.*

8. Describe the principle involved in the method of assay of the following :
   (a) boric acid,
   (b) borax and
   (c) mild silver protein.

9. Give method of preparation, properties, uses and assay for :
   (a) yellow mercuric oxide and
   (b) ammoniated mercury.

10. What are astringents ? How are they useful topically ? List the compounds of aluminium as astringent. How are these compounds assayed ?

11. Give method of preparation, uses and assay of :
    (a) zinc chloride,
    (b) zinc sulphate and
    (c) zinc stearate.

12. Describe preparation, properties and pharmaceutical uses of the following :
    (a) precipitated sulphur,
    (b) sublimed sulphur and
    (c) selenium sulphide.

# 10

## DENTAL PRODUCTS

Importance of dental hygiene has been recognised since long. A large number of dental products are available in the market and various chemicals are used in their preparation as well employed in dentistry.

Though it is recognised that clean teeth helps good health and a clean tooth cannot decay; it is impossible to keep ones teeth continuously clean all the years. Various factors contribute to dental decay and the problem of oral hygiene arises.

A wide variety of inorganic compounds (and some organic also) are used in dentistry and in dental products. These includes mainly :

(a) anticaries,

(b) cleaning and

(c) polishing agents.

A brief account of these is presented here.

### ANTICARIES AGENTS

Dental caries or tooth decay has been defined as a disease of the teeth caused by acids formed by the action of microorganisms on carbohydrates and is characterised by decalcification of tooth accompanied by foul mouth odour. Though the exact cause and mechanism of dental caries is not known it is believed that dental caries begin on the surface of the teeth. Acids produced by bacterial metabolism of fermenting carbohydrates act on teeth, produce lesions where bacterias get localised and dental caries is produced.

In order to prevent dental caries and to maintain clean and healthy teeth it is necessary to use dentifrices. Primary function of dentifrice is to clean the accessible surface of the teeth. There are substances with known therapeutic value. Use of ammoniated toothpaste, urea-ammonia containing powders, antibiotic containing mixtures and antienzyme compounds have been in use. These compounds have their advantages and limitations.

Role of fluoride in preventing dental caries is well accepted. Administration of traces of fluoride containing salts or their use in topical use to the teeth have found to give encouraging results

When a fluoride containing salt or solution is taken internally, it gets readily absorbed, transported and deposited in the bone or developing teeth and remainder is excreted by the kidneys. The deposited fluoride on the surface of teeth prevent the action of acids or enzymes in producing lesions. A small quantity (1 ppm) of fluoride is thus necessary to prevent caries, but when more quantity of fluoride (more than 2-3 ppm) is ingested it is carried to bones and teeth and produces mottled enamel known as dental fluorosis.

Fluoride is administered by two routes (i) orally and (ii) topically. The use of fluoridation of public water supply is the most common and effective way of oral administration. Water supply containing about 0.5 to 1 ppm is provided which is sufficient. Alternatively, it can be given in drinking water or fruit juice in such a concentration to have about 1 ppm per day. Sodium fluoride tablets or solution of sodium fluoride in a dose of 22 mg per day is employed. For topical application 2% solution is used on teeth.

Besides fluoride inorganic phosphate salts have been considered to be useful in reducing the dental caries. Phosphate ions are required for stronger bones as well healthy teeth. Phosphate salts both in soluble and insoluble forms are consumed through normal diets. The phosphates are normally given in deficiencies. Role of phosphate as cleaning agent is also important.

## CLEANING AGENTS

A good cleaning agent generally has coarse to fine particle size and satisfactory abrasive property. Cleaning agents must remove stains from teeth and to achieve this, adequate abrassiveness is essential. It is difficult to evaluate abrassiveness. Some tests have been designed for this but those are not comparable when tested *in vivo*. The role of phosphate as anticaries and cleaning agent is well-known. Calcium phosphate dibasic and tribasic, sodium metaphosphate are common cleaning agents in toothpaste and tooth powders. Similarly, calcium carbonate, pumice powder also serve as cleaning agents.

## POLISHING AGENTS

One of the requirements of good dentifrice is to have polishing effect on the cleaned teeth. The polishing effect is achieved by abrasive action. The overall effect is giving whiteness to the teeth. Besides, having polishing effect some densitizing agents are added in dentifrices to reduce sensitivity of teeth to heat and cold. The numbning effect is of short duration like that of local anaesthetic. This property is shown by astringent type compounds and due to which they are incorporated in dental products.

Some important compounds of dental products are discussed here :

**Sodium Fluoride :**

NaF $\hspace{4cm}$ **Mol. Wt. 42**

Contains not less than 98.0% of NaF, calculated with reference to the dried substance.

**Preparation :** It is commonly obtained by neutralizing hydrofluoric acid with sodium carbonate.

$$2HF + Na_2CO_3 \longrightarrow 2NaF + H_2O + CO_2\uparrow$$

Another method is the double decomposition of calcium fluoride with sodium carbonate wherein insoluble calcium carbonate is filtered out.

$$CaF_2 + Na_2CO_3 \longrightarrow 2NaF + CaCO_3\downarrow$$

**Properties :** It occurs as colourless, odourless crystals or as white powder. It is soluble in water but is insoluble in alcohol. Aqueous solutions of the salt corrode ordinary glass bottles and hence the solution should be made in distilled water and stored in dark, pyrex bottles.

On acidification of salt solution, hydrofluoric acid is produced. This is weak acid and is poisonous. Aqueous solution of salt gives alkaline reaction.

**Action and Uses :** Sodium fluoride because of its fluoride ion is an important agent in dental practice for retarding or preventing dental caries. Areas wherein the drinking water lacks fluoride ions, sodium fluoride in 1 ppm concentration is used. Higher levels than 1 ppm causes mottling of teeth.

Sodium fluoride in 2% aqueous solution is widely used topically, occasionally the solution is applied to the surface of dry teeth periodically over several times in a year. Fluoride ion enters the enamel of teeth and becomes part of enamel structure and thus becomes effective.

**Assay :** It is assayed by complexometric titration method using disodium edetate.

A weighed quantity is dissolved in water, small amount of sodium chloride and alcohol is added, contents heated to boiling and dropwise excess lead nitrate is added with stirring. On cooling, coagulated precipitate is filtered, residue washed with dilute alcohol and the combined filtrate and washings are titrated with disodium edetate using xylenol orange as indicator.

**Storage :** It should be kept in well-closed containers.

## Stannous Fluoride :

$SnF_2$ $\qquad$ **Mol. Wt. 157**

Tin fluoride solution is prepared from using Tin fluroride capsules by dissolving in water. A fresh solution (about 8%) is used in dentistry.

**Properties :** It is a white crystalline powder with unpleasant astringent-salty taste. It is soluble in water but insoluble in alcohol and organic solvents. Aqueous solution of stannous fluoride deteriorates rapidly on standing due to oxidation of stannous cation to stannic form resulting in turbidity.

**Uses :** Stannous fluoride is used in fluoride treatment of teeth. Because of instability of prepared aqueous solutions, fresh solutions are prepared at the time of application. A freshly prepared 8% solution of stannous fluoride is applied to the cleaned dry teeth. A single application is sufficient for six to twelve months.

Following cleaning agents are used in dental produces :

## Calcium Carbonate :

This compound is already discussed under 'Antacid'.

**Uses :** The precipitated chalk is used externally as a dentifrice because it has mild abrasive quality. It forms a common ingredient of tooth powder and toothpaste.

## Dibasic Calcium Phosphate :

It is a calcium monohydrogen phosphate $CaHPO_4$, anhydrous or dihydrate. This compound is discussed under calcium compounds.

**Uses :** This calcium salt has 1:1 ratio of calcium to phosphorus and is most frequently recommended for oral administration as an electrolyte replenisher. As a salt it supplies both calcium and phosphorus which is required for growth in children and as supplements to pregnant woman and lactating mothers.

Externally it is used as dentifrices having cleaning action. The moderate abrasive quality makes it suitable for toothpaste and tooth powders.

### Sodium Metaphosphate :
**NaPO₃**  **Mol. Wt. 102**

It is a sodium salt of metaphosphoric acid HPO₃. It is known as Graham's salt. It occurs as colourless, glassy hygroscopic sticks or powder, odourless, tasteless and gritty in nature. It is soluble in water. A polymeric form is insoluble in water which acts as a very good cleaning agent. It occurs in polymeric form and one of the form known as calgon is used in water-softening. It prevents and removes boiler scales also.

### Pumice :
Pumice is a substance of variable composition consisting of complex silicates of aluminium, potassium and sodium. It is a product obtained from volcanic origin.

**Properties :** It occurs as odourless, tasteless, very light, hard, grayish-white powder with fineness. It is gritty in nature, stable in air and is insoluble in water. On sifting it is categorised into superfine, fine and coarse pumice powder.

**Uses :** Depending upon the particle size it is employed in industry as a filtering and distributing medium. It is also used as abrasive in metal polishes. Because of its grittiness, it is used in soaps and cleaning powders. It forms an ingredient in dental preparation as dental abrasive.

## DESENSITISING AGENTS

Generally, teeth are sensitive to heat and cold. During teeth decay, or in toothache the perception to heat and cold is felt strongly. Some denensitising agents are incorporated in dental preparations to reduce sensitivity of teeth to heat and cold. Their exact mechanism is not known. However, they are effective probably acting like local anaesthetic. The compounds known as desensitisors are strontium chloride and zinc chloride.

### Strontium Chloride :
**SrCl₂·6H₂O**

**Preparation :** It is prepared by adding strontium carbonate to hydrochloric acid until effervescence has ceased. The solution is filtered concentrated and allowed to crystallise.

**Properties :** It occurs as colourless crystals or white granules. It effloresces in dry air. It is soluble in water and alcohol.

**Uses :** It acts as desensitising agent in dental remedies.

### Zinc Chloride :
**ZnCl₂**

This compound is discussed under 'Astringent'.

**Uses :** As discussed earlier, it is a good astringent when used in solution for topical applications. It is used in 10% solution to be applied to the teeth as desensitising agent.

### EXERCISE

1. What are anticaries agents ? Discuss the role of fluoride as anticaries.
2. Describe the method of preparation, uses and assay of :
   (a) sodium fluoride and
   (b) dibasic calcium phosphate.

# 11

# INHALANTS

Inhalants are the drugs or chemicals which in vapour form are inhaled in the body. Some chemicals act as anesthetics in vapour form. These are administered by inhalation by a closed-mask method. However, use of gases as inhalant is a major consideration for discussion of this chapter.

Inhalation of gases cause changes in physiological functions and brings about pharmacological actions. This depends upon the gas, its concentration and the condition in which it is used. Thus, action and effect of gas will be different under different conditions.

**Role of Oxygen :**

Oxygen is important to the living cells. It is necessary for normal oxidative metabolic processes in a cell, for the production of energy. This energy is used by cells to synthesize Adenosine Triphosphate (ATP). When ATP is hydrolysed, energy is released. Enzymes like NADH and FADH play an important role in the reaction.

Transport of oxygen (after it has been inhaled) is carried by hemoglobin, a constituent of blood. Concentration of hemoglobin in blood is important in transport mechanism. Oxygen combines with hemoglobin reversibly as :

$$Hb + O_2 \rightleftharpoons HbO_2$$

wherein $Hb$ = deoxyhemoglobin
and $HbO_2$ = oxyhemoglobin

This loose combination readily dissociates and releases oxygen into the medium of cell. Number of factors affect the formation and dissociation of oxyhemoglobin. These include temperature, electrolytes, effect of carbondioxide, carbon-monoxide, pH, etc.

Under physiological conditions, the action of electrolyte and $CO_2$ on the liberation of oxygen from oxyhemoglobin is important.

Similar to oxygen, carbon monoxide also combines with hemoglobin and forms carboxyhemoglobin. The formation of carboxyhemoglobin is a very fast process. The formation of carboxyhemoglobin reduces the amount of hemoglobin available to carry oxygen. Hemoglobin also has remarkable buffering capacity. In oxyform it is a stronger acid than in its reduced (doxy) form. When the $H^+$ ion (from the dissociation of carbonic acid in cell) is accepted by the reduced hemoglobin, the buffering effect occurs.

By inhalation during respiration, oxygenation of blood takes place in alveoli of lungs. In different conditions, the requirement of oxygen by body varies. Thus, when more oxygen supply needed as in asphexia, or in anoxic conditions, oxygen is supplied by inhalation method.

**Role of Carbondioxide :**

Carbondioxide is readily absorbed and carried by blood, both in the cells and in the plasma. Besides, it is also produced in the body during metabolic process. A large quantity of carbondioxide produced is eleminated by lungs in the expired air. A large quantity of carbondioxide cannot remain in the dissolved form in plasma. It exists in three major forms, (i) as a carbonic acid, after combining with water, (ii) as a carbamino bound form in which it combines with proteins, again mainly with hemoglobin and (iii) carried as bicarbonate in combination with other cations.

In utilization of carbondioxide, under normal physiological conditions, the pH of blood is maintained via carbonic acid formation, and its conversion into bicarbonate ions, etc. The normal $CO_3/HCO_3^-$ ratio is 1/20 and from equation

$$pH = pKa - \log \frac{[H_2CO_3]}{[HCO_3^-]}$$

change in pH is calculated.

It is seen that an increase of bicarbonate (systemic) ions, results in increase in pH of body fluids, while increase in carbondioxide levels via carbonic acid decreases it. Both effects are interbalanced by excretion process.

The interchange and transport mechanism for carbondioxide and oxygen occurring in lungs, tissue and blood is shown diagrammatically in Fig. 11.1 (a) and (b).

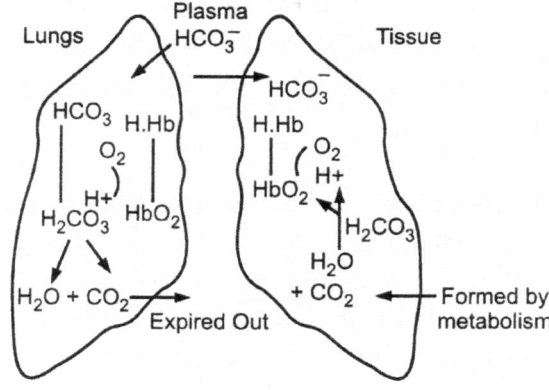

(a)

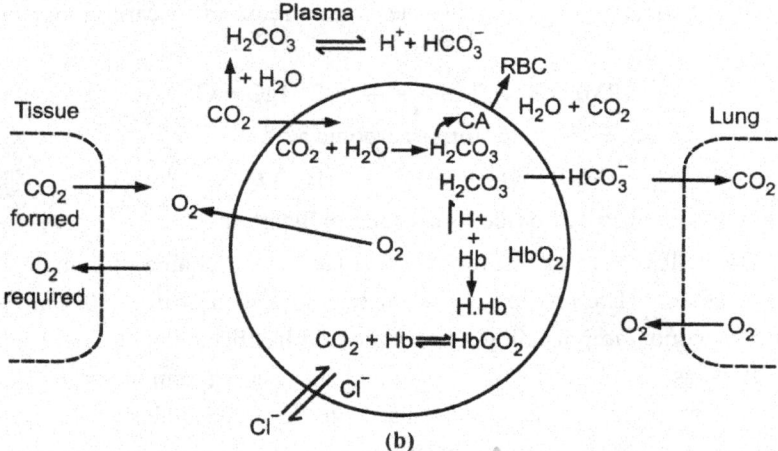

Fig. 11.1 : Transport mechanism for $CO_2$ and $O_2$ in lungs, tissue and blood

In addition to carbondioxide, production of ammonia in kidneys by the deamination of amino acid also plays an important role in maintaining acid-base balance in the body. Detailed discussion of this is beyond the scope of this book.

**Carbondioxide :**

$CO_2$ Mol. Wt. 44.01

Carbondioxide contains not less than 99% v/v of $CO_2$. For convenience it is stored and supplied in metal cylinders under compression.

**Preparation :** It is obtained by many methods.

1. Compounds containing carbon-like materials, like coal, coke, oil etc. are burned with an access of oxygen.

$$C + O_2 \longrightarrow CO_2 \uparrow$$

2. When carbonate is treated with acid, carbondioxide gas is evolved.

$$CaCO_3 + 2HCl \longrightarrow H_2CO_3 + CaCl_2$$

$$H_2CO_3 \rightleftharpoons H_2O + CO_2 \uparrow$$

2. Calcium carbonate or sodium bicarbonate when heated, gives out carbondioxide.

$$CaCO_3 \longrightarrow CaO + CO_2 \uparrow$$

$$2NaHCO_3 \rightleftharpoons Na_2CO_3 + H_2O + CO_2 \uparrow$$

Carbondioxide under pressure may be dissolved in cold water. It forms carbonic acid ($H_2CO_3$) from which carbon dioxide is liberated when pressure is released.

**Properties :** Carbondioxide is a colourless, odourless gas with faintly acidic taste. It is soluble in water. Carbondioxide does not support combustion. However, when a magnesium ribbon burns in an atmosphere of carbondioxide, it gets reduced to carbon and metal oxide is formed.

$$2Mg + CO_2 \longrightarrow 2MgO + C$$

Carbondioxide when passed in water forms carbonic acid.

$$H_2O + CO_2 \longrightarrow H_2CO_3$$

This on addition to sodium hydroxide forms sodium bicarbonate.

**Action and Uses :** It is used as respiratory stimulant when inhaled, it stimulates respiratory and cardiovascular centers. The mixture of $CO_2$ with 5% oxygen or upto 10% air is used in the treatment of carbon monoxide poisoning. Carbondioxide has been found useful in treatment of drug addiction. It is used to prepare dry ice which is used in minor surgical operation for destroying tissue. Carbondioxide is widely used in beverage industry for preparation of concentrated soft drinks. Pharmaceutically it is used to displace air in some parenteral preparations.

**Assay :** It is assayed by gasometric method. The apparatus consists of nitrometer connected by rubber tubing to a balancing tube. The absorbing liquid is 50% KOH solution. The decrease in volume of gas, when passed through the absorbing liquid after correction to standard conditions of temperature and pressure, is measured. Not more than 1 ml of gas remains in the tube.

**Storage and Labelling :** Carbondioxide is supplied in metal cylinders. The shoulder of cylinder is painted grey and has the name and symbol of $CO_2$ stencilled on it.

### Nitrous Oxide :

$N_2O$                                                                **Mol. Wt. 44.01**

It contains not less than 95% v/v of $N_2O$. The gas is supplied and stored in metal cylinder. It is also called as "Launching gas" as it produces an exhilarating effect when inhaled.

**Preparation :** It is prepared by thermal decomposition of ammonium nitrate. The gas is purified by washing with sodium chromate, sodium hydroxide and water and filled in cylinder.

$$NH_4NO_3 \longrightarrow 2H_2O + N_2O$$

**Properties :** It is a colourless gas with a slight sweetish odour and taste. It dissolves in water and is soluble in alcohol. At a high temperature (500°C) it decomposes.

$$N_2O \xrightarrow{\Delta} N_2 \; (O)$$

The liberated oxygen assists in burning.

**Action and Uses :** It is used by inhalation for operation of short duration like dental extractions, minor operations of boils and abscesses. It produces anaesthesia with analgesia. It is also effective in calming excited mental patients. Nitrous oxide is given by inhalation in 60-80% or with oxygen 20-40% as required.

**Assay :** It is assayed by using a special apparatus as described by pharmacopoeia. The apparatus consists of gas burettes connected to a condenser-monometer (Refer details in pharmacopoeia). Volume of gas in liquid nitrogen is measured. Not less than 95% v/v is condensed.

**Storage and Labelling :** The gas is stored in metal cylinders under pressure and at a temperature not exceeding 37°C. The cylinder is painted blue and carries a label stating the name of gas and symbol $N_2O$ stencilled in paint.

**Oxygen :**

$O_2$  Mol. Wt. 32

Oxygen is an important constituent of air and constitutes about 21% by volume of atmosphere. According to the Indian Pharmacopoeia, oxygen contains not less than 99% v/v of $O_2$ with traces of other gases like argon, nitrogen or hydrogen. It is available and supplied in metallic cylinders in a compressed form.

**Preparation :** Oxygen is manufactured mainly by two methods : (1) by fractionation of liquid air and (2) by electrolysis of water.

In the former method, air is purified by removing moisture, carbondioxide, dust, etc. and then compressed to get liquid air. The liquid air is fractionated by distillation, to get oxygen which is then filled under pressure in metallic cylinders.

In the electrolysis method, a direct current is passed through a cell between the iron or steel electrodes immersed in about 10% of aqueous solution of sodium or potassium hydroxide. Oxygen is liberated at the anode and hydrogen at the cathode. The liberated oxygen is suitably collected.

**Properties :** Oxygen is a colourless, odourless, tasteless gas and has a density of 1.105. Oxygen dissolves in about 32 volumes of water, 36 volumes of alcohol at 1 atmospheric pressure. Oxygen is reactive chemically and primarily functions as an oxidizing agent.

Non metals like sulphur, carbon and phosphorous combine with oxygen when heated to form oxides

1. $S + O_2 \longrightarrow SO_2$
2. $C + O_2 \longrightarrow CO_2$
3. $4P + 5O_2 \longrightarrow 2P_2O_5$

Oxygen does not combine directly with halogens and inert gases. Most metals when heated, combine with oxygen and forms oxide

For example :

$4Fe + 3O_2 \longrightarrow 2Fe_2O_3$

$2Mg + O_2 \longrightarrow 2MgO$

Oxygen gas for medicinal use should not contain impurity of carbonmonoxide (not more than 5 ppm), carbondioxide (not more than 30 ppm) and halogens.

**Action and Uses :** Oxygen is required by living cells. In blood, it combines with haemogloblin and carried to the cells.

Oxygen is widely used in treatment of hypoxia. It is usually administered by oxygen tent or mask in a concentration ranging from 40–100% of oxygen. It gives relief in the treatment of anoxia which arises due to inadequate oxygenation of blood. Oxygen is useful in treatment of carbonmonoxide poisoning.

Industrially oxygen is used in oxy-acetylene flames required for welding or cutting metals. Liquid oxygen is used as a Fuel in rocket technology.

**Assay :** It is assayed by gas measurement method. A specified apparatus (as described in pharmacopoeia) is used.

The apparatus comprises a gas-burette of 100 ml capacity having two way capillary tap at upper end. One of which is used for introducing gas in apparatus and other connected to a gas pipette having two bulbs of suitable size. The pipette is filled with absorbing reagent.

After introduction of gas in apparatus, it is allowed to come in contact with absorbing liquid. When most of the gas is absorbed by liquid. The residual gas is brought back in burette by adjusting mercury reservoir and the volume of residual gas in burette is measured. It should not exceed 1% v/v.

**Storage and Labelling :** Oxygen is stored and supplied in metal cylinders under pressure. The shoulder of the cylinder is painted white (as an international colour code) and the remainder part of cylinder is painted black. The name and symbol of oxygen ($O_2$) is stencilled on the shoulder of the cylinder.

### EXERCISE

1. *Discuss the role of oxygen and carbondioxide in biological system.*
2. *Give method of preparation, properties, uses and assay technique for :*
   *(a) nitrous oxide and*
   *(b) oxygen.*

■■■

# 12

# EXPECTORANTS, EMETICS AND RESPIRATORY STIMULANTS

Expectorants are the drugs that remove sputum from the respiratory tract. These drugs either increase the fluidity (or reduce the viscosity) of sputum or increase the volume of fluids that are to be expelled from the respiratory tract by coughing.

Expectorants are classified according to their mechanism of action into two categories viz. (i) sedative type and (ii) stimulant type.

The sedative type of expectorants are stomach irritants. They produce their effect through stimulation of gastric reflexes. Drugs that are bitter like ipecac, senega, Indian squill and compounds like antimony potassium tartrate, ammonium chloride, sodium citrate and potassium iodide are sedative type expectorants.

In stimulant type, the drugs bring about a stimulation of the secretory cells of the respiratory tract directly or indirectly. Since the drug stimulates secretion, more fluid is produced in respiratory tract and sputum gets diluted. Turpenoid oils like Eucalyptus, Lemon, Anise and active constituents of oil like terpine hydrate, anethole are stimulant expectorants. Emetics are the drugs that remove fluid from respiratory tract. Some inorganic compounds act directly by stimulating secretions of respiratory tract. The emetics are added in cough syrups preparations.

The inorganic compounds of recognisable expectorant and emetic activities are given below :

**Ammonium Chloride :**

**$NH_4Cl$** **Mol. Wt. 53.5**

It contains not less than 99.5% of $NH_4Cl$, calculated with reference to substance dried over silica gel for four hours.

**Preparation :** Commercially it is prepared by the interaction of ammonia gas with hydrochloric acid. The solution is evaporated to dryness.

$$NH_3 + HCl \longrightarrow NH_4Cl$$

The salt is purified by crystallisation and sublimation. During purification, it is mixed with 5% calcium phosphate to prevent sublimation of any volatile iron salts during sublimation process. The sublimation is carried out in cast iron pots lined with fire clay and having a dome of glass. It may also be prepared by treating ammonia gas liquors with lime and the liberated ammonia is passed into hydrochloric acid.

**Properties :** Ammonium chloride occurs as a white or colourless crystalline or a coarse powder. It is almost odourless and has a cooling, saline taste. It is slightly hygroscopic, very soluble in water, sparingly soluble in alcohol but freely soluble in glycerin.

Freshly prepared aqueous solutions are neutral to litmus but become quickly acidic on standing due to hydrolysis.

$$NH_4Cl + 2H_2O \rightleftharpoons NH_4OH + H_3O^+ + Cl^-$$

Ammonium chloride solutions are incompatible with alkalis, carbonates of alkaline earths and lead salts.

**Action and Uses :** Ammonium chloride exhibits three principle pharmacological actions. These actions are dose dependant.

1. It acts in maintaining acid-base equilibrium of body fluids. Deamination of amino acids produce ammonia which is exerted in kidney and in the process sodium ion is retained.

2. The diuretic effect is due to utilization of ammonium cation in conversion into urea and in the process proton $H^+$ and $Cl^-$ ions are produced. The hydrogen ion reacts with bicarbonate and $CO_2$ and water is produced. In the process, bicarbonate ion is lost and alkali reserve of body is reduced. On continued use, it increases acidity of urine and metabolic acidosis is produced.

3. Ammonium chloride acts as mild expectorant and diaphoretic when administered in small doses. It does so because of local irritation which produces increasing secretion of respiratory tract, and makes the mucus less viscous. Ammonium chloride and ammonium carbonate are therefore used in cough preparations.

Usual dose as systemic acidifier is 1 to 2 g four times a day. The administration is in the form of injection or tablets. For expectorant action, 0.3-0.5 g dose is employed.

**Assay :** The compound was previously assayed by Volhard's method based on precipitation titration. In the assay, an excess of silver nitrate solution is added to the ammonium chloride solution (prepared by weighing the substance and dissolving in water). The residual silver nitrate is determined by titrating it with standard ammonium thiocyanate using ferrium ammonium sulphate as indicator.

The assay of ammonium chloride now is based on formal titration principle. The formaldehyde which is added to the ammonium chloride solution endows acidic properties to the compound and hence it can be titrated with standard alkali solution using phenolphthalein as indicator.

**Storage :** It is stored in tightly closed containers.

## Ammonium Acetate :

### CH₃COONH₄              Mol. Wt. 78

**Preparation :** It is a salt prepared by neutralizing acetic acid with ammonia solution.

**Properties :** It occurs as colourless crystals or crystalline masses, and is deliquescent. It gives the smell of acetic acid. It is very soluble in water and alcohol.

**Uses :** Ammonium acetate has slight diaphoretic action. It is used in the form of dilute solution as mild expectorant and diuretic. The action is due to ammonium ions, similar to that of ammonium chloride.

## Ammonium Carbonate :

### NH₄CO₃

Ammonium carbonate is salt of variable composition of ammonium bicarbonate ($NH_4HCO_3$) and ammonium carbamate ($NH_2CONH_4$). It contains equivalent of not less than 30% of $NH_3$.

**Properties :** It occurs as translucent crystalline masses with ammoniacal odour when exposed to air it partly dissociates and volatilises giving white powder. It is very soluble in water and sparingly in alcohol.

**Uses :** It acts as respiratory stimulant and expectorant because of ammonium ion.

## Potassium Iodide :

### KI              Mol. Wt. 166

It contains not less than 99% KI, calculated with reference to the substance dried to a constant weight at 105°C.

**Preparation :** Two different processes are used for preparation of potassium iodide on industrial scale.

1. It is prepared by the action of iodine on moist iron filing to form ferro-ferric iodide ($FeI_3 \cdot FeI_2$) which is then decomposed with potassium carbonate.

$$Fe + I_2 \longrightarrow FeI_2, \quad 3FeI_2 + I_2 \longrightarrow FeI_2 \cdot FeI_3$$

$$FeI_2 \cdot 2FeI_3 + 4K_2CO_3 \longrightarrow 8KI + FeO \cdot Fe_2O_3 + 4CO_2 \uparrow$$

Ferro-ferric oxide is filtered out and the filtrate is concentrated to obtain potassium iodide. It is purified by recrystallisation.

2. Alternatively it is prepared by adding excess of iodine to the solution of potassium hydroxide. Potassium iodide and iodate are formed. The potassium iodate is reduced to potassium iodide with carbon.

$$6KOH + 3I_2 \longrightarrow 5KI + KIO_3 + 3H_2O$$

$$KIO_3 + 3C \xrightarrow{\Delta} KI + 3CO \uparrow$$

**Properties :** It is colourless transparent or opaque salt. It is odourless and has a saline bitter taste. The salt is deliquescent in moist air. It is soluble in water, alcohol and glycerine. When KI is added to water to prepare solution, the temperature of solution lowers. Aqueous solution of potassium iodide take up iodine and forms $KI_3 KI_4$ etc.

**Uses :** It acts as an expectorant because of iodide ions. The action is rapid and produces bronchial fluid which dilutes sputum. It is used either in tablet form or in solutions. Usual dose is 0.3 g. The tablets are enteric coated to overcome the unpleasant bitter metallic taste.

It is also used as a source of iodine and potassium. It is employed as stabilizer in preparation of iodine solutions. It is also employed as a reagent in pharmacy.

**Assay :** It is assayed by titrating with potassium iodate as oxidising agent. A weighed quantity is dissolved in water, acidified with hydrochloric acid and the contents titrated with standard potassium iodate solution using chloroform (to detect the disappearance of iodine) as indicator solvent.

**Storage :** It is stored in well closed containers.

Ammonium iodide also acts as expectorant due to both ammonium and iodide ions.

**Antimony Potassium Tartrate :**

$C_4H_4KO_7Sb$

It is known as "tartar emetic".

**Preparation :** It is prepared by mixing antimony trioxide $Sb_2O_3$ (5 parts) with potassium acid tartrate (6 parts) in a fine paste and left aside for a day. It is then boiled with water for fifteen minutes while stirring. The liquid is then filtered hot and the filtrate left for crystallization. The crystals are collected on filter and dried.

**Properties :** It occurs as colourless, odourless with sweetish taste. It effloresces on exposure to air. It is soluble in water and is insoluble in alcohol.

**Uses :** It acts as expectorant-emetic due to its irritant action on mucosa. Now-a-days it is not used because of availability of better effective drugs. The drug has central depressant action and hence is not suitable as general purpose emetic.

**Assay :** The assay is based upon the oxidation-reduction reaction. Iodine solution is used as an oxidising agent, which converts antimony to antimonic state ($Sb_2O_5$). The titration is carried out in presence of an excess of sodium potassium tartrate and borax. The sodium potassium tartrate prevents the precipitation, of antimonious hydroxide. In the reaction (which is reversible) hydroiodic acid is neutralised by borax in the analysis. Strong alkalies like sodium hydroxide or sodium carbonate is not used, as it would react with iodine to form hypoiodate.

$$2NaOH + I_2 \longrightarrow NaOI + NaI + H_2O$$

$$2C_4H_4O_7SbK + 3H_2O + 2I_2 \longrightarrow 2KHC_4H_4O_6 + Sb_2O_5 + 4HI$$

Antimony sodium tartrate also acts similarly as emetic agent.

## Copper Sulphate :

**$CuSO_4 \cdot 5H_2O$**  Mol. Wt. 249.7

It contains not less than 98.5% and not more than 101% $CuSO_4.5H_2O$.

**Preparation :** It is prepared by roasting copper containing sulphide ore in presence of air or by heating copper in a furnace with sulphur. The mixture of copper sulphate and copper oxide obtained in the above process is treated with dilute sulphuric acid. The resulting solution is filtered, concentrated and allowed to crystalise.

It is also prepared by treating granulated copper in the presence of air with sulphuric acid.

$$2Cu + 2H_2SO_4 + O_2 \longrightarrow 2CuSO_4 + 2H_2O$$

**Properties :** It occurs as deep blue, triclinic crystals of pentahydrate or as blue crystalline granules or powder. It effloresces slowly in dry air and the crystals become covered with a white anhydrous salt. It is soluble in water, almost insoluble in alcohol. Aqueous solutions are acidic to litmus paper and produces blue green colour.

**Uses :** It was (as it is no longer used) used as an emetic in a dose of 300 mg in 30 ml of water. It activates the vomitting center very rapidly and hence is employed as emetic in chemical poisoning. It is also used externally as astringent and also as a fungicide (1 - 5%). It is an ingredient of Benedict and Fehling reagent.

## Zinc Sulphate

**$ZnSO_4 \cdot 7H_2O$**

It is already discussed under 'Astringents'. Zinc sulphate activates the vomitting reflex because it causes irritation of mucosa. As an emetic 1 to 2 g in about 200 ml of water is used of emptying stomach contents.

# RESPIRATORY STIMULANTS

Respiratory stimulants belong to the class known as Central Nervous System Stimulants. Drugs which increase the activities of various functions of the CNS are called as central nervous system stimulants or stimulants or analeptics. One of the important features of stimulant activity is 'respiratory stimulation'. This action is brought through stimulation of chemo-receptors and the vasomotor centres by various agents.

Various drugs and chemicals stimulate respiratory function by different mechanisms. The role of gases like carbondioxide, oxygen is discussed under inhalants. The pH or hydrogen ion concentration of blood and various chemicals which alter the pH also affect respiration. (This is mainly through chemo-receptors). Inorganic compounds act as respiratory stimulant by reflex mechanism. The epithelial cells of trachea, bronchial and bronchiolae get stimulated by irritation by drugs. This in turn leads to respiratory stimulation.

Ammonical salts and preparation are in general considered as respiratory stimulants because they give off ammonia gas which irritates respiratory tract and acts as reflex stimulant. Some important and useful compounds are covered below.

## Ammonium Carbonate :

This compound is discussed under expectorant category.

The compound is a mixture of ammonium bicarbonate and ammonium carbonate. It is volatile and gives smell of ammonia. The ammonia gas when inhaled stimulatus respiratory center and thus acts as respiratory stimulant.

## Ammonium Solution Dilute :

It contains approximately 10% w/w of $NH_3$ and is prepared by diluting a strong ammonia solution with purified water.

Ammonia gas is a reflex stimulant. It acts directly by irritation of the trigeminal nerve. A dilute ammonia solution being alkaline in nature is not used directly.

## Aromatic Spirit of Ammonia :

It contains 1.12–1.25% w/v of free ammonia and 2.76–3.24% w/v of ammonium carbonate.

Composition :

| | | |
|---|---|---|
| Ammonium bicarbonate | ... | 25 g |
| Ammonia solution strong | ... | 70 ml |
| Lemon oil | ... | 5.1 ml |
| Nutmeg oil | ... | 3 ml |
| Alcohol (90%) | ... | 750 ml |
| Purified water to produce | ... | 1000 ml |

**Preparation :** Lemon oil, nutmeg oil, alcohol and about 375 ml of water is placed in a distillation assembly and about 875 ml of distillate is collected. In addition, 35 ml of distillate is collected separately and to it ammonium bicarbonate and ammonia is added. The contents are warmed on water-bath at 60°C, stirred, filtered through cotton wool and filtrate added gradually to first distillate. Sufficient water is added to produce the desired volume.

**Action and Uses :** It is supplied in single-dose thin walled glass vials wrapped in cotton envelop. On breaking, the contents are absorbed by cotton and on inhalation respiratory stimulation is produced.

**Assay :** The preparation is analysed for alcohol, ammonium carbonate and for free ammonia content.

**Storage :** It should be preserved in well-closed stoppered containers and kept in a cool place.

### EXERCISE

1. *What are expectorants ? How do they act ? Discuss the role of ammonium compounds as respiratory stimulants.*
2. *Give the method of preparation, action, uses and assay for the following compounds :*
    *(a) ammonium chloride,*
    *(b) potassium iodide,*
    *(c) antimony potassium tartrate.*
3. *Outline the principle involved in the assay of the following compounds :*
    *(a) antimony potassium tartrate,*
    *(b) ammonium chloride,*
    *(c) potassium iodide,*
    *(d) copper sulphate.*
4. *Give method of preparation and assay for the aromatic spirit of ammonia.*

■■■

# 13

# MAJOR INTRA AND EXTRACELLULAR ELECTROLYTES

## (A) MAJOR INTRA AND EXTRACELLULAR ELECTROLYTES

There are various inorganic and organic compounds present in the body fluids and the concentration of these, in various compartments, is balanced in such a way that the body cells and tissue always have the same environment. There are various regulatory mechanisms which control the ionic balance, osmotic balances and the pH, which in turn maintain the concentration of solutes in various body fluids. Generally, in the body, the electrolyte concentration is maintained, but if the body cannot maintain or correct the electrolyte balance, then it is done by external administration, which is known as replacement therapy. Various products like electrolytes, acids and bases, carbohydrates, proteins, amino acids and blood products are used as replacement therapy as per need of the patient, when the balance of the fluids are disturbed. In this chapter we are only going to consider the electrolytes used in replacement therapy and for correction of the acid-base balance in various body fluids.

The electrolyte concentration of body fluids differ in various fluid compartments. The various body fluid compartments are as follows :

1. **Intracellular fluid :** The fluid present inside the cell, e.g. cytoplasm.
2. **Interstitial fluid :** The fluid present between the cells and,
3. **The plasma (vascular fluid) :** The fluid present within the blood vascular system. The second and the third category are termed as 'Extracellular fluid'.

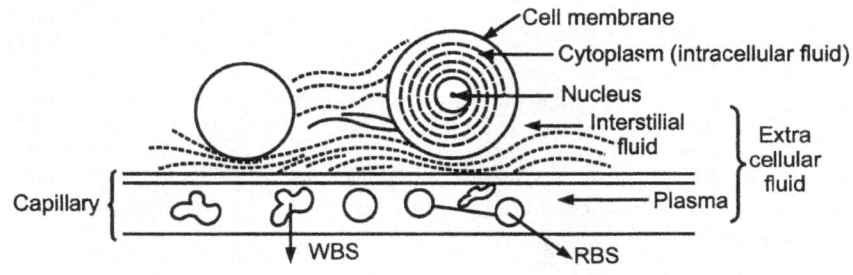

Fig. 13.1 : Diagrammatic representation of various body fluids

The three fluid compartments are separated by from each other by membranes. These membranes are permeable to water and certain inorganic and organic components present in the body fluids. These membranes do not allow the transfer of certain molecules like proteins, as a result they are impermeable to these molecules. For certain ions like sodium, potassium and magnesium the membranes shows selective permeability. Thus the composition and concentration of various solutes in body fluids is definite and differ from one another.

The body fluids contain various inorganic ions which are either anionic, or cationic in character. Examples of anionic electrolytes are $HCO_3^-$ (bicarbonate), $Cl^-$ (chloride), $SO_4^{--}$ (sulphate) and $HPO_4^-$ (phosphate) and that of cationic electrolytes are sodium, potassium, calcium and magnesium etc. The fluids in each compartment are ionically balanced.

The concentrations of some important electrolytes in the intracellular, extracellular and plasma are given in the following table.

**Table 13.1 : Concentration of Important Electrolytes**

| Ions | Extracellular electrolytes mEq/L | Intracellular electrolytes mEq/L | Plasma (range) mEq/L |
|---|---|---|---|
| Cations : | | | |
| 1. $Na^+$ | 142 | 10 | 135 – 145 |
| 2. $K^+$ | 4 | 140 | 4.5 – 5.5 |
| 3. $Ca^{++}$ | 2.4 | 0.0001 | 2.1 – 2.6 |
| 4. $Mg^{++}$ | 1.2 | 58 | 1.5 – 3.0 |
| Anions | | | |
| 1. $Cl^-$ | 103 | 4 | 98 – 105* |
| 2. $SO_4^{--}$ | 1 | 2 | 0.3 – 1.5 |
| 3. $HCO_3^-$ | 28 | 10 | 25 – 31* |
| 4. Phosphates | 4 | 75 | 1.2 – 3.0* |

* The values given are range in adults.

From the table it can be seen that the 'extracellular fluid' contains large quantities of sodium and chloride ions and reasonably large quantities of bicarbonate ion, but small quantities of potassium, calcium, magnesium, phosphate and sulphate ions. Whereas intracellular fluids contain small quantities of sodium and chloride ions, very very small quantity of calcium ions but the quantities of potassium and phosphate are very large and a moderate quantities of sulphate and magnesium ions.

As one can see from the table given above the concentration of electrolytes is expressed in terms of mEq/L i.e. milliequivalent per litre and not as w/v i.e. weight/volume. When the electrolytes are administered, usually salt solutions are given and their strength is expressed as w/v unit. The usual doses of electrolytes are generally expressed as m. Eq/L. Thus a pharmacist should know how to convert mEq/L to w/v and vice versa.

Equivalent weight expresses the combining powder and can be obtained by dividing atomic or molecular weight by valency, thus one can easily calculate the concentration in terms of mEq/L by the following equation.

$$mEq/L = \frac{mg \text{ of substance}/L}{\text{Equivalent weight}} = \frac{mg \text{ of substance}/L}{\frac{\text{Molecular weight}}{\text{Valency}}}$$

**Example :** Calculate the number of mEq of sodium chloride in one litre of a 0.45% w/v solution.

0.45% sodium chloride = 4.5 g sodium chloride/L using the equation given above

$$mEq/L = \frac{4500 \text{ mg}}{58.5} = 76.9 \text{ mEq NaCl/L}$$

As the number of sodium ions is necessarily equal to the number of chloride ions thus concentration of each ion is equal i.e. 76.9 mEq $Na^+$/L and 76.9 mEq $Cl^-$/L.

The weight of the substance required to prepare the solution in terms of mEq can be calculated as follows :

$$mg/\text{Litre} = (mEq/L)(Eq.wt) = mEq/L \left(\frac{\text{Mol. Wt.}}{\text{Valency}}\right)$$

**Example :** How much of calcium chloride as dihydrate will be needed to prepare one litre of solution containing 12 mEq $Ca^{++}$/L ?

$$mg/L = \frac{(12)(147)}{2} = 882 \text{ mg}$$

The various electrolytes present in the intracellular or extracellular fluids in the body are associated with various metabolic functions. Following is the discussion in brief about the major physiological ions associated with electrolyte replacement therapy and the correction of acid-base balance therapy.

## MAJOR CATIONS

**1. Sodium :** Normally human body contains about 1.8 g/kg of sodium ions ($Na^+$) and adequate amount of sodium are present in the daily diet. The good food sources for sodium are table salt, milk, baking powder, meat and some vegetables. Daily requirement is about 3–5 g for a normal adult. It is absorbed nearly completely from diet in the intestinal tract. Normally kidneys excretes the excess of the sodium and regulates the sodium content in the body. The sodium from the glomerular filtrate is reabsorbed, hormonal control. Prostaglandin is also said be responsible for the reabsorption of sodium.

**Functions :** Major cation component of the extracellular fluid is sodium ions. It is associated with chloride and bicarbonate in regulating the acid-base equilibrium. Another important function served by sodium is maintenance of osmotic pressure of various body fluids, thus protecting the body against excessive fluid loss. It plays an important role in preserving normal elasticity of muscles and the permeability of cell.

Conditions under which there is low serum sodium level (hyponaturemia) can be summarised as follows :

1. Loss due to excessive urination as in case of 'diabetes inspidus'.
2. Excessive sodium excreation in 'metabolic acidosis'.
3. Diarrhoea and vomiting.
4. In "Addison's disease" in which there is a decreased excreation of hormone aldosterone which is antidiuretic in nature.

Conditions under which there are high serum sodium levels (hypernaturemia) are as follows :

(i) severe dehydration (ii) hyper adrenalism (Cushing syndrome) (iii) certain types of brain damage and (iv) excessive treatment with sodium salts.

Low serum sodium levels leads to dehydration, acidosis and excess leads to edema and hypertension. In case of low sodium levels, sodium salts are administered and in case of high sodium levels treatment involves low salt diet and diuretics. If heart is affected, then cardiotonics in combination with diuretics are given.

**2. Potassium :** Human body usually contains about 2.6 g per kg body weight of potassium ($K^+$). The daily requirement is about 1.5 to 4.5 g. The good sources of potassium in food are milk, certain vegetables, meat and whole grains. Its deficiency generally does not occur except in certain pathological conditions. It is rapidly absorbed from diet from gastrointestinal tract and is rapidly excreted through kidneys. The potassium is also excreted in the digestive fluids but is reabsorbed. The excretion of potassium through kidney is influenced by changes in acid-base balance and activity of adrenal cortex.

**Functions :** It is a principal cation of intracellular fluid, but also a important constituent of extracellular fluid as it influences the muscle activity particularly that of cardiac muscle. Intracellular potassium serves similar function as that of extracellular sodium i.e., it influences the acid-base balance, osmotic pressure and water retention.

Elevated serum potassium levels (Hyperkalemia) are usually seen in patients with renal failure, advanced dehydration or shock. In 'Addison's disease' there is an adrenal insufficiency which elevates, the serum potassium along with a high intracellular potassium. Symptoms of hyperkalemia are mainly cardiac and C.N.S. depression. In hyperkalemia there are signs of bradycardia, poor heart sound, peripheral vascular collapse and lastly cardiac arrest. It also causes electrocardiographic changes. Extracellular elevation of potassium level causes mental confusion; weakness of respiratory muscles and flaccid paralysis of extremeties.

Low serum potassium levels (Hypokalemia) develop in various conditions, which can be summarised as follows :

(a) Illness in which postoperative treatment which includes intravenous administration of solutions not containing potassium for a prolonged period.

(b) They are associated with malnutrition, gastrointestinal losses, as in diarrhoea and in metabolic alkalosis.

(c) Use of diuretics such as acetazolamide and chlorothiazide increases the excretion of potassium in urine. Potassium salts are given if these drugs are to be used for a longer duration.

(d) In case of heart disease, the potassium content of myocardium is depleated, with heart recovery the potassium becomes normal. However, during intracellular depletion of calcium, the myocardium becomes sensitive to digitilis intoxication and arrhythmia.

(e) During correction of dehydration or acidosis or alkolosis with sodium and water the depletion of potassium becomes apparant.

3. **Calcium** : The total calcium ($Ca^{++}$) content in body is about 22 g per kg body weight and daily requirement is about 0.8 g. Most of the calcium is found in bones and remaining is largely found in extracellular fluid compartments. The biochemical role, its absorption, metabolism and other aspects are discussed under "compounds of calcium".

4. **Magnesium** : The total magnesium ($Mg^{++}$) content in body is about 0.5 g per kg body weight and about 70% of this is present in complex form with calcium and phosphorous in bones. The remaining is distributed in soft tissues and body fluids. The daily requirement is about 350 mg. Good food source for magnesium are various nuts, soyabeans, whole grains and sea foods. The magnesium ingested with food is absorbed from duodenum in acidic media and this absorption is not related to magnesium stores in body. The main functions are (i) it is a cofactor for phosphate $\left(PO_4^-\right)$ transferring enzymes, (ii) constituent of teeth and bones and (iii) it decreases neuromuscular irritability. Magnesium is essential for protein synthesis and for smooth functioning of the neuromuscular system.

Magnesium depletion can occur due to malnutrition, dietary restriction and chronic alcoholism, faulty absorption and gastrointestinal diseases. Its deficiency may lead to muscular tumour, confusion, vasodilation and hyper irritability etc.

There are other cations like iron ($Fe^{++}$) (discussed under "compounds of iron") and cation like zinc ($Zn^{++}$), copper ($Cu^{++}$), cobalt ($Co^{++}$), Manganese ($Mn^{++}$), chromium ($Cr^{+++}$) are called essential trace ions and their discussion is beyond the scope of this book.

## MAJOR ANIONS

1. **Chloride** : The total chloride ion present in the body is about 50 mEq per kg body weight and daily body requirement is about 5 to 10 g as sodium chloride. The dietary source for chloride ion is common table salt used in cooking. It is readily absorbed throughout gastrointestinal tract. Chloride ions are excreted mainly through urine and sweat. It is present in all body secretions. It is a major anion of all body fluids and constitutes nearly 66% of the anions present in plasma as chloride ion.

Chloride ions do not exert any important pharmacological action. However, it serve two important functions. Osmotic balance between different body fluids is maintained by chloride ions along with sodium ions. It is also responsible for maintaining the balance of charges between the body fluids, i.e. intracellular and extracellular both, as they can pass through all membranes. When carbon-dioxide from an actively metabolising tissue enters R.B.C. and gets converted to bicarbonate, equivalent amount leaves cells and thus charge neutrality is maintained. Chloride ions are involved in formation of gastric hydrochloric acid and also in maintenance of acid-base balance. Under the normal physiological conditions there is no deficiency of chloride ion, but if there is more utilization then, deficiency can lead to 'hypochloremic alkalosis' causing vomiting.

**2. Sulphate** : Very small quantity of this ion is present in plasma and interstitial fluids. Good diatery sources are animal and plant proteins, having sulphur containing amino acids like cystein and methionin. They are derived from metabolism of the above two amino acids. The organic sulphur is oxidised to sulphate. Sulphur containing compounds are important in detoxication mechanism and SH group containing organic compounds in tissue respiration.

**3. Bicarbonate** : It is the second largest anion present in the extracellular fluid compartment. The bicarbonate ion along with carbonic acid acts as one of the important buffer systems in maintenance of the acid-base balance. If there is excess of bicarbonate it produces metabolic alkalosis and depletation causes metabolic acidosis. The details of the above will be discussed under physiological acid-base balance and electrolytes.

**4. Phosphate** : Phosphate ion is a major anion of the intracellular fluid compartment. The main dietary sources are milk, milk products, whole grains legumes, nuts etc. All cells in the body contain phosphorous and nearly 4/5th of phosphorous is present in teeth and bones along with calcium. It is also present in combination of proteins, carbohydrates and fats. Daily requirement of phosphate is nearly same as that of calcium, particularly in pregnant and lactating mothers and in children.

Metabolism of phosphate is quite complex and involves many processes. Its metabolism is related with that of calcium. Usually, the ratio of calcium to phosphorous in diet affects the absorption and excretion, i.e. if calcium is in excess than it increases the excretion of phosphate and vice-versa. Vitamin D affects the metabolism of calcium which is concerned with phosphate. In the body fluids it is present as monohydrogen phosphate and dihydrogen phosphate. The ratio $H_2PO_4^-/HPO_4^{--}$ serves as buffer system of the body fluids. One of the important metabolic processes in the body is 'phosphorylation' which converts many organic compounds into phosphate esters. It is essential for the proper calcium metabolism and thus for proper development of teeth and bones. Glucose and other hexoses are metabolised through phosphorylation and similarly many vitamins after phsophorylation functions as co-enzymes. Phosphate ester bonds in the body is a source of energy. With balanced diet generally there is no possibility of hypophosphatemia, but its deficiency affects the utilisation of glucose in erythrocytes. Its deficiency rarely leads to osteomalecia and renal rickets.

## (B) ELECTROLYTES USED IN REPLACEMENT THERAPY

Under the normal physiological conditions body mechanism adjusts the electrolyte balance and no replacement is necessary. However, under some conditions (including pathological or disease) there results deficiency of particular electrolyte. Administration of that electrolyte in appropriate concentration of tonocity becomes necessary. Usually, electrolyte salts of sodium, potassium, calcium, etc. are used singly or in combination with other constituents (like dextrose, invert sugar, mannitol, etc.). A brief account of such electrolytes as a replacement ions is presented here with.

## REPLACEMENT OF SODIUM

The most commonly used salt for sodium ion is sodium chloride.

### 1. Sodium Chloride :

**NaCl** Mol. Wt. 58.54

It contains not less than 99.5% and not more than 100.5% of NaCl, calculated with reference to substance dried at 130°C.

**Preparation :** In laboratory, it can be obtained by passing HCl gas in aqueous solution of common salt, when the crystals are precipitated out.

Industrially it is obtained (i) by evaporation of sea water and then purification and (ii) by purifying rock salt.

**Properties :** It is a white crystalline powder or colourless crystals, odourless and has saline taste. It is freely soluble in water slightly more in boiling water, soluble in glycerine.

It can be oxidised chemically and liberates chlorine gas.

$$2Cl^- + MnO_2 + 2H_2SO_4 \longrightarrow Mn^{++} + SO_4^{--} + 2H_2O + Cl_2 \uparrow$$

It gives a white water insoluble precipitate of silver chloride when aqueous solutions are treated with solution of silver nitrate.

**Assay :** Earlier it was analysed by precipitation titration technique using Mohr method, in which aqueous solution is directly titrated with standard silver nitrate solution using potassium chromate as indicator.

$$NaCl + AgNO_3 \longrightarrow AgCl\downarrow + NaNO_3$$

Now-a-days it analysed by Volhard's precipitation method with modification. In this method the aqueous solution is acidified with nitric acid, excess of standard silver nitrate is added. Silverchloride gets precipitated. Then nitrobenzene is added and excess of silver nitrate is determined by titrating with standard ammonium thiocynate using ferric ammonium sulphate as indicator. Nitrobenzene prevents interaction of silverchloride with ferric thiocynate.

**Storage :** It is stored in tightly closed containers in dry place as it absorbs moisture.

**Uses :** It is a source of both sodium and chloride ions. The dosage forms are solutions, tablets and parenteral solutions. 0.9% w/v solution is isotonic and is used as wet dressing and irrigating body cavities or tissues. In the form of injections and infusions it is used alone or in combination with other salts or glucose when body fluid electrolytes are depleted. Such preparations find use as electrolyte replenisher. Hypertonic solutions are used in conditions when there is excessive loss of sodium along with water. When hypertonic solution is given orally it induces vomiting and thus can be used in case of poisoning as a first aid. It is a constituent of Ringer's solution, Ringer's injection, lactated Ringer's injection, sodium chloride and potassium chloride intravenous infusion and oral rehydration salt.

When sodium chloride is used in combination, such preparations are discussed under "Electrolyte combination Therapy". The formulations of sodium chloride alone or with glucose are given below.

### 2. Sodium Chloride Eye Lotion (B.P.) :

It contains 0.85 to 0.95% w/v of NaCl.

It is prepared by dissolving sodium chloride in purified water, filtered, transferred to final container, avoiding the entry of microorganisms and sterilised by heating in an autoclave.

### 3. Sodium Chloride Solution (B.P.) :

It contains 0.9% w/v sodium chloride, prepared in purified water and clarified by filtration.

When normal saline is prescribed then above solution is dispensed. If the label states that it is sterile solution, then it should comply with the test for sterility.

### 4. Sodium Chloride Injection (I.P., B.P.) : (Sodium chloride intravenous infusion) :

It is a sterile isotonic solution of sodium chloride in water for injection. It contains between 0.85–0.95% w/v of NaCl (I.P.), whereas B.P. states sodium chloride content between 95–105% w/v of the stated amount.

One should take care in labelling the above product. As per I.P. the label should indicate that (i) The injection contains 150 millimoles of sodium and chloride ions per litre and (ii) The injection should not be used if it contains visible solids particles.

As per B.P. sodium chloride injections are available in various strength containing 0.9%, w/v of sodium chloride in 2, 5, 10, 20, 50, 100, 500 and 1000 ml containers. Other strengths available are 0.18, 0.225, 0.45, 1.8, 2.7 and 5% w/v solution of sodium chloride in 500 ml container.

When sodium chloride injection is required as diluent for pharmacopoeial injections, sodium chloride intravenous infusion (0.9% w/v) is to be used.

### 5. Sodium Chloride Hypertonic Injection (I.P.) (Hypertonic saline) :

It is a sterile solution of sodium chloride in water for injection and contains not less than 1.52% and not more than 1.68% w/v of sodium chloride. It contains no antimicrobial agent.

This preparation contains 270 millimoles of sodium and chloride ions per litre.

### 6. Sodium Chloride Tablets (B.P.) :

It contains NaCl, 95.0 to 105% w/w of the stated amount. They are usually available in the following strength, tablets containing 180, 300 and 500 mg of NaCl.

### 7. Sodium Chloride and Dextrose Injection (I.P.) :
### (Sodium chloride and dextrose intravenous infusion)

It is a sterile solution of sodium chloride and dextrose in water for injection and contains between 95 to 105.0% of the stated amount of sodium chloride and dextrose ($C_6H_{12}O_6$).

This preparation is available in various strengths.

(a) Containing, 0.11, 0.18, 0.2, 0.225, 0.3 and 0.33% of sodium chloride and 5% w/v dextrose.

(b) Containing 0.45% sodium chloride with 2.5%, 5.0% and 10% dextrose.

(c) Containing 0.9% sodium chloride with 2.5, 5.0, 10 and 25% dextrose.

The above preparations are used as fluid nutrient and electrolyte replenishers. The label must state the % w/v of both ingredients and also the miliequivalent of sodium and chloride ions as it is used as intravenous infusion.

### 8. Mannitol and Sodium Chloride Injection (U.S.P.) :

It is a sterile solution of sodium chloride and mannitol in various proportions of the above ingredients e.g. 5 and 10% mannitol with 0.3% NaCl, 15 and 20% mannitol with 0.45% NaCl.

The above preparation is used as diuretic.

All sodium chloride formulations are analysed for NaCl content by method used for sodium chloride, the glucose is analysed using polarimeter.

## REPLACEMENT OF POTASSIUM

The most commonly used salt is potassium chloride.

### 1. Potassium Chloride :

KCl                                                                 Mol. Wt. 74.55

It contains not less than 99% KCl, calculated with reference to the dried substance.

**Preparation :** It is obtained from the natural mineral 'Carnallite' ($KCl.MgCl_2.6H_2O$). The raw salt deposit is ground and treated with hot water when less soluble KCl crystallises out from mother liquor.

In laboratory it can be prepared by the action of HCl on potassium carbonate or bicarbonate.

$$K_2CO_3 + 2HCl \longrightarrow 2KCl + H_2O + CO_2 \uparrow$$
$$KHCO_3 + HCl \longrightarrow KCl + H_2O + CO_2 \uparrow$$

**Properties :** It is available as colourless prismatic or cubical crystals or as a white grannular powder. It is odourless and possesses a saline taste. It is freely soluble in water and aqueous solutions are neutral to litmus. In qualitative analysis chloride is precipitated by $Ag^+$, $Hg_2^{++}$ and $Pb^{++}$ as insoluble chlorides.

**Assay :** As per I.P. it is analysed by 'Mohr' method in which the aqueous solution is directly titrated with standard silver nitrate solution using potassium chromate as indicator.

As per B.P. it is analysed on lines of the principle used for analysis of sodium chloride, with exception that, the nitrobenzene is replaced by dibutyl phthalate.

**Uses :** The salt is most widely used for oral replacement of potassium in the form of solution. However, the aqueous solution causes irritation of gastro intestinal tract. It is used intravenously if person can not take it orally or in cases of sever hypoptassemia. It finds use as adjunct in treatment of 'Myasthenia gravis', (severe muscular weakness).

It is a constituent of oral rehydration salt, sodium chloride and potassium chloride intravenous infusion, sodium and potassium chloride and glucose intravenous infusion, 'Ringer's injection' and 'Ringer's solution'.

2. **Potassium Chloride and Glucose Intravenous Infusion (B.P.) :**

It is a sterile solution in water for injection containing KCl 95 - 105% and glucose 95 to 105% of the stated amount on label. Usual strength available are intravenous infusions containing 0.15, 0.2 and 0.3% w/v of KCl, each containing 5% w/v of glucose in 500 ml and 1000 ml containers.

3. **Potassium Chloride and Sodium Chloride Intravenous Infusion (B.P.) :**

**(Potassium chloride and sodium chloride injection)**

It is a sterile solution containing 95 to 105% of the stated amount of sodium chloride and potassium chloride. The solution is prepared in water for injection and sterilised by heating in an autoclave. Usual strengths available are infusions containing 0.15, 0.2 and 0.3% w/v KCl, each containing 0.9% w/v of NaCl in 500 ml and 1000 ml containers.

4. **Potassium Chloride, Sodium Chloride and Glucose Intravenous Infusion (B.P.) :**

It is sterile solution in water for injection containing KCl, 95 to 105% w/v of stated amount on label, sodium chloride 0.17 to 0.19% w/v and glucose ($C_6H_{12}O_6$) 3.8 to 4.2 % w/v. Usual strength available are infusions containing 0.15, 0.2 and 0.3% w/v KCl, each containing 0.18% w/v NaCl and 4% w/v glucose.

## REPLACEMENT OF CALCIUM

This has already been discussed under the title official "compounds of calcium".

## (C) ELECTROLYTE COMBINATION THERAPY :

Usually, when patient is unable to take normal diet before or after surgery, an electrolyte combination therapy is given. Infusions containing glucose and normal saline are used. But when the patient has vitamin deficiency or has protracted illness, other electrolytes are also needed and in such cases the combination of electrolytes are prepared and given as per the need of the patient. Various combinations of electrolytes, varying in concentration are available commercially.

Electrolyte combination products are divided in two categories (i) Fluid maintenance and (ii) Electrolyte replacement. In the former the fluid or solutions of electrolytes are administered intravenously which provide the normal requirement of water and electrolytes to patients who can not take food orally. All the fluid maintenance of electrolyte infusions contain at least 5.0% glucose, which helps to reduce certain metabolites like urea, ketonebodies and phosphate, which are usually associated with starvation.

When there is a heavy loss of water and electrolytes for e.g. in excessive vomiting, diarrhoea, or prolonged fever, electrolyte combinations are used as replacement therapy. Various electrolyte combinations and varying concentrations are commercially available as dry powders to be dissolved in specified amount of water or in the form of prepared solutions "oral electrolyte solutions".

Some important products used in electrolyte combination therapy are as follows :

1. **Sodium Lactate Injection (I.P., B.P.) :**

   **(Sodium lactate intravenous infusion)**

   It is a sterile solution containing 1.75 to 1.95% w/v of sodium lactate ($C_3H_5NaO_3$) prepared in water for injection, using lactic acid and sodium hydroxide in such a manner that there is conversion of any lactid present. It is sterilised by heating in an autoclave.

   It is a 1/6 molar solution and is given at a rate of 5 ml or less per minute. The label also states its contains approximately 167 millimoles of sodium and of bicarbonate ions (as lactate) per litre. It is used as fluid and electrolyte replenisher.

2. **Compound Sodium Chloride Injection (I.P.) :**

   **(Ringer's injection)**

   It is a sterile solution prepared in water for injection containing NaCl, 0.82 to 0.90% w/v; KCl, 0.0285 – 0.0315% w/v, and $CaCl_2 \cdot 2H_2O$, 0.03–0.036% w/v. It does not contain antimicrobial agent. It is sterilised by heating in an autoclave.

3. **Compound Sodium Lactate Injection (I.P.)**

   **Compound Sodium Lactate Intravenous Infusion (B.P.) :**

   **(Ringer lactate solution for injection, Hartmann's solution for injection)**

   It is sterile solution prepared in water for injection containing, total chloride (Cl) 0.37–0.42% w/v; $CaCl_2.2H_2O$, 0.025 – 0.029 % w/v and lactic acid ($C_3H_6O_3$), 0.23–0.28% w/v. The formula for preparing above solution is :

   | | | |
   |---|---|---|
   | Lactic acid | ... | 2.4 ml |
   | Sodium hydroxide | ... | 1.15 g |
   | Dilute HCl | ... | quantity sufficient |
   | Sodium chloride | ... | 6.0 g |
   | Potassium chloride | ... | 0.4 g |
   | Calcium chloride | ... | 0.27 g |
   | Water for injection | ... | to produce 1000 ml. |

The label also states the approximate milliequivalent of ions present per litre. It contains sodium 131, Potassium 5, calcium 4, chloride 111, and carbonate (lactate) 29 milliequivalent per litre.

### 4. Oral Rehydration Salts :

A large number of formulations of oral rehydration preparations are available in the market, which contains anhydrous glucose (or glucose), sodium chloride, potassium chloride, and either sodium bicarbonate or sodium citrate. These dry powder preparations are to be mixed in specific amount of water and are used for oral rehydration therapy. These preparations may contain a flavouring agent and a suitable agent for free flow of the powder.

The following three formulations are usually prepared. When glucose is used, sodium bicarbonate is packed separately. The quantities given below are for preparing 1 litre solution.

| Ingredient | Formula I | Formula II | Formula III |
|---|---|---|---|
| Sodium chloride | 1.0 g | 3.5 g | 3.5 g |
| Potassium chloride | 1.5 g | 1.5 g | 1.5 g |
| Sodium bicarbonate | 1.5 g | 2.5 g | – |
| Sodium citrate | – | – | 2.9 g |
| Anhydrous glucose | 36.4 g | 20.0 g | 20.0 g |
| or Glucose | 40.0 g | 22.0 g | – |

The formula II and III are recommended by WHO and UNICEF for control of diarrhoel diseases.

Various oral electrolyte solutions are also available in market.

## (D) PHYSIOLOGICAL ACID-BASE BALANCE

The acid-base balance in the body is well regulated by intricate mechanisms. Number of chemical reactions take place in the cell and the activity of cell and the reactions occurring inside is greatly influenced by pH or hydrogen ion concentration. The hydrogen ion concentration in the extra-cellular fluid is regulated at a value of approximately $4 \times 10^{-8}$ Eq/lit.

The pH of blood of healthy person remains constant around 7.35. This is because of various mechanisms. If the pH of blood is low (high hydrogen ion concentration) 'acidosis' and when pH is high (low hydrogen ion concentration) 'alkalosis' results.

The control of hydrogen ion concentration (pH) is mainly carried by three mechanisms viz.

**1. Buffering system :** Three major systems of buffering in the body are (i) carbonic acid/bicarbonate $\left(H_2CO_3/HCO_3^-\right)$ which mainly occurs in plasma and kidney, (ii) monohydrogen phosphate/ dihydrogen phosphate $\left(HPO_4^{2-}/H_2PO_4^-\right)$ found in cells and kidney and (iii) Protein buffer system. Proteins are composed of aminoacids bound together by peptide linkage. However, some amino acids like histidine have free acidic group which on dissociation form base and $H^+$ which participates in buffering of the body fluids.

2. The other important pH control is through the control of "respiratory centre". When this is stimulated it alters the rate of breathing. Through the rate, the removal of $CO_2$ from body fluids lead to the changes in pH of blood carbonic acid.

3. The third mechanism is via elimination of some ions through urine by kidney. Absorption of certain ions and elimination of others control the acid-base balance of blood and thus of body fluids.

## METABOLIC ACIDOSIS AND ALKALOSIS

Metabolic acidosis can result from (i) failure to excrete metabolic acids by kidney (ii) formation of excessive quantities of metabolic acids (like carbonic acid) (iii) absorption or administration of excess metabolic and other acids (iv) loss of base from body fluids under certain conditions. Metabolic acidosis results due to diarrhoea, vomiting, uremia or diabetes mellitus.

Metabolic alkalosis does not normally occur. However, it may result under certain conditions like administration of diuretics or excessive ingestion of alkaline drugs or due to loss of chloride ions etc.

When the conditions of acidosis or alkalosis result, certain drugs are administered to control the acid-base balance. Following drugs are used and a brief account of these is presented.

## ELECTROLYTES USED IN ACID-BASE THERAPY :

Generally potassium/sodium compounds like bicarbonates, lactate, acetate are used to treat metabolic acidosis, whereas metabolic alkalosis is treated with ammonium salt, important being ammonia chloride.

**1. Potassium Acetate (B.P.) :**

$C_2H_3O_2K$  Mol. Wt. 98.14

It contains between 99–101% of $C_2H_3O_2K$, calculated with reference to the dried substance.

**Preparation :** It is prepared by neutralising acetic acid with potassium carbonate or bicarbonate till the effervescence ceases. The solution is evaporated to dryness and then fused and allowed to solidify. It is powdered and bottled immediately. If it is required in crystalline condition, then it is stirred continuously during concentrating the solution. The crystals so formed are removed by centrifugation and dried in warm air.

$$2CH_3COOH + K_2CO_3 \longrightarrow 2CH_3COOK + H_2O + CO_2 \uparrow$$

**Properties :** It is a white crystalline powder or colourless crystals, almost odourless. It has saline and slightly alkaline taste. When exposed to air it absorbs moisture rapidly and thus stored in air tight containers. It is soluble in water and alcohol but insoluble in ether. Aqueous solution has alkaline reaction. When heated strongly it gives inflammable vapour and leaves residue of potassium carbonate.

$$2CH_2COOK + 4O_2 \xrightarrow{\Delta} K_2CO_3 + 3H_2O + 3CO_2 \uparrow$$

**Aasay :** It is assayed by non-aqueous titration method, by dissolving it in glacial acetic acid and titrating with standard perchloric acid using crystal violet as indicator.

**Uses :** The aqueous solutions of acetate are oxidised by body tissue to bicarbonate after absorption and thus function as alkali. It is used as urinary alkaliser. It also has diuretic action. It is a systemic alkaliser similar to sodium bicarbonate. The acetate ion also acts as antacid in stomach by combining with hydrogen ion to form slightly ionisable acetic acid.

2. **Potassium Citrate :**

$$C_6H_5K_3O_7, H_2O \begin{bmatrix} CH_2COOK \\ | \\ HO - C - COOK \\ | \\ CH_2COOK \end{bmatrix} \quad \text{Mol. Wt. 324.4}$$

It is a tripotassium salt of citric acid and is associated with one molecule of water. It contains not less than 99% and not more than 101% of $C_6H_5K_3O_7$, calculated with reference to anhydrous substance.

**Preparation :** It is prepared by neutralising a solution of citric acid with potassium carbonate or bicarbonate. The solution is then evaporated to dryness with constant stirring. A fine powder is obtained by trituration in a warm mortor.

$$3KHCO_3 + C_6H_8O_7 + H_2O \longrightarrow C_6H_5K_3O_7 \cdot H_2O + 3H_2O + 3CO_2\uparrow$$

**Properties :** It is available as colourless crystals or a white grannular powder, odourless and has a cooling saline taste. The salt is deliquescent in moist air and thus stored in air tight containers. It is soluble in water but is insoluble in alcohol. When heated at 100°C, it looses water and becomes anhydrous at about 200°C. On further heating it carbonises and gives out inflammable gases and residue of potassium carbonate is obtained.

$$2K_3C_6H_5O_7 \cdot H_2O + 9O_2 \longrightarrow 3K_2CO_3 + 7H_2O + 9CO_2\uparrow$$

**Assay :** It is analysed by non-aqueous titration method, by dissolving it in glacial acetic acid and titrating with standard perchloric acid using 1-naptholbenzein as indicator.

**Uses :** It has diuretic, expectorant and diaphoratic action. These actions are greater than other alkali salts and ammonium compounds. It has a slight laxative action. The citrate ion is readily oxidised by tissue to $CO_2$ and water and equivalent sodium bicarbonate is formed and thus functions as systemic alkalinising agent. It has anticoagulant action also.

3. **Sodium Acetate :**

$CH_3COONa \cdot 3H_2O$            Mol. Wt. 136.1

It is a sodium salt of acetic acid and is obtained as trihydrate. It contains not less than 99% and not more than 101% of $C_2H_3NaO_3 \cdot 3H_2O$.

**Preparation :** It is prepared by neutralising acetic acid with sodium carbonate or bicarbonate. The solution is filtered, concentrated and allowed to crystallise.

It is also manufactured by neutralising the wood vinegar by sodium carbonate. In this case the impurities are removed by various treatments and the crystals are obtained by evaporating the solution

$$2CH_3COOH + Na_2CO_3 \longrightarrow 2CH_3COONa + H_2O + CO_2\uparrow$$

**Properties :** It is obtained as colourless crystals or white granular crystalline powder. It has a slight odour and a slightly saline and bitter taste. It is soluble in water and alcohol. Its aqueous solutions are alkaline in nature.

**Assay :** It is assayed by non-aqueous titration method by dissolving it in glacial acetic acid and acetic anhydride (10:1 ratio) and titrated with perchloric acid using 1-naphthol benzein as indicator.

**Uses :** It is an ingredient of peritoneal dialysis fluid. The tissue oxidises it to bicarbonate and thus acts as alkalinising agent. It also causes hypertonic condition of extracellular fluid and result of this is diuretic action.

### 4. Sodium Bicarbonate :

The method of preparation, properties and uses of this compound are discussed under "Antacid". Some important uses are as follows : Medicinally it is used to combact systemic acidosis, and also used as antacid to neutralise gastric hyperacidity. As it causes alkalinisation of urine it is administered along with sulpha drugs to prevent crystal urea. Its continuous use as antacid has serious drawback as it can cause "rebound acidity".

### 5. Sodium Citrate :

$$C_6H_5Na_3O_7\cdot 2H_2O \quad \begin{bmatrix} CH_2COONa \\ | \\ HO-C-COONa\cdot 2H_2O \\ | \\ CH_2COONa \end{bmatrix} \qquad \text{Mol. Wt. 294.1}$$

It contains not less than 99% and not more than 101% of $C_6H_5Na_3O_7$, calculated with reference to anhydrous substance.

**Preparation :** It is prepared by neutralising solution of citric acid with sodium carbonate or bicarbonate. When the effervescence ceases, the solution is evaporated to crystallise the product.

$$\begin{array}{c} CH_2COOH \\ | \\ HO-C-COOH \\ | \\ CH_2COOH \end{array} + 3NaHCO_3 \longrightarrow Na_3C_6H_5O_7\cdot 2H_2O + 3CO_2\uparrow + 2H_2O$$

**Properties :** It is available as colourless crystals or white crystalline powder, freely soluble in water, but insoluble in alcohol and ether. It has a saline taste. The salt effloresces on exposure to dry air and has to be stored in air-tight container.

When heated to about 150°C, it becomes anhydrous, and on further heating it chars and leaves a residue of sodium carbonate.

$$2Na_3C_6H_5O_7\cdot 2H_2O + 9O_2 \longrightarrow 3Na_2CO_3 + 9CO_2\uparrow + 9H_2O$$

**Assay :** It is analysed by non-aqueous titration method, by dissolving it in glacial acetic acid and titrating with standard perchloric acid. In this case the end point is determined potentiometrically.

**Uses :** In solution form it ionises to liberate sodium and citrate ion. The citrate ion can take up hydrogen ion from highly ionisable hydrochloric acid and thus acts as buffer against acid. Like other citrates, when taken orally, it is oxidised to sodium bicarbonate and thus used as systemic alkaliser. It has anticoagulant and good sequestring properties.

### 6. Sodium Phosphate :
### (Disodium hydrogen phosphate)

This compound has already been discussed under 'laxative'. Besides being a laxative, it can be used as a source of phosphate in phosphorous deficiency in diabetic acidosis. It acts as buffer.

### 7. Ammonium Chloride :

The preparation and properties of this compound has already been discussed under 'Expectorant'.

The ammonium ion is important in maintenance of acid base equilibrium of the body, and used in metabolic alkalosis. Actually it reduces the alkali reserve of the body. In large doses it produces diuresis and makes the urine acidic. For treating severe alkalosis it can be administered in a 2% solution intravenously along with glucose. Ammonium chloride formulations like tablets and capsules are available in market.

## EXECISE

1. *Make a list of major intra and extracellular electrolytes, categorising them as anionic and cationic.*
2. *Explain the term milliequivalent. Calculate the number of mEq of potassium chloride in one litre of a 0.48% w/v solution.*
3. *Discuss the important functions of sodium ion in the body.*
4. *Describe the conditions leading to hypokalemia and hyperkalemia.*
5. *Give the important functions served by chloride and bicarbonate ion.*
6. *Make a list of sodium chloride formulations used in electrolyte replacement therapy.*
7. *Give method of preparation, properties and uses of potassium chloride.*
8. *Give a brief account of electrolyte combination therapy.*
9. *How the acid-base balance of the body is maintained ?*
10. *Explain the terms metabolic acidosis and alkalosis. How are these corrected ? Give method of preparation and uses of potassium acetate or sodium bicarbonate.*

# 14

# OFFICIAL COMPOUNDS OF IRON

**IRON COMPOUNDS**

In medicine, iron is used in the form of its compounds as Ferric salts ($Fe^{+++}$), Ferrous salts ($Fe^{++}$) and complexed. Iron compounds such as ferric ammonium citrate.

Iron is one of the essential constituents of the body and the usual contents are about 45 mg/kg body weight. Iron plays a very important role in body functions. It is an essential constituent of blood system and tissues where it plays a very specific role. Iron is usually associated with the types of proteins : (i) hemoproteins, (ii) iron storage and/or transport proteins.

Hemoproteins are responsible for respiration and for carrying oxygen. Amongst the cytochromes, cytochrome C is important. In this, iron is complexed in porphyrin ring system and functions as electron carrier either as $Fe^{++}$ or $Fe^{+++}$ as it can take up or loose electron in the process of electron transfer. Other important enzymes which contains iron are catalase and peroxidase. Hemoglobin and myoglobin are other important hemoproteins which stores and/or transports oxygen. In hemoglobin, iron is present in ferrous from and it complexes with molecular oxygen. The uptake or release of oxygen in turn depends on various factors like pH, carbondioxide, concentration etc. Iron deficiency anemies are characterised by decreased capability of oxygen transport.

The second category of proteins Ferritin and Hemosiderin are the important ironstore proteins which are found in liver, spleen and bone marrow. In ferritin, the complexed iron is present as a ferric ($Fe^{+++}$) form, but it is incorporated or released in ferrous ($Fe^{++}$) form. Hemosiderin is considered as dehydrated form of ferritin by some Scientists. Solubilities of these two proteins differ, ferritin is water soluble whereas hemosidarin is water insoluble. Transferrin, a glycoprotein present in blood plasma as the major iron transport protein. Two atoms of ferric iron are bound to each molecule of glycoprotein. This binding is firm so that practically no free iron is present in the plasma. The protein releases iron to precursor of red cell for the production of R.B.C.

The contents of iron in body is controlled by regulating the absorption and not by excretion, as body recycles the iron obtained from breakdown of R.B.C. and thus daily requirement of iron is quite low. Iron requirement increases during pregnancy, growth and lactation (about 10-12 mg for male and 12-18 mg for female). Large amount of iron is lost in haemorrhage and in menstrual flow. The iron loss is more in case of females compared to males. Iron loss is still more during pregnancy as it is transported to placenta, thus iron preparations are generally given during pregnancy. A small amount of iron is excreted into urine and faeces (about 1 mg daily) and the bulk of iron excreted through faeces is from unabsorbed iron from food.

Food is the common source for iron for most people. The treatment of anemia, starts with treatment of the pathological condition causing anemia, along with supplemental iron therapy. This is in conditions of insufficient iron intake or excessive loss of iron due to bleeding or inadequate iron absorption. In treating macrolytic anemia, iron preparations are used as supplement along with cyanocobalamine. A large number of iron preparations are available in market like liquids, capsules, tablets, or injectables. Injectables are rarely used, as oral therapy gives satisfactory results. The oral preparations can sometimes cause constipation, gastrointestinal irritation leading to vomiting and diarrhoea. The above side affects can be controlled by regulating the time of administration and dose.

Over doses of oral iron preparations can cause serious problems leading to death particularly of young patients. Iron poisoning progresses in various stages.

Iron poisoning is usually treated by gastric lavarage, followed by giving sodium bicarbonate and sodium dihydrogen phosphate which converts iron into insoluble iron salt. If there is no evidence of kidney damage, then deferoxamine is orally administered to prevent absorption of iron. Deferoxamine when administered parenterally causes chelation of iron which passes through urine. It is used only when unbound iron is indicated to be present in serum. It is important to keep iron preparations away from childrens.

Important iron compounds and preparations are as follows :

## 1. Ferric Ammonium Citrate :

It is a complex salt and contains not less 20.5% and not more than 22.5% Fe. This is known as "scale preparation" of iron. This compound is no more official in I.P. and B.P.

**Preparation :** This is prepared using ferric sulphate, sodium hydroxide, ammonia and citric acid. In the first step, ferric hydroxide is freshly prepared by adding the ferric salt solution to alkali (NaOH) by constant stirring (and not adding alkali to ferric salt which may result into precipitate containing basic ferric salt, which subsequently prevent the formation of transparent scales).

$$Fe_2(SO_4)_2 + 6NaOH \longrightarrow 2Fe(OH)_3 + 3Na_2SO_4$$

The precipitate of ferric hydroxide is collected, washed and added as such, without drying, by stirring into solution of citric acid. Most of it gets dissolved. A slight excess of ammonia is then added and any undissolved ferric hydroxide is filtered out. The clear reddish-brown filtrate is evaporated to a syrup (little ammonia is added during this process to maintain any loss during evaporation). The syrup is then painted on glass plates and dried at 40°C. The dried scales are scraped-off and packed.

The characteristic brownish-red colour of ferric ammonium citrate is due to basic complexes of variable composition which may be represented by general formula, $FeC_6H_5O_7 \cdot XFe(OH)_3$, where 'X' is greater than one but less than two.

**Properties :** It occurs as bright brownish-red scales with slight astringent taste. It is freely soluble in water but insoluble in alcohol. This preparation is deliquescent in air and is affected by light and thus stored in well-closed containers, protected from light and moisture.

## 2. Ferrous Fumarate :

$$\left[ \begin{array}{c} H-C-COO^- \\ \| \\ \bar{O}OC-C-H \end{array} \right] Fe^{++}$$

$C_4H_2FeO_4$      Mol. Wt. 169.9

It contains not less than 93% of $C_4H_2FeO_4$, calculated with reference to the dried substance.

**Preparation :** It is prepared by double decomposition. A hot aqueous solution of ferrous sulphate is added to a solution of sodium fumarate with constant stirring. The sparingly soluble ferrous fumarate separates, which is filtered and dried.

**Properties :** It is a reddish-orange or reddish-brown powder. It may contain soft lumps which produce yellow streaks when crushed. It has a light odour and astringent taste. It is slightly soluble in water and still less in alcohol.

One of the important tests is, that the content of ferric iron be not more than 20%. For this, about 3 g of compound is dissolved in 200 ml water and 20 ml hydrochloric acid by heating. To the cooled solution is then added 3 g potassium iodide and allowed to stand for 15 minutes in dark and the liberated iodine is titrated with 0.1 N sodium thiosulphate using starch solution as indicator. A blank determination is carried out (without ferrous fumarate). The difference gives the amount of iodine liberated by ferric iron.

Each ml of 0.1 N sodium thiosulphate = 0.005585 g of ferric iron.

**Assay :** It is based on oxidation-reduction reaction. About 0.3 g sample is dissolved in 15 ml of dilute sulphuric acid by gentle warming, cooled, 50 ml water is added and immediately titrated with 0.1 M ceric ammonium sulphate using ferroin sulphate solution as indicator.

$$Fe^{2+} + Ce^{4+} \longrightarrow Fe^{3+} + Ce^{3+}$$

Each ml of 0.7 M ceric ammonium sulphate = 0.01699 g of $C_4H_2FeO_4$.

## 3. Ferrous Fumarate Tablets :

These are official in I.P. and B.P. Each average weighing tablet contains not less than 90% and not more than 105% of ferrous fumarate ($C_4H_2FeO_4$) of the stated amount. Usually tablets, each containing 200 mg and 304 mg of ferrous fumarate, equivalent to 65 mg and 100 mg of ferrous iron, are available.

### 4. Ferrous Gluconate :

$$\left[ HOCH_2 - \underset{\underset{OH}{|}}{\overset{\overset{H}{|}}{C}} - \underset{\underset{OH}{|}}{\overset{\overset{H}{|}}{C}} - \underset{\underset{H}{|}}{\overset{\overset{OH}{|}}{C}} - \underset{\underset{H}{|}}{\overset{\overset{OH}{|}}{C}} - COO^- \right]_2 Fe^{++}$$

$C_{12}H_{22}O_{14}Fe, 2H_2O$            Mol. Wt. 602

It is iron (II) di (D-gluconate). It contains not less than 95% $C_{12}H_{22}O_{14}Fe$, as per I.P., whereas B.P. standards states that it contains not less than 11.8% and not more than 12.5% of iron (II), both calculated with reference to the dried substance.

**Preparation :** It is obtained by reacting ferrous carbonate with gluconic acid, which is obtained by fermentation of glucose. Gluconic acid is treated with ferrous carbonate and from the resulting solution ferrous gluconate crystallizes out usually as dehydrate.

$$C_6H_{12}O_6 \xrightarrow{O_2} C_6H_{12}O_7$$
Glucose    Fermentation    Gluconic acid

$$2C_6H_{12}O_7 + FeCO_3 + H_2O \longrightarrow Fe(C_6H_{11}O_7)_2 \cdot 2H_2O + CO_2\uparrow$$

**Properties :** It is a yellowish-grey or pale greenish - yellowish fine powder with odour of burnt sugar. It is soluble in water, more soluble in boiling water but insoluble in alcohol. The aqueous solution is acidic in nature.

**Assay (I.P.) :** It is based on redox titration method. About 1.5 g of substance is dissolved in a mixture of 75 ml water and 15 ml of 2 N sulphuric acid. About 0.75 g of zinc powder is added, the flask stoppered and set aside until the solution is decolourised. It is filtered through sinter glass, the precipitate washed with 20 ml water, and the combined filtrate and washing is titrated with 0.1 M ceric ammonium sulphate using ferroin sulphate solution as indicator until the colour changes from orange to green. A blank is performed to make any necessary correction.

Each ml of 0.1 M ceric ammonium sulphate ≡ 0.04461 g of $C_{12}H_{22}FeO_4$.

### 5. Ferrous Gluconate Tablets :

Tablets are official both in I.P. and B.P. As per I.P., the contents of ferrous gluconate in each average weight of the tablet is not less 95.0% and not more than 105% of the stated amount, whereas B.P. states the ferrous iron ($Fe^{++}$) content to be between 90 to 105% of the stated amount. The tablets are prepared by the compression method and are usually coated. Usual strength of tablet is 300 mg of ferrous gluconate.

### 6. Ferrous Succinate :

This is official in B.P. It contains not less than 34% and not more than 36% of $Fe^{++}$, calculated with reference to dried substance.

**Preparation :** It is manufactured by the interaction of sodium succinate and ferrous sulphate in boiling aqueous solutions. After cooling the product precipitates.

**Properties :** It is a brownish yellow to brown amorphous powder, odour slight. It is practically insoluble in water and alcohol, but dissolves in dilute mineral acids.

**Assay :** Principal involved is that of redox titration and the procedure is similar to that of ferrous fumarate.

### 7. Ferrous Succinate Tablets and Capsules :

Ferrous succinate is used in the form of both tablets and capsules and are official in B.P. Each average weight of the tablet or capsule contains 90 to 105%o of stated amount of Fe (II). Usual strength is 100 mg of ferrous succinate equivalent to 35 mg of ferrous iron.

### 8. Ferrous Sulphate :

$FeSO_4.7H_2O$                                                                                                       Mol. Wt. 278.0

It contains not less than 98% and not more than 105% of $FeSO_4 \cdot 7H_2O$.

**Preparation :** It is prepared by dissolving iron (in excess) in dilute sulphuric acid. After the effervescence has stopped, the liquid is filtered, concentrated and cooled. The crystals formed are separated by filtration. In all the operations undue exposure to air is prevented.

$$Fe + H_2SO_4 + 7H_2O \longrightarrow FeSO_4 \cdot 7H_2O + H_2\uparrow$$

**Properties :** It is a pale bluish-green crystalline powder or transparent, green crystals, odourless with metallic astringent taste. It effloresces in air. On exposure to moist air it undergoes oxidation rapidly and thus is coated with brownish yellowish basic ferrous sulphate. It is freely soluble in water but insoluble in alcohol. Ferrous sulphate when heated decomposes to ferric oxide, sulphur dioxide and sulphuric acid.

$$2(FeSO_4 \cdot 7H_2O) \xrightarrow{\Delta} Fe_2O_3 + SO_2\uparrow + H_2SO_4 + 13H_2O$$

Ferrous sulphate reduces the salts of gold and silver to the metals and mercuric chloride to mercuric chloride.

$$Ag^+ + Fe^{++} \longrightarrow Ag\downarrow + Fe^{+++}$$
$$Au^{+++} + 3Fe^{++} \longrightarrow Au\downarrow + 3Fe^{+++}$$
$$2HgCl_2 + 2Fe^{++} \longrightarrow Hg_2Cl_2 + 2Fe^{+++} + 2Cl^-$$

**Assay :** It is based on redox principle. Previously, it was assayed by titrating with potassium permanganate in acidic media.

$$2FeSO_4 + 2KMnO_4 + 4H_2SO_4 \longrightarrow K_2SO_4 + 2MnSO_4 + Fe_2(SO_4)_3 - 4H_2O$$

Now, it is titrated with ceric ammonium sulphate.

An accurately weighed quantity of about 1 g of substance is dissolved in a mixture of 30 ml water and 20 ml dilute sulphuric acid and the contents titrated with 0.1 M ceric ammonium sulphate using ferroin sulphate solution as indicator.

Each ml of 0.1 M ceric ammonium sulphate = 0.0278 g of $FeSO_4.7H_2O$

9. **Dried Ferrous Sulphate :**

It is ferrous sulphate deprived of part of its water of crystallization by drying at 40°C. It contains not less than 80% and not more than 90% of $FeSO_4$.

**Properties :** It is a greyish-white powder with an astringent and a metallic taste. It dissolves slowly in freshly boiled and cooled water, practically insoluble in alcohol. It is more stable in air than ferrous sulphate heptahydrate and conveniently used in the preparation of tablets and capsules.

**Assay :** Method is similar to ferrous sulphate using 0.5 g of substance.

10. **Ferrous Sulphate Tablets :**

It contains a quantity of $FeSO_4$, equivalent to not less than 80% and not more than 90% of the stated amount of dried ferrous sulphate. The tablets are coated and are prepared by-wet granulation method. Usual strength is 200 mg and 300 mgg of dried ferrous sulphate in each tablet.

11. **Ferrous Sulphate Mixture Paediatric :**

This preparation is official in B.P. It is a solution containing 1.1 to 1.3% w/v of $FeSO_4$. $7H_2O$ containing a suitable antioxidant (ascorbic, acid) in a suitable vehicle and a flavouring agent (orange flavour).

12. **Iron and Dextran Injection (I.P., B.P.) :**

It is a sterile colloidal solution containing a complex of ferric hydroxide with dextrans of low molecular weight (B.P. 80 specifies molecular weight of dextran between 5000 to 7000) in water for injection. It contains not less than 4.75% and not more than 5.25% w/v of iron. It is sterilized by heating in an autoclave. It is administered by deep intramuscular injection and usual dose is 1-2 ml daily.

13. **Iron Sorbitol Injection (B.P.) :**

It is sterile colloidal solution of complex of ferric iron, sorbitol and citric acid, stabilised with dextrin and sorbitol. It is sterilised by heating in an autoclave. The content of Fe are between 4.75 to 5.25% w/v.

Both the above injections are used in prevention and treatment of anaemia.

## INCOMPATIBILITIES AND STORAGE OF IRON SALTS

Most of the iron compounds and preparations are oxidised by air and thus are stored in airtight containers in cool and dark place.

Ferric ammonium citrate is incompatible with mineral acids, alkali, alkali-carbonates and tannates.

Ferrous glucoalate is more stable in solutions buffered with citrate buffers to pH 3.5 to 4.5. In alkaline and neutral solutions, it undergoes rapid oxidation. The solutions are incompatible with ascorbic acid, glycin and pyridoxine. With vitamin C and glycine the solutions develop a dark colour, whereas in presence of pyridoxine they becomes greenish.

Ferrous sulphate is incompatible with alkali and gets oxidised in air easily in presence of arsinates and mercuric salts. It is also incompatible with phosphates, tannates and benzoates. Sugars, glycin and alkali citrates prevent the precipitation of ferric salts.

**Action and Uses :** Iron-deficiency anemia occurs due to a inadequate dietary intake of iron to meet the normal iron requirements. In some cases, requirement of iron increases because of blood loss or because of interference with iron absorption. The iron compounds and preparations are generally used as hematinic (substances that increase the haemoglobin content). The choice of use of various iron salts and their preparations and dose depends on extent of iron deficiency anemia and as prescribed by physician. Ferrous sulphate is one of the most commonly used iron preparations in the form of tablets, which are coated or mixed with glucose or lactose, to prevent its oxidation. Ferrous sulphate mixture is used for paediatric purpose. Ferrous gluconate and ferrous succinate are used in the form of tablets and/or capsules similar to ferrous sulphate, but they have less side effects as compared to ferrous sulphate, particularly the gastrointestinal disturbances. Ferric ammonium citrate is relatively free from astringent properties of ferrous sulphate and is less constipating than inorganic form of iron and has less irritating action.

Some of the iron preparations are used parenterally, e.g. iron and dextran injection and iron sorbitol injection. They are alternatives to oral preparations. They have a distinct advantage that the iron store is rapidly created, which otherwise takes months to achieve by oral administration. They are also used in diseases like sprue in which iron absorption from G.I.T. is prevented, or in cases of inflammatory diseases of the bowel where oral administration can have adverse effect.

**Doses :** These also depends upon the need of the patient and the iron content of the preparation and are as follows :

Ferrous fumarate 100 mg contains about 32.5 mg iron and usual dose is 200 to 600 mg daily.

Ferrous gluconate 100 mg contains about 11.6 mg iron and usual dose is 600 mg daily as prophylactic and 1.2 to 1.8 g daily as therapeutic in divided doses.

Ferrous sulphate heptahydrate 100 mg, contains 20 mg iron and usual dose is 200 to 300 mg daily as prophylactic and 400-600 mg daily as therapeutic in divided doses.

Ferrous succinate 100 mg contains about 35 mg of iron.

The other less commonly used iron salts are :

**1. Ferro Cholinate :** It is ferric iron chelate, available as tablets and pediatric drops. This preparation is said to be less toxic than ferrous sulphate and gluconate.

$$\begin{array}{c} H_2O \\ H_2O-Fe^{++} \\ H_2O \end{array} ---- O-\underset{\underset{OOC^-}{|}}{\overset{\overset{^-OOC-CH_2}{|}}{C}}-CH_2COO^- -\overset{CH_2CH_2OH}{\underset{|}{N^+}}-(CH_3)_3$$

2. **Ferric Cacodylate :** $(Fe(CH_3)_2 AsO_3)_3$ (Mol. Wt. 455). This compound is source of iron and is claimed to be useful in treatment of leukemia because of arsenic.
3. **Ferric Citrate :** Its approximate composition is $C_6H_5FeO.5H_2O$. (Mol. Wt. 239)
4. **Ferric Glycerophosphate :** It is often included in tonics and is an ingredient of glycerophosphate elixirs.
5. **Ferric Hypophosphite :** It is usually an ingredient of some hypophosphite syrups.

### EXERCISE

1. *Discuss the source and biological importance of iron.*
2. *Give preparation, properties and uses of the following iron compounds :*
   *(a) ferrous fumarate,*
   *(b) ferrous gluconate and*
   *(c) ferrous sulphate.*
3. *Describe the method of preparation of ferric ammonium citrate and give its use and assay.*
4. *Discuss the principle and procedures of assay for the following :*
   *(i) ferrous succinate and*
   *(ii) ferrous sulphate tablets.*
5. *Write brief account on the following :*
   *(i) Iron and dextran injection.*
   *(ii) Official formulations of iron compounds.*
   *(iii) Incompatibilities of iron compounds.*

■■■

# 15

# OFFICIAL COMPOUNDS OF IODINE

Iodine (as iodide) is one of the essential trace element. Iodine, its compounds and preparations have to be considered from the following points (a) Its systemic use and biochemical role and (b) Iodine and its preparation for topical applications. The later part has been already dealt in detail under the category of topical agents. In this chapter, we will mainly deal with iodine and iodine compounds from the point of its systemic use and biochemical role.

The inorganic iodide ingested along with food after absorption reaches blood circulation and plays an important role in the synthesis of two important thyroid hormones known as thyroxine and triiodothyronine which are essential for the normal growth and development and play an important role in the energy metabolism.

Thyroxine                       Triiodothyronine

There is an evidence that thyroxine is a storage form of hormone while triiodothyronine is a circulating form.

The important function of thyroxine is to increase the metabolic rate through increasing the oxidative processes in the body. Deficiency of thyroid hormones causes 'hypothyroidism' a condition in which all metabolic processes are slowed down and gaiter (enlargement of thyroid gland) characterised by swelling of neck. Cretinism (mental retardation, dwarfism) is a clinical condition of deficiency of thyroid hormones since birth.

Hyperthyrodism results from the excessive secretion of thyroid hormones and the severe form of this malady is manifested by Exopthalmos (enlargement of eye balls). To treat both, hypothyrodism and goiter, thyroid hormones or suitable iodine compounds like sodium iodide or potassium iodide are used. Whereas for hyperthyrodism, antithyroid drugs like carbimazole and methimazole are used.

The usual requirement of iodine in an average male is about 140 micrograms and for female about 100 micrograms daily which is usually obtained from diet. Iodine can be administered internally which is reduced to iodide in the intestinal track, but because of insolubility of iodine, the salt of iodine like sodium iodide are preferred for internal administration. The iodine in the form of iodide is normally utilised for the synthesis of thyroid hormone. The iodide is oxidised to iodine which is then incorporated into an amino acid tyrosine to form monoiodo and diiodo tyrosine. These are then converted to triodo and tetraiodo thyronine by coupling reactions. Using radioactive iodide, it has been shown that the iodine is incorporated in thyroid gland only for the purpose of forming the thyroid hormones.

After the administration of iodine (iodide) its uptake is governed by various factors like : (a) condition of local thyroid tissue. If it is tumorous then the uptake is slower than normal tissue. (b) The concentration of inorganic iodide in blood, as high blood levels keep the iodine in high level in colloids and thus only small part of the administered iodide is utilized, (c) an anterior pituitary hormone thyrotropin levels in blood, as it is directly related in utilization of iodine in the formation of iodinated hormones. It also controls the release of thyroid hormones from thyroid gland.

Dietary deficiency of iodine results in endemic goiter, if the soil is deficient in iodine. Now-a-days sufficient intake of iodine is easily achieved by using iodised table salt or iodised sodium chloride with 0.01% sodium iodide.

## IODINE

$I_2$             **Mol. Wt. : 253.8**

It contains 99.5 to 100.5% w/w of iodine.

**Preparation :** Iodine is manufactured by extracting kelp (seaweed ash) with water and the, solution is concentrated. The sulphate and chloride of sodium and potassium are crystallised out, leaving freely soluble sodium and potassium iodides in the mother liquor. Sulphuric acid is added to the mother liquor and sulphur, which is liberated from small amount of thiosulphate and sulphide is allowed to settle. The mother liquor is decanted and to this $MnO_2$ is then added and the iodine is distilled out.

$$2NaI + 3H_2SO_4 + MnO_2 \longrightarrow MnSO_4 + 2 NaHSO_4 + I_2 + 2H_2O$$

Impurities like ICl, IBr and ICN are removed by heating crude iodine with potassium iodide.

$$ICl + KI \longrightarrow KCl \quad I_2$$

**Properties :** Iodine occurs as a heavy, bluish-black rhombic prism or plates with metallic luster. It has a peculiar odour and volatilises at ordinary temperature. At higher temperature it melts. It is practically insoluble in water but soluble in alcohol. It is freely soluble in chloroform and solvent ether. The chemical properties are as under :

1. It combines directly with some non-metals and with many metals.

$$2P + 3I_2 \longrightarrow 2PI_3$$

$$Fe + I_2 \longrightarrow FeI_2$$

2. Reducing agents react with aqueous iodine solution and gets oxidised.

$H_3ASO_3 + I_2 + H_2O \longrightarrow 2 HI + H_3ASO_4$

$H_2S + I_2 \longrightarrow 2 HI + S$

$2Na_2S_2O_3 + I_2 \longrightarrow 2 NaI + Na_2S_4O_6$
(sodium tetrathionate)

3. Iodine reacts with alkali to form an iodide and iodate especially when heated.

$3 I_2 + 6 NaOH \longrightarrow 5 NaI + NaIO_3 + 3 H_2O$

4. Potassium iodide dissolves large quantities of iodine because of the formation of $I_3^-$ ion.

$KI + I_2 \longrightarrow KI_3$

5. Iodine adds to unsaturated compounds and also to the unsaturated acids present in the oil. This principle reaction is used in the preparation of non-staining iodine ointment.

$RCH = CH - COOH + I_2 \longrightarrow RCHICHI - COOH$

**Assay :** Iodine is analysed by oxidation - reduction titration method. About 0.5 g of iodine is dissolved in a solution of potassium iodide in 5 ml of water in an iodine flask, diluted with 50 ml water, acidified with 1 ml of acetic acid and titrated with 0.1 N sodium thiosulphate solution, using starch solution as indicator.

Each ml of 0.1 N sodium thiosulphate = 0.01269 g of Iodine

**Uses :** Element iodine as such is used in the form of its aqueous and alcoholic solutions as germicide and fungicide. This has already been discussed under topical agents. Strong solution of iodine is used in many conditions in which the action of the iodide ion is required. In the treatment of 'thyrotoxicosis', it is used to reduce the metabolic rate prior to operation of thyroid. Elemental iodine is effective in purification of drinking water. In emergencies, few drops of tincture are added to water and allowed to stand. It is both bactericidal and amoebicidal. Iodine causes precipitation of alkaloids and thus tincture can be used as a chemical antidote for alkoloidal poisoning. In thin layer chromatography elemental iodine is used as locating agent. It also finds application in analytical chemistry in oxidation-reduction titrations.

**Incompatibilities :** As iodine is a oxidising agent, it oxidises, hypophosphite, sulphites, some metals and reducing agents and gets itself reduced to iodide. The reaction of iodine with turpentine is violent. It reacts with ammonia or ammoniated mercury to form explosive iodide of nitrogen. It reacts with alkali hydroxide and carbonates to form iodide or iodates. If aqueous solution of alkaloidal salts is treated with iodine, alkaloids are precipitated.

**Storage :** Iodine is stored in amber-coloured bottles with a tight glass stopper or earthenware containers and kept in a cool place.

## COMPOUNDS CONTAINING IODINE

Under this category the important compounds are sodium iodide, potassium iodide and radioactive iodine and iodine containing compounds.

## 1. Sodium Iodide :

**NaI**  Mol. Wt. 149.9

Sodium iodide is official in B.P. 1988. It contains not less than 99% and not more than 100.5% of NaI, calculated with reference to the dried substance.

**Preparation :** It is prepared by adding slight excess iodine to the concentrated solution of sodium hydroxide. This gives a mixture of sodium iodide and sodium iodate. The reaction mixture is evaporated to dryness and the residue is treated (reduced) with carbon to convert sodium iodate into sodium iodide.

$$6\ NaOH + 3\ I_2 \longrightarrow 5\ NaI + NaIO_3 + 3H_2O$$
$$NaIO_3 + 3C \longrightarrow NaI + 3\ CO\uparrow$$

**Properties :** It is a white crystalline powder or colourless crystals and odourless. It is hygroscopic in nature and stable in dry air but may decompose on storage and develops brown colour (air, oxidation causes liberation of free iodine). Sodium iodide is soluble in water and alcohol. The aqueous solution gives yellow precipitate with silver nitrate and oxidising agents liberate iodine in acidified solution.

$$NaI + AgNO_3 \longrightarrow AgI\downarrow + NaNO_3$$
$$2NaI + H_2SO_4 + H_2O \longrightarrow I_2 + 2H_2O + Na_2SO_4$$

**Assay :** The principal involved is direct titration involving oxidation with potassium iodate.

When sodium iodide solution is titrated with potassium iodate solution in acidified media, iodine is liberated. Under high concentration of hydrochloric acid, the liberated iodine is converted into iodine monochloric. The end-point of this titration is indicated by disappearance of iodine colour from chloroform layer.

**Method :** About 1.3 g of sodium iodide is dissolved in 100 ml of water. 20 ml of this solution is taken in iodine flask, 40 ml concentrated hydrochloric acid added and contents titrated with 0.05 M potassium iodate until the colour changes to yellow. 5 ml chloroform is added and titration continued with shaking against potassium iodate until chloroform layer is colourless.

Each ml of 0.05 M $KIO_3$ = 0.01499 g of NaI.

## 2. Potassium Iodide :

**Incompatibilities :** Both iodides get decomposed in presence of acid with liberation of iodine. Sugar retards this reaction. Oxidising agents also liberate iodine with simultaneous reduction of the agent, for example, cupric sulphate liberates iodine and cupric iodide is precipitated. The iodides also precipitate many alkaloids.

**Storage :** Sodium and potassium iodides are deliquescent in moist air and are oxidised giving yellowish or brown colour due to liberation of iodine and thus stored in a well closed container and kept in a dry place.

**Uses :** Sodium iodide or potassium iodide is the oldest remedy for disorders of thyroid gland. Before the discovery of antithyroid drugs, they were used for symptoms of hyperthyroidism also. The iodide acts as fibrolytic agent in syphilis and leprosy. Now due to use of antibiotics in syphilis, iodides are not used. Iodides do not have curative properties nor do they influence resistance. In fungal infections and in actinomycosis small doses are found to be useful.

Due to their fibrolytic action, iodides are contraindicated in treatment of tuberculosis. However, it is also claimed that use of iodides improves the accessibility of chemotherapeutic anti-tubercular agents to the causative organism.

Potassium iodide is present in number of cough mixtures as expectorant. It liquifies the tenacious secretions, thus finding use in asthma and chronic bronchitis.

If iodides are used in excessive doses, the toxic symptoms are irritation of skin and mucous membrane, which is termed as 'iodism', characterised by coryza, rashes, headache, laryngitis. Sometimes, it causes gastrointestinal effects like nausea and vomiting. If iodism or segastic disturbances are observed, the treatment is discontinued and sodium chloride is administered for rapid removal of iodide.

## RADIOACTIVE IODINE AND SODIUM IODIDE

There are several radioactive isotopes of iodine and out of which, the irradiation is most abundantly used. $^{131}I$ is obtained by neutron irradiation of tellarium and used in the form of sodium iodide ($^{131}I$).

The solution of sodium iodide ($^{131}I$) is official in B.P. 1988. It is an aqueous solution containing iodine – $^{131}I$ in the form of sodium iodide and contains sodium thiosulphate or any other reducing agent and may be suitably buffered. The activity of the given contents of I-131 should not be less than 90 and not more than 110 of the stated amount of the label at any given date and hour. Not less than 95% of the radioactivity corresponds to iodine-131 in the form of iodide. The specific activity is not less than 185 GB 9 per mg of iodine at the date and hour stated on the label.

**Properties :** It is a clear colourless solution. Iodine - 131 has a half life of 8.04 days and emits beta and gamma radiations. As the half life is of eight days over 99% of its radiant energy is expended within 56 days. The solution has a pH between 7 to 10.

**Assay :** The activity is determined by comparison with a standardised iodine-131 solution, using any suitable counting instrument. Besides this, it is also tested for Radionuclide purity and Radiochemical purity.

**Uses :** Radioactive iodine is most widely used for the diagnosis of disorders of thyroid function and for the treatment of hyperthyroidism. For diagnostic purpose, tracer studies with radioactive iodine helps in measurement of thyroidal accumulation of tracer dose. It helps in diagnosis of hypothyroidism, hyperthyroidism and goiter and also the response of thyroid to thyrotropic can be evaluated. As far as its therapeutic uses are concerned, in many cases of hyperthyroidism, it is considered as a choice treatment. Course of Grave's disease can be followed by using radioactive iodine. In metastatic thyroid cancer patients accumulate very little iodine. In the above condition, it can prolong the life particularly of a young patient.

Iodine-123 has a half life of only 13 hours and it emits X-rays. Because of brief exposure to radiation, it is used for thyroid scans.

## EXERCISE

1. Discuss the biochemical role of iodine in the body. Describe deficiency symptoms of iodine.
2. Give commercial method of obtaining iodine and outline some of its important chemical properties.
3. Give method of preparation, properties, uses and assay of (a) sodium iodide or potassium iodide.
4. Outline importance of radioactive sodium iodide.

# 16

# OFFICIAL COMPOUNDS OF CALCIUM

Calcium is one of the essential elements required for various functions of the body. About 90% of the body calcium is found in bones as calcium carbonate and phosphate. The remaining calcium is found in the extracellular fluids in the form of soluble salts and in combination with serum protein (in the undissociated form) and soluble calcium form. In the body, there is a balance in various forms of calcium. The ionic form of calcium is involved in the various physiological activities.

Generally, sufficient calcium is ingested through the normal diet. Daily body requirement is about 450 mg. It is absorbed from upper intestinal tract and is excreted through urine and faeces. As in the upper portion of intestine, the condition is acidic, it favours absorption of calcium as calcium salts have better solubility. Alkaline conditions cause the precipitation of calcium salts and thus the adsorption is retarded. Higher fatty acid contents also lessen the absorption due to formation of calcium salts of fatty acids which are insoluble.

The calcium ions are essential for maintenance of some of the important body functions for example :

1. The cation is essential for normal functioning of autonomic nervous system and voluntary systems.
2. For normal cardiac function.
3. It is important factor in coagulation of blood and
4. For the formation of certain tissues and bones.

When there is deficiency of ionised calcium in blood, the condition is known as hypocalcemia which may be due to various reasons and produces syndromes known as tetany and related phenomenon. It is characterised by increased neuromuscular excitability, muscle cramps and convulsions etc. Hypocalcemia may be due to the following :

(i) Nutritional deficiencies of calcium leads to faulty growth. If the body is deprived of calcium and vitamin D, due to inadequate diet particularly in infants, it results in bone disease known as rickets; and low calcium in the skeleton in adults, results in osteomalacia. Vitamin D is essential for the proper absorption of calcium from diet and thus many marketed calcium preparations contain vitamin D.

(ii) Hypoparathyroidism causes hypocalcemia which may be associated with opacity of lens, calcification of basal gangalion, etc.

(iii) Hypocalcemia is frequently associated with advanced renal insufficiency with hyperphosphatemia.

(iv) Neonatal tetany is caused if the mothers of new born have hyperparathyroidism.

(v) Hypocalcemia can occur if large volumes of transfusion with citrated blood are administed.

Administration of large quantities of calcium can cause hypercalcemia. Hypercalcemia is condition in which high concentration of calcium ions are present in blood. It is characterised by loss of weight, bradycardia, muscular pain, arrhythmia and kidney impairment, etc. Hypercalemic condition can be associated with various clinical conditions.

(a) Hyperparathyroidism and hyperthyroidism.

(b) Hypercalcemia known as milk alkali syndrome is caused by excess of milk and alkalinising agents.

(c) Mild hypercalcemic condition is associated with administration of benzothiazide diuretics.

(d) Excess of vitamin D administration can also lead to hypercalcemic condition.

(e) Sarcoidosis is associated with hypercalcemia which is due to increased production of calcitrol which in turn increases the intestinal absorption of calcium.

Number of drugs are used in the treatment of various hypercalcemia conditions :

1. Prednisolone and some steroids are used if hypercalcemia is a consequence of sarcoid.
2. Indomethacin is used if hypercalcemia is a result of excess production of prostaglandins.
3. If plasma calcium levels are to be lowered rapidly, then disodium edetate is used which acts by chelating.
4. Calcitonin and phosphates are orally administered in hypercalcemic condition.

Calcium compounds in general are given in deficiency state or as dietary supplement, if diatary intake is inadequate. Calcium salts are useful in immediate treatment of low calcium tetany and are best controlled by intravenous administration. If the tetany symptoms are milder or in cases of latent tetany calcium salts are orally administered.

The official compounds of calcium are discussed below :

## 1. Calcium Acetate (B.P.) :

$C_4H_6CaO_4$                                                                                     Mol. Wt. 158.2

It contains not less than 98% and not more than 100.5% of $C_4H_6CaO_4$, calculated with reference to the anhydrous substance.

**Preparation :** It is prepared by neutralising acetic acid solution with suitable calcium salts like calcium carbonate or calcium hydroxide.

$$2\ CH_3COOH + CaCO_3 \longrightarrow (CH_3COO)_2\ Ca + CO_2 \uparrow + H_2O$$

**Properties :** It is a white powder; almost colourless and hygroscopic in nature. It is soluble in water but slightly soluble in alcohol. Aqueous, solutions are slightly alkaline in nature.

**Assay :** It is assayed by complexometric titration method. The salt is dissolved in water, buffered with diethylamine and titrated with 0.1 M disodium edetate using methyl thymol blue mixture as indicator.

Each ml of 0.1 M disodium edetate ≡ 0.01582 g of $C_4H_6CaO_4$.

**Storage :** As it is hygroscopic in nature, it is kept in a well closed container in dry place.

**Uses :** It is one of the ingredients of solutions used for haemodialysis and peritoneal dialysis. The haemodialysis solutions are solutions of electrolytes in concentrations similar to those of normal extracellular body fluids and glucose may be included in such formulations. These, solutions are intended for use in a haemodialyser for blood purification. As large volumes are used during dialysis, they are prepared by diluting the concentrated haemodialysis solutions.

## 2. Calcium Carbonate (Precipitated Chalk) :

This has already been discussed under the category of "antacids" and 'protective agent and dentifries'.

## 3. Calcium Chloride :

**$CaCl_2 \cdot 2H_2O$**  Mol. Wt. 147.02

It contains not less than 97% and not more than 103% of $CaCl_2 \cdot 2H_2O$.

**Preparation :** It is obtained as a by-product of ammonia soda process for the manufacture of sodium carbonate. Calcium chloride is prepared by adding pure calcium carbonate to hot dilute hydrochloric acid. The alkali is added in slight excess and after the reaction is over, it is removed by filtration. The filtrate is evaporated to syrupy liquid. As crystallisation is difficult, the liquid is cooled from 0-10°C and the separated crystals are removed by filtration using suction and kept in well stoppered bottles.

**Properties :** It is available as white crystalline powder, fragments or granules. It is odourless and is hygroscopic in nature. It is soluble in water and alcohol. Because of its high solubility in water, it forms an excellent freezing mixture with ice. When one part of the salt is mixed with two-third of its weight of crushed ice, it has a temperature of − 45°C. An aqueous solution is slightly acidic in nature.

It reacts with ammonia to form $CaCl_2 \cdot 8NH_3$ and with ethylalcohol to form $CaCl_2 \cdot 2C_2H_5OH$. Calcium chloride forms several hydrates, e.g. monohydrate, dihydrate, tetrahydrate and hexahydrate. When aqueous solutions are evaporated, large prisms of hexahydrate are formed. When heated, all hydrates lose some of their water of hydration and a porous mass results, which is used for drying gases and liquids. While heating, some calcium oxide is formed as follows :

$$CaCl_2 \cdot H_2O \longrightarrow Ca(OH)_2 + 2\,HCl$$

$$Ca(OH)_2 \xrightarrow{\Delta} CaO + H_2O$$

**Assay :** It is assayed by direct complexometric titration method. The sample solution is adjusted to the desired pH using sodium hydroxide solution and titrated with disodium edetate solution using calcon mixture as indicator.

Each ml of 0.1 M disodium edetate is ≡ 0.01470 g of $CaCl_2.2H_2O$.

**Storage :** As it is hygroscopic in nature, it should be kept in a well closed container.

**Uses :** It is one of the important calcium salts used in therapy. When administered orally, the chloride portion acts similar to hydrochloric acid and produces acidic urine or acidosis (as in the treatment of calcium tetany). It is generally not used as a source of calcium as better calcium salts are available. It is not suitable for oral administration because of unpleasant taste and irritating nature. Intramuscular or subcutaneous administration is not done because of its irritating and corrosive nature. It is one of the ingredients of "Ringers solution" and the "Compound Sodium Lactate intravenous Infusion". The later is official in B.P. 1980.

**4. Calcium Gluconate :**

$$\left[ OOC - \underset{\underset{OH}{|}}{\overset{\overset{H}{|}}{C}} - \underset{\underset{H}{|}}{\overset{\overset{OH}{|}}{C}} - \underset{\underset{OH}{|}}{\overset{\overset{H}{|}}{C}} - \underset{\underset{H}{|}}{\overset{\overset{OH}{|}}{C}} - CH_2OH \right]_2 Ca \cdot H_2O$$

It is a calcium D-gluconate monohydrate and contains 98-102% of $C_{12}H_{22}CaO_{14} \cdot H_2O$.

**Preparation :** It may be prepared either by the oxidation of glucose to gluconic acid in presence of calcium carbonate or by first preparing gluconic acid then adding calcium carbonate to form the salt. In the former method, the oxidation of glucose is effected either by bromine or by electrolytic oxidation in presence of sodium bromide. In the later procedure, the gluconic acid is usually obtained by the action of various moulds or bacteria of the Acetobactor group on glucose.

**Properties :** It is available as white crystalline or granular powder, odourless and tasteless. It is stable in air. It is sparingly soluble in water, freely soluble in boiling water and insoluble in alcohol. If the aqueous solution is treated with hydrochloric acid or other acids, gluconic acid is formed which is said to be converted to D-gluconolactone.

**Incompatibilities :** It is incompatible with oxidising agents and solution of calcium gluconate gives a precipitative with oxalates and borates.

**Assay :** It is assayed by direct complexometric titration methods. As the salt has low solubility in water, it is dissolved by boiling in sufficient water, cooled. The pH is adjusted with sodium hydroxide solution and titrated with standard disodium edetate solution using calcon carboxylic acid mixture as indicator (B.P. 1980).

As per I.P., it is assayed by complexometric titration involving replacement with magnesium, using 5 ml of standard magnesium sulphate solution. The pH is adjusted with ammonia-ammonium chloride buffer. The volume of disodium edetate equivalent to magnesium sulphate solution is substrated from total disodium edetate used and then results are calculated.

Each ml of remainder of 0.05 M disodium edetate ≡ 0.02242 g of $C_{12}H_{22}CaO_{14} \cdot H_2O$.

Following formulations of calcium gluconate are official :

**(a) Calcium Gluconate Injection :** It is a sterile solution of calcium gluconate in water for injection. It contains a quantity of calcium equivalent to not less than 8.5% and not more than 9.4% of the stated amount of calcium gluconate. Not more than 5% of calcium gluconate be replaced with suitable calcium salt like calcium D-saccharate which acts as stabilizer. It functions as a sequestering agent, increases the solubility in water and prevents precipitation of calcium gluconate. It is sterilised by heating in an autoclave. The usual strength available in market are, equivalent of 0.5 g and 1 g of calcium gluconate in 5 ml the equivalent of 1 g of calcium gluconate in 10 ml and equivalent of 1 g and 2 g calcium gluconate in 20 ml.

The lable on the container should state :
1. The strength as percentage w/v of calcium gluconate equivalent to the total amount of calcium.
2. That solutions containing visible solid particles must not be used and
3. The percentage of any added stabilizing agent.

It is assayed for the content of calcium by following B.P. or I.P. procedure, discussed under calcium gluconate.

**(b) Calcium Gluconate Tablets :** Each average weight of the tablet contains not less than 95% and not more than 105% of the stated amount of calcium gluconate $C_{12}H_{22}O_{14}Ca$, $H_2O$ stated on label. These tablets are generally, intended to be chewed before swallowing and are generally prepared in suitably favoured base. Usual strengths available are 0.325 g, 0.5 g, 0.65 g and 1 g.

The tablets are assayed for calcium gluconate content following the I.P. or B.P. procedure discussed under calcium gluconate.

Another formulation which is official in B.P. is effervescent calcium gluconate tablets, which are prepared by using suitable effervescent base.

**Uses :** Calcium gluconate and its preparations are used as a source of calcium in calcium deficiency. It is the drug of choice for severe hypocalcemic tetany. Calcium gluconate tablets are administered orally which do not cause irritation of gastroinestinal tract. Usual dose is 3 to 4 g. The tablets are also used in supplementing diet of convalescent and expectant mothers. Injections are used intravenously. The intramuscular route should not be used particularly in children as it causes abscess at the site of injection.

## 5. Calcium Hydroxide :

$Ca(OH)_2$                                                                 Mol. Wt. 74.09

It contains not less than 99% $Ca(OH)_2$

**Preparation :** It is commonly called 'hydrated lime' and is manufactured by addition of limited amount of water to lime (CaO). The process is called 'slaking'. During this process, water is absorbed by calcium oxide to form calcium hydroxide and is accompanied by evolution of heat and the swelling of CaO lumps, which usually disintegrates, to a fine powder. The quality of the finished product depends upon the purity of the starting material.

$$CaO + H_2O \longrightarrow Ca(OH)_2$$

**Properties :** It is soft white powder, with an alkaline and slightly bitter taste. It is very slightly soluble in water, less in boiling water, soluble in glycerine and aqueous solutions of sugars, but insoluble in alcohol.

When three-four times, its own weight of water is added, it forms 'milk of lime' which is different from 'lime water'. Calcium hydroxide solutions are basic and can neutralise acids to form salts. These solutions absorb $CO_2$ with the formation of precipitate of calcium carbonate.

$$Ca(OH)_2 + 2HCl \longrightarrow CaCl_2 + 2H_2O$$

$$H_2O + CO_2 \longrightarrow H_2CO_3$$

$$Ca(OH)_2 + H_2CO_3 \longrightarrow CaCO_2 \downarrow + H_2O$$

When heated strongly it looses water and gets converted to CaO.

$$Ca(OH)_2 \xrightarrow{\Delta} CaO + H_2O$$

**Assay :** It is assayed by following principles of acid-base titration. About 1.5 g of sample is wettened with 5 ml of neutralised alcohol and about 250 ml of neutralised sucrose solution is added and shaken vigorously for 5 minutes and then at frequent intervals for four hours. The volume is made to 500 ml with sucrose solution and filtered. The sucrose solution helps to solubilize the calcium hydroxide. 250 ml of filtrate is titrated with 1 N hydrochloric acid using phenolphthatein as indicator.

Each ml of 1 N HCl = 0.03705 g Ca(OH)$_2$.

## 6. Calcium Hydroxide Solution (B.P.) (Lime Water) :

It contains not less than 0.15% w/v of $Ca(OH)_2$.

**Preparation :** It is prepared by shaking 10 g $Ca(OH)_2$ thoroughly with 1000 ml of freshly boiled and cooled water. It is allowed to stand and the cleared liquid is syphoned as required.

**Properties :** It is a clear colourless liquid, absorbs carbon dioxide and forms a film of calcium carbonate at the surface of the liquid. On boiling, it becomes turbid which on cooling becomes clear.

**Assay :** It is analysed by titration with standard hydrochloric acid using phenolphthalein as indicator.

**Storage :** This solution should be kept in a well-filled and in tightly closed container.

**Uses :** Calcium hydroxide is generally not used as source of calcium. It acts as a antacid and used as a astringent in infantile diarrhoea and vomiting, in the form of lime water. It reacts with fatty acids, forming calcium soaps, which acts as emulsifying agent. It is a ingredient to some skin lotions.

## 7. Calcium Lactate :

$$\left( \begin{array}{c} CH_3 - CH - COO \\ | \\ OH \end{array} \right)_2 Ca \cdot XH_2O \qquad \text{Mol. Wt. 218.2 (anhydrous)}$$

It is a hydrated calcium-2-hydroxy propionate or a mixture of calcium (RS) and (R), (S) -2-hydroxypropionate. In B.P. 1988 pentahydrate and trihydrate forms are official.

It contains not less than 98% and not more than 101% of $C_6H_{10}CaO_6$, calculated with reference to dried substance.

**Preparation :** It is obtained by neutralising a hot solution of lactic acid with calcium carbonate. It is removed by filtration and the salt is crystallised from the filtrate.

Industrially, it is prepared by mixing a monosacchoride ($C_6H_{12}O_6$) solution with milk and chalk and inducing lactic acid fermentation by putrid cheese which is rich in lactic acid bacilli. The mixture is digested for a week at about 30°C. The product obtained is purified by recrystillisation.

**Properties :** It is available as nearly odourless and tasteless, crystalline or granular powder. The pentahydrate effloresces slightly. When heated at 120°C, loses its molecule of water. It is soluble in water, more in boiling water, but insoluble in alcohol. Aqueous solutions are acidic in nature and slowly evolves carbon dioxide.

$$C_6H_{12}O_6 \xrightarrow{\text{Fermentation}} 2CH_3 - \underset{\underset{OH}{|}}{CH} - COOH$$

$$2CH_3 - \underset{\underset{OH}{|}}{CH} - COOH + CaCO_3 \longrightarrow (CH_3CH(OH)COO)_2Ca + CO_2\uparrow + H_2O$$

**Assays :** The method is similar to calcium gluconate, using 0.3 g of sample.

Each ml of remainder of 0.05M disodium edetate $\equiv$ 0.01091 g of $C_6H_{10}O_6Ca$.

## 8. Calcium Lactate Tablets :

Average weight of every tablet contains not less than 95% and not more than 105% of stated amount, calculated as $C_6H_{10}CaO_6 \cdot 5H_2O$. The usual strength available are tablets containing 300 mg and 600 mg of calcium lactate pentahydrate or equivalent amount of calcium lactate trihydrate.

**Usual Dose :** 1 to 5 g.

**Uses :** It is used as a source of calcium and hence used orally as electrolyte replenisher or as calcium replacement therapy. It is said to less be irritant than calcium chloride, but more than calcium gluconate.

## 9. Calcium Levulinate (I.P.) :

$(CH_3COCH_2CH_2COO)_2Ca \cdot 2H_2O$ \qquad **Mol. Wt. 306.33**

It is a dihydrate of Ca, 4-Oxo-pentanoate. It contains not less than 97.5% and not more than 100.5% of $C_{10}H_{14}CaO_6$ calculated with reference to the dried substance.

**Preparation :** It is manufactured by the interaction of levulinic acid with calcium chloride or lime water or calcium carbonate. The levulinic acid is usually obtained by heating sugars. The solution is concentrated and allowed to crystallise.

**Properties :** It is a white crystalline or amorphous powder. It is freely soluble in water and slightly in alcohol and insoluble in ether and chloroform. As it contains a carbonyl function, it reacts with 2, 4-dinitrophenyl hydrazine to form corresponding hydrazone. Because of presence of $CH_3CO$ group, it reacts with iodine solution in alkaline media to form iodoform.

**Assay :** The procedure is similar to calcium gluconate using 0.6 g sample. Each ml of remainder of 0.05 M disodium edetate $\equiv$ 0.01351 g of $C_{10}H_{14}CaO_6$(I.P.).

### 10. Calcium Levulinate Injection (I.P.) :

It is a sterile solution of calcium levulinate in water for injection and contains not less than 95% and not more than 105% of the stated amount of $C_{10}H_{14}CaO_6 \cdot 2H_2O$. Usual strength is 100 mg per ml.

**Uses :** Calcium Levulinate is another calcium salt which produces less irritation than calcium chloride and because of its high solubility in water, it can be used in more concentrated aqueous solution. As a source of calcium, it is used intravenously or subcutaneously. Its usual dose is 1 g daily.

### 11. Calcium Pantothenate :

$$\left[ HO-CH_2-\underset{\underset{CH_3}{|}}{\overset{\overset{CH_3}{|}}{C}}-\underset{\underset{H}{|}}{\overset{\overset{OH}{|}}{C}}-CONHCH_2CH_2COO \right]_2 Ca^{++} \qquad \text{Mol. Wt. 476.54}$$

It is a calcium salt of dextrorotatory isomer of (R)-3- (2, 4 dihydrogen 3, 3-dimethyl butyramido) propionic acid. The I.P. and B.P. standards differ for the products. As per I.P., it contains between 90-110.0% and as per B.P. between 98 - 101% of $C_{18}H_{32}CaN_2O_{10}$, calculated with reference to dried substance.

**Properties :** It is a white hygroscopic powder and has a bitter taste. It is freely soluble in water and slightly soluble in alcohol.

**Assay :** I.P. uses a microbial method of analysis whereas B.P. analysis is by non-aqueous titration method, determining the end-point potentiometrically.

**Uses :** It is never used as a source of calcium but it is a vitamin B coenzyme factor and is one of the ingredient of some multivitamin preparations.

### 12. Calcium Phosphate Dibasic (I.P.)

**$CaHPO_4$**                                                                              **Mol. Wt. 136.06**

**$CaHPO_4 \cdot 2H_2O$**                                                  **Mol. Wt. 172.09**

It is anhydrous or a dihydrate. It contains not less an 30.9% and not more than 31.7% of calcium (Ca), calculated with reference to the ignited substance.

**Preparation :** It is prepared from animal bones as described under calcium phosphate tribasic or from mineral apatite, which is powdered and digested with sulphuric acid.

Calcium sulphate is precipitated and phosphoric acid is formed. Calcium sulphate is filtered off and calculated amount of $Ca(OH)_2$ is added to the filtrate to form dibasic salt.

$Ca_3(PO_4)_2 + 3H_2SO_4 \longrightarrow 2H_3PO_4 + 3CaSO_4$
(Apatite)

$NaPO_4 + CaCl_2 \longrightarrow CaHPO_4 + 2H_2O$

In laboratory, it can be prepared by reaction between secondary sodium phosphate and calcium chloride in neutral media.

$NaHPO_4 + CaCl_2 \longrightarrow CaHPO_4 + 2NaCl$

**Properties :** It is a white powder, odourless and tasteless. It is practically insoluble in water and alcohol. It is easily soluble in dilute hydrochloric and nitric acid.

**Assay :** It is analysed by direct complexometric titration method. The substance is dissolved in a mixture of hydrochloric acid and water. Small quantity of triethanolamine is added and titrated with 0.05 M disodium edetate using hydroxynapthol blue as indicator nearing end point. Then pH is adjusted with sodium hydroxide solution (till colour of indicator changes from red to clear blue). Titration is continued till colour changes to violet then again blue which persists for 60 seconds.

Each ml of 0.05 M disodium edetate ≡ 0.002004 g Ca.

**Uses :** As the salt supplies both the calcium ions and phosphorus, it is administered orally to children, for bone growth and to pregnant women and lactating mothers. It also finds use in tablets as excepient.

## 13. Calciun Phosphate Tribasic

It mainly consists of tricalcium diorthophosphate $Ca_3(PO_4)_2$, together with calcium phosphates of more acidic or basic character. I.P. and B.P. prescribes different standards in their monograph. As per I.P., it contains calcium (Ca) between 34 – 40% and phosphate, $(PO_4)$, not less than 90% of Calcium phosphate $Ca_3(PO_4)_2$, calculated with reference to the ignited substance, while as per B.P., it contains not less than 90% of calcium phosphate calculated as $Ca_3(PO_4)_2$.

**Preparation :** Usually, bones are calcined until white, powdered and digested with sulphuric acid. This converts the insoluble phosphate into soluble phosphoric acid and insoluble calcium sulphate. The solution is filtered and the filtrate is treated with calculated quantity of calcium hydroxide, when the product is precipitated.

$Ca_3(PO)_4 + 3H_2SO_4 \longrightarrow 2H_3PO_4 + 3CaSO_4\downarrow$

$2H_3PO_4 + 3Ca(OH)_2 \longrightarrow Ca_3(PO_4)_2\ 6H_2O$

The white precipitate is collected washed with hot water and dried.

**Properties :** It is a white amorphous powder, odourless. It is stable in air, insoluble in water and alcohol but soluble in dilute hydrochloric and nitric acid.

**Assay :** As per I.P., it is analysed for content of calcium and for contents of calcium phosphate $Ca_3(PO_4)_2$. Calcium content is determined by following the method content given under dibasic calcium phosphate. In determining the phosphate, as $Ca_3(PO_4)_2$, the sample is dissolved in a mixture of water and dilute nitric acid, filtered, filtrate made basic with ammonia till slight precipitation occurs. It is again dissolved by adding nitric acid, then precipitated as phosphomolybdate by treating the solution with ammonium molybdate solution. The so formed phosphomolybdate is filtered, washed till free from acidity and dissolved in known volume of 1 N sodium hydroxide and the excess of sodium hydroxide is back titrated with 1 N sulphuric acid using phenolphthalein as indicator.

Each ml of 1 N NaOH $\equiv$ 0.006743 g of $Ca_3(PO_4)_2$.

B.P. uses the principle of complexometric titration following back titration technique. The sample is dissolved in a hydrochloric acid and diluted with water. A known volume is taken, a known excess volume of 0.05 M disodium adetate is added; pH adjusted with ammonia buffer and the excess of disodium edetate is determined by titration with 0.05 M zinc chloride solution using mordent black 11 mixture as indicator.

Each ml of 0.05 M zinc chloride $\equiv$ 0.005170 g of $Ca_3(PO_4)_2$.

Both B.P. and I.P. states water contents not more than 2.5%. The I.P. standards for contents of calcium and calcium phosphate are with reference to loss on ignition at 800°C (which is not more than 8%) but this criteria is not in B.P.

**Uses :** Similar to dibasic calcium phosphate.

### 14. Calcium Sodium Lactate (B.P.) :

It contains between 7.5–8.5% w/w calcium and between 8.5–10% w/w of sodium.

**Properties :** It is a white powder or granules and has a slight characteristic odour. It is soluble in water, in boiling alcohol but insoluble in ether. The aqueous solution is very slightly acidic or alkaline.

**Assay :** It is analysed for its calcium and sodium content. Calcium is directly titrated by complexometric titration method. Whereas for determination of sodium, sample is first carbonised. The residue contains both Calcium and Sodium in the form of oxide, which is taken in known volume of standard acid and the excess of acid is back titrated using standard sodium hydroxide solution using methyl orange as indicator. Contents of calcium are calculated after subtraction of one fifth of the volume of standard disodium edetate that would be required by the calcium in the weight of the sample taken.

**Uses :** It is used in the treatment of calcium deficiency.

**Storage :** This salt being deliquescent, it is kept in a well-closed container in a dry place.

## 15. Calcium Sulphate Dried (B.P.) :

**(Exsiccated calcium sulphate, plaster of paris)**

$CaSO_4 \cdot 1/2 \, H_2O$                                                                                   Mol. Wt. 145.1

Calcium sulphate is found in the natural state with two molecules of water ($CaSO_4 \cdot 2H_2O$) as 'gypsum' and 'selenite' in crystalline form and as grannular masses called as 'Alabstar'.

**Preparation :** It is usually prepared by heating gypsum at a controlled temperature at about 150°C, till three quarters of water of crystallization is lost, with minimum formation of anhydrous calcium sulphate.

Calcium sulphate dihydrate can be prepared by adding soluble sulphate like sodium sulphate to calcium chloride solution. The precipitate formed is filtered, washed throughly and dried properly.

$$Na_2SO_4 + CaCl_2 + 2H_2O \longrightarrow CaSO_4 \cdot 2H_2O + 2NaCl$$

The B.P. states it may contain suitable setting accelerator or deccelerator.

**Properties :** It is a white or almost white powder, odourless and hygroscopic in nature. It is sparingly soluble in water, but soluble in dilute mineral acids and insoluble in alcohol. When mixed with water, it forms a mass that 'sets quickly'. If overheated during drying, it forms a product which does not set properly and thus becomes unfit for use.

**Uses :** It is used in dentistry for taking impressions and in surgery for making casts. It is used as the plaster in fixing bone fractures. It also finds use for making plaster of paris bandages.

**Storage :** Being hygroscopic, it is stored in a tightly closed container, protected from moisture and heat.

## 16. Sodium Calcium Edetate (B.P.) :

It is a calcium complex with ethylenediaminetetracetic acid disodium salt (Sodium edetate) and contains between 98–102% of $C_{10}H_{12}CaN_2Na_2O_8$, calculated with reference to the anhydrous substance.

**Preparation :** It is prepared by the interaction between soluble calcium salt and disodium edetate solution. The product is obtained by evaporating the solution.

**Properties :** It is a almost white crystalline powder or granules powder, freely soluble in water, insoluble in ether, alcohol and chloroform. As it is hygroscopic in nature, it is stored in a tight container in dry place.

### 17. Sodium Calcium Edetate Intravenous Infusion (B.P.) :

It is a sterile solution of sodium calcium edetate, prepared immediately before use by diluting a 'strong sterile sodium calcium edetate solution' with 'sodium chloride' intravenous infusion or with 'Glucose Intravenous Infusion'. The strong sterile sodium calcium edetate solution contains equivalent of 20% w/v of anhydrous sodium calcium edetate. This solution can be sterilised by autoclaving.

**Storage :** This solution is to be stored in lead-free glass container.

**Uses :** It is used in the form of infusion in cases of lead poisoning. It can also be used in case of metal poisoning due to copper, nickel, zinc, chromium etc. However, it is not useful if metal poisoning is due to arsenic, mercury or gold.

### 18. Calcium Amino Salicylate (I.P.) (Calcium PAS) :

$C_{14}H_{12}CaN_2O_6 3H_2O$     Mol. Wt. 398.38

It is calcium 4-amino-2-hydroxybenzoate with 3 molecules of water of crystallization.

It contains between 98–101% of $C_{14}H_{12}CaN_2O_6$, calculated with reference to anhydrous substance.

**Preparation :** It is prepared by neutralising p-amino salicylic acid with required quantity of lime. The solution is filtered and the product is crystallized by evaporation and cooling or by precipitation with water miscible solvents like alcohol.

**Properties :** It is a white to cream-coloured crystalline powder, some what hygroscopic in nature. It is soluble in water, slightly soluble in alcohol and nearly insoluble in ether. Its solution decomposes slowly and darkens in colour. Its aqueous solution with drop of ferric chloride gives purple red colour, due presence of phenolic group. Aqueous solution on addition of few drops of acid gives a precipitate of 4-amino salicylic acid.

**Assay :** The principle involved is diazotization of the primary aromatic amino group in acidic media with sodium nitrite. Earlier the end-point was detected with starch iodide paper which turns blue due to nitrous acid, as it liberates iodine from KI, which gives blue colour with starch. Now the end-point is detected potentiometrically. This titration of primary aromatic amino group with sodium nitrite is known as 'Nitrite titration'.

**Storage :** It is stored in a tightly closed container, as it is slightly hygroscopic and also sensitive to light or denatured on exposure to light.

**Uses :** In the form of tablets (official in I.P.), it is used in treatment of tuberculosis. It causes less gastric irritation than free acid, usual dose is 10-20 g daily in divided doses.

There are certain calcium salts, some of which are used as source of calcium and some for other purposes, but are not official in I.P. or B.P. are discussed below in short.

### 19. Calcium Mandelate :

$C_{16}H_{14}O_6 \cdot Ca$ Mol. Wt. 324.4

**Preparation :** It is prepared by the action of suitable alkali on mandelic acid, the solution is evaporated and dried. Mandelic acid is prepared by the action of cyanide on benzaldehyde as follows :

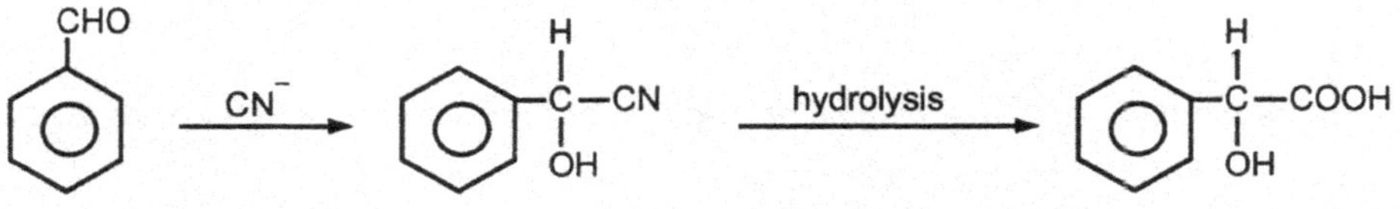

$$C_6H_5CHO \xrightarrow{CN^-} C_6H_5CH(OH)CN \xrightarrow{hydrolysis} C_6H_5CH(OH)COOH$$

Mandelic acid

**Properties :** It is a white crystalline powder, odourless or slightly aromatic with saline taste. It is slightly soluble in cold water, more in boiling water and insoluble in alcohol.

**Uses :** It is used as antibacterial agent.

### 20. Calcium Glycerophosphate :

**Preparation :** It is prepared by adding phosphoric acid slowly to glycerine and heated when glycerophosphoric acid is formed. This is dissolved in water and treated with milk of lime. The calcium phosphate formed is removed by filtration, the excess of calcium hydroxide is converted to calcium carbonate by passing $CO_2$, which is also removed by filtration. The filtrate is concentrated in vacuum to get the product.

**Properties :** It is a fine white powder, practically odourless and is slightly hygroscopic in nature. It is soluble in large quantities of water but insoluble in alcohol.

### 21. Calcium Hypophosphite :

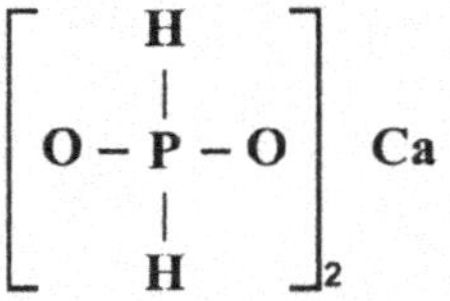

$[O-PH(H)-O]_2 Ca$ Mol. Wt. 170.06

**Preparation :** It is prepared by the action of lime water, on a partially oxidised phosphorus. It is filtered, the residue is washed with water. The filtrate and washings are concentrated under reduced pressure with stirring when the product crystallizes out.

$$3Ca(OH)_2 + 8P + 6H_2O \longrightarrow 3Ca(PH_2O_2)_2 + 2PH_3$$

**Properties :** It occurs as white crystalline powder or as colourless crystals and has a bitter taste. It is soluble in water but insoluble in alcohol. As it undergoes oxidation easily, it should not be heated with oxidising agents like potassium permanganate, nitrate or perchlorates, it may cause explosion.

**Uses :** Both the above salts are used in the form of syrup as a source of calcium, but are not useful in treating nerve disorders as was thought, because of its phosphate or phosphite part.

## 22. Bleaching Powder (Chlorinated Lime) :

This compound was official in earlier editions of I.P. and B.P. but is no more official. However, it has been already discussed under the category of "Topical Agents".

### EXERCISE

1. *Give list of official compounds of calcium and their formulations.*
2. *Describe the biological importance of calcium ions and discuss its deficiency symptoms.*
3. *Give method of preparation and uses of :*
   *(i) Calcium acetate,*
   *(ii) Calcium carbonate,*
   *(iii) Calcium gluconate and*
   *(iv) Calcium phosphate dibasic.*
4. *Outline the principle and assay procedure for the following calcium compounds :*
   *(i) Calcium gluconate,*
   *(ii) Calcium hydroxide and*
   *(iii) Calcium amino salicylate.*

# 17

# RADIOPHARMACEUTICALS AND CONTRAST MEDIA

## (A) RADIOACTIVITY AND RADIO PHARMACEUTICALS

Many heavy elements like uranium, thorium, radium and their compounds emit radiations spontaneously. These radiations can penetrate through solid material, can ionise gases, produce a glow on zinc sulphide paint or affect the photographic plates. The substances which emit such radiations are called radioactive substances and the phenomenon of spontaneous and continuous emission of such radiations is called as radioactivity. These radiations are emitted without any help from external agencies and are independent of temperature, pressure, concentration or catalyst. Radioactive substance may exist in the form of element or its compound.

**Radioisotopes :**

It is known that every atom of an element is composed of nucleus containing protons and neutrons, surrounded by electrons. If the atom is electrically neutral then the number of protons in nucleus is same as that of electrons. It is also known that the number of protons in the nucleus is equal to atomic number which determines its properties. The atomic number of the atom is characteristic of that element. Various atomic species are known as nuclides and are often represented simply by the name or symbol e.g. carbon, $^{12}_{6}C$ where superscript is the mass number and the subscript is the atomic number of the element. Number of elements contains a certain percentage of atoms which differ in atomic weight or mass from majority of atoms present. Elements having the same atomic number but different atomic weight or mass are known as isotopes e.g. $^{14}_{6}C$, $^{14}_{7}N$ etc. Isotopes of particular element have same chemical and physical properties, with a difference in the kinetics or rates of reactions as it depends upon mass.

There are two major type of isotopes found in nature :

(a) The stable isotopes (nuclide) which do not decompose to other isotopic form of the element.

(b) The unstable or radio active isotopes (radionuclide) which decomposes or decay by emitting the nuclear particles into the other isotope or different elements. The decomposition is characteristic of each isotope and it continues till stable isotopic level is achieved.

Some radioactive isotopes are found naturally in elements, but a large number of unstable isotopes, which finds wide applications in the field of chemistry, medicine, geology, etc. are produced synthetically. The unstable isotopes are usually produced by bombardment of atomic nuclei with neutrons or electrons to produce unstable nuclei of the same element or a different element (radionuclides).

**Radioactive Decay :**

A Radioactive substance disintegrates or decays with the emission of certain particles or certain quantities of energy which is always characteristic of the isotope. The important emissions are the alpha particles ($\alpha$), the beta particles ($\beta$) and the gamma ($\gamma$) rays.

**Alpha particles :** When a radioactive element emits alpha particles from the nucleus of the atom the resulting nucleus will have two positive charges less than the original nucleus and thus it will correspond with the element having its atomic number less than two units. The mass number of the new nucleus will be less than 4 amu as compared to original. This can be examplified by decay of radium nucleus to give randon nucleus by emission of alpha particles.

$$^{226}_{88}Ra \longrightarrow ^{222}_{88}Ra^{222} + ^{4}_{2}He$$

The alpha particles are the heaviest and slowest of the radioactive emissions. They are helium ions $He^{++}$ with a relative of +2 charge, containing two protons and two neutrons and has 4 amu mass and atomic number 2. Their velocity is about $1/10^{th}$ that of light which varies from element to element. There penetrating power is least as compared to other emissions. Because of low penetrating power of alpha particles, elements which emits these do not find any use in biological applications as they cannot penetrate tissue. Alpha particles are affected by strong magnetic field.

**Beta particles :** These can be described as electrons of nuclear origin. They have a mass of 1/1836 of the mass of hydrogen atom and a relative charge of $-1$. As these radiations are lighter, they travel with the velocity little less than that of light. They have much more penetrating power and can penetrate an aluminium sheet upto 3 mm thick. As these particles carry a negative charge, they cause ionization of molecules when they passes through various media. These particles are affected by strong magnetic field. Number of isotopes emitting beta particles are useful in biological applications because of their high penetration power. They can penetrate tissue.

The emission of beta particles from an element does not alter the atomic mass, but alters the atomic number and is converted to element with next highest atomic number for e.g. :

$$^{14}_{6}C \longrightarrow ^{14}_{7}N + \beta^{-}$$

Beta particles are sometimes referred to as negations, which are emitted by unstable nuclei, in which the neutron/proton ratio exceeds the stability limit. In such cases, neutrons are transformed into protons with beta emissions.

$$^{1}_{0}n \longrightarrow ^{1}_{1}p + B^{-}$$

There are another type of beta emissions which are called as positrons ($\beta^{+}$). These are not very common and as they are short lived. They do not find application in biological field.

**Gamma radiations :** These radiations do not have any charge and thus are not affected by electric or magnetic field. They have properties of both, a wave and particle. They do not have mass and charge but have very high energy and thus have excellent penetrating power. Only a very thick lead sheet or concrete shield affords protection from these radiations. They are of very short wavelength resembling X-rays and travel with the velocity of light. Being uncharged, they have poor ionising power but they can interact with molecules and atoms in specific media, and can produce ions and free radicals by dislodging electrons from orbitals.

When gamma rays are emitted from an element, there is lowering of nuclear energy level but no elemental change is noted unless other types of radiations are emitted, which is usually the case.

## Unit of Radioactivity :

The basic unit of radioactivity is "Curie" symbolised as 'C'. Curie is defined as "the quantity of any radioactive substance undergoing the same number of disintegrations in unit time as of 1 g of pure radium". One Curie is equal to $3.7 \times 10^{10}$ disintegrations per second. The subunits of curie are called as millicurie (mC) $1 \times 10^{-3}$ of curie = $3.7 \times 10^7$ disintegrations per second and microcurie ($\mu$C) = $1 \times 10^{-6}$ or $3.7 \times 10^4$ disintegrations per second.

The Roentgen '$\gamma$' is unit of measurement of radiation mainly for X-rays. It measures the ionizing effect of given radiation and its damaging effect on biological matter. Approximately 1 $\gamma$ is equivalent to about 930 erg/g of tissue or water.

The rad (radiation absorbed dose) is another unit of measuring the radiation absorbed and is defined as the quantity of radiation which releases or absorbs 100 erg/g of a specified medium.

Since, the effect of given radiation on biological system depends upon the type of radiation a unit known as Relative Biological Effectiveness or RBE has been introduced. This expresses the relative effects of radiation $\alpha$, $\beta$ and $\gamma$ on the biological system.

## Half-life of Radioelement :

Radioactive isotopes or nuclides continue to decay for a particular period of time. During a given time, a particular number of atoms originally present decay. The half-life is used to designate this part of time, which refers to the time required for one half of atoms originally present to complete their emission of radiation.

Half-life is defined as the time in which the amount of radionuclide decays to half its initial value. It is related to decay constant $\lambda$ by equation,

$$t/2 = \frac{0.693}{\lambda}$$

Half life for various radioactive elements varies considerably, e.g. $^{212}$Po has half-life $3 \times 10^{-7}$ seconds, $^{131}$I has 8 days, $^{32}$P has 14.3 days, $^{65}$Zn has 150 days, $^{22}$Na has 2-6 years while $^{238}$U has $4.5 \times 10^4$ years.

## Properties of Radiation :

Radiation emitted by atoms of radio active material is a form of energy. This energy can be divided into two categories : (i) particulate and (ii) electromagnetic. The two categories are interchangeable.

The particulate radiations are in the form of alpha and beta radiations emitted by disintegrating atoms of radioactive material. These are the beams of high speed charged particles which (a) can be detected by electrical or magnetic field, (b) can penetrate matter, (c) can ionise matter (e.g. gas) through which they pass, (d) cause certain substances to emit flashes of light (scintillation) and (e) can darken a photographic plate. Some of these properties are utilised in their detection and estimation or measurement The ionizing effect is measured in ionization chambers and Geiger Muller Counters, the scintillation effect in scintillatiom counters and the photographic effect in autoradiography.

## Detection and Measurement of Radiation :

The several kinds of particles and rays produced during the disintegration of a radioactive material leave number of ions along their paths. It is these ions that are normally detected and measured. The method adopted for the measurement of radioactivity depends upon the extent of penetrability and dissipation of energy. Following are the various devices used in measurement.

**1. Ionization Chamber :** The detector of this type makes use of the electrical conductivity of a gas that has been partially ionized by radiation passing through it. This is carried out in an ionization chamber. Ionization chambers are of various shapes and sizes. A chamber is filled with gas and is fitted with two electrodes kept at different electrical potentials (50 to 100 volts for each centimeter of distance between the two electrodes). It is connected to a measuring instrument to indicate flow of electric current. Radiation causes ionization of gas molecules or produce ions which results in emission of electrons. This shows change in electrical current which is measured. The current produced is of the order of 10-15 amps.

**2. Proportional Counters :** It is a modified ionization method in which, at an applied potential, ionization of primary electrons produce a very large number of free electrons which are carried to the anode. Since, for each primary electron liberated, a large number of secondary electrons are liberated, the current pulse through electrical circuit is greatly amplified. The voltage range over which gas ionization takes place is known as the proportional region and the counters working in this region are known as proportional counters.

**3. The Geiger Counters :** This is commonly known as Geiger-Muller (GM) counter and is the best known of all radiation detector.

It consists of a cylinder of stainless steel or glass coated with silver on the innerside which acts as cathode. A fine metal wire is mounted coaxially inside the tube as anode. The chamber is filled with a mixture of argon, which provides ionizable substance and some heavier gas like alcohol, methane, etc. Radiation enters the tube through a thin section of outer wall called as window. It causes ionization of the gas atoms. A high voltage (800-1300 V) is maintained between the electrodes. Due to ionization of gas, the electrons and the positively charged ions are attracted and collected by the anode and cathode respectively. The passages of these ions trough the tube constitutes the flow of current. Each particles of radiation causes a brief flow or pulse of current which is recorded by a device known as the scalar, which shows the total number of pulses.

**4. Scintillation Counters :** The three types of radiations, viz. alpha, beta and gamma, can be detected by scintillation counters. The detector works on the principles that when ionizing radiation strikes certain substances like phosphorus (or a flurogenic material), a flash of light is given out. This flash is collected by photomultiplier tube which produces electric impulse. This impulse on further amplification is recorded by the scalar.

The counter consists of a scintillation crystal coupled with photomultiplier tube, an amplifier and scaler. For gamma radiations (as they have high penetrating power), the phosphor in crystal is sodium iodide activated with about 1% of thallium to enhance the degree of fluorescence. The gamma radiations passing through a small window enter the crystal, [NaI (TI)] where it produces a small flash of light. This is brought to the photomultiplier tube which in turn detects the flash, and amplifies it into an electrical impulse. The impluse is recorded by means of a scalar.

For counting beta particles, crystals of anthracene or stilbene, or solution of stilbene in xylene, boron or cadmium compounds are used. Commercially the solutions called as 'scintillation cocktails' are also available.

**5. Semiconductor Detectors :** These are of several types. They are useful for measuring X-rays and gamma rays. In these detectors, the charge carriers produced by ionizing radiation, are electron-hole pairs (and not ion-pairs). These travel towards the positive electrode with high velocities.

**6. Photographic Plate Method :** An ionising particle will cause an activation and subsequent darkening of a photographic plate. The degree of darkening gives the measure of the total activity. This method is used to locate the exact distribution of radioactive material in a thin section. This technique is mainly used for detecting gamma radiations in pysiological studies of plants and animals.

### Handling and Storage of Radioactive Materials :

Great care must be taken in handling and storage of radioactive materials. This is to protect people and personnel who handle it, from harmful radiations which the radioactive material emits. Certain precautions to be taken while working with materials, detectors, in experiments, in radio assays and in handling are as follows :

(a) Radioactive materials should never be touched with hand, but should be handled by means of forceps or suitable instruments.

(b) Smoking, eating or drinking should be prohibited in the laboratory, where radioactive materials are present.

(c) Sufficient protective clothing or shields must be used while handling the materials.

(d) Radioactive materials should be kept in suitable, labelled containers, shielded by lead bricks and preferably in a remote area.

(e) Areas where radioactive materials are stored or used, should be monitored (tested regularly for radioactivity).

(f) There should be a proper disposal method for radioactive materials.

**Applications of Radioisotopes :**

Radioisotopes are used in medicine in two different ways. They may be :

1. Radiation source in therapy;
2. Radioactive tracers for diagnostic purposes. In therapeutic use of radioisotopes, the radiations emitted produce destructive effects on existing cells and prevent the formation of new cells and tissues. For this reason, the radioisotope therapy is used only in those disease conditions, in which extensive cellular metabolic malfunction exists.

The therapeutically used radioisotopes depend mainly on their ability to ionise atoms. The measurement of the energy involved in radiations and which results in ionizing is expressed in millions of electron volts called as MeV. The strength or the energy of alpha, beta and gamma is expressed as MeV. All radiations cause ionization of atoms in their paths. The radiations of short wavelength (gamma rays) have high penetrating power than those of long wavelength (beta rays). Besides, the greater the MeV of the rays the more destructive it becomes to the surrounding tissues.

Some important radioisotopes used in medicine are :

**Calcium ($^{44}$Ca and $^{45}$Ca) :** The radioactive calcium is used to study bone structure and in the treatment of carcinoma of bone.

**Carbon ($^{14}$C):** It is the most widely used isotope in various studies, for e.g. in reaction mechanism, metabolism of carbohydrate and fats, drug excretion, decomposition of pharmaceutical products.

**Cobalt ($^{60}$Co) :** This radioactive agent emits beta and gamma rays and is used in therapy where X-rays are used. It is also used for the sterilization of surgical materials and dressings by its gamma radiation.

**Cyanocobalamine ($^{57}$Co) :** It is radioactive Cyanocobalamine $^{57}$C. The half life of $^{57}$Co is 270 days. This is used in the diagnosis of pernicious anemia.

**Gold ($^{198}$Au) Solution :** It is a cherry red, colloidal solution of radioactive gold ($^{198}$Au) which is sterilised by autoclaving. It emits beta particles (0.96 MeV) and gamma rays (0.41 MeV) and has a half life of 207 days. It is used as neoplastic suppressant. It is also used in estimation of reticuloendothelial activity.

Hydrogen ($^{2}$H and $^{3}$H) : The deuterium ($^{2}$H) and tritium ($^{3}$H) are useful to determine total body water.

**Iron (Fess and $^{59}$Fe) :** It emits beta particles and high energy gamma rays. The half life of $^{59}$Fe is 45 days. It is used in research studies about utilization and absorption of iron salts. It is also used to measure red cell life span.

**Nitrogen ($^{13}$N and $^{15}$N) :** It is useful in investigations of amino acids and protein metabolism and also in studies of nitrogen fixation by plants.

**Oxygen ($^{7}$O and $^{18}$O) :** These are useful in studies in organic reactions and photosynthesis etc.

**Sodium ($^{22}$Na and $^{24}$Na)** : It is employed in estimation of extra cellular fluid, blood circulation rate, studies in cell permeability, excretion and distribution of water, etc.

**Sodium Chromate ($^{51}$Cr) Solution** : It is a radioactive $^{51}$Cr ion in the form of $Na_2^{51}CrO_4$. It has a half life of 26.5 days. It is used to study red cell volume and its survival time.

**Sodium Iodide ($^{131}$I) Capsule and Solution** : It is a radioactive isotope of $^{131}$iodine in the form of sodium iodide$^{131}$. It emits beta and gamma rays (energy 0.364 MeV). It has a biological half life of 8 days. It is mainly used as a diagnostic and therapeutic agent in thyroid related diseases and in myxedema.

**Sodium Phosphate ($^{32}$P) Solution** : The radioactive isotope of $^{32}$P is in the form of sodium acid phosphate ($NaH_2^{32}PO_4$) and sodium basic phosphate ($NaH^{32}PO_4$). It emits beta particles. It has a half life of 14.3 days and is used in the treatment of polycythemia vera to decrease the rate of formation of the erythrocytes. It is also used in the treatment of 'chronic granulocytic leukemia'.

## (B) RADIO-OPAQUE CONTRAST MEDIA

Radio-opaque substances are those compounds, both inorganic and organic, that have the property of casting a shadow on X-ray films. These substances have the ability to stop the passage of X-rays and hence appear opaque on X-ray examination. Such compounds and their preparations are called as X-ray constrast media.

X-ray are electromagnetic radiations of short wavelength and thus have high penetrating power. The electrons of high atomic number element can interact with X-rays. The interaction causes interference in their passage through the medium.

In diagnostic study using X-rays, the soft tissues are permeable to the passage of X-rays (as the tissues are mostly composed of elements of low atomic numbers like carbon, hydrogen, oxygen and nitrogen) and hence cause darkening on X-ray film. The bony structure casts a shadow on the film, as the bones contain elements having high atomic number like calcium and phosphorus. As a result bony tissues can be distinguished on an exposed X-ray film.

Inorganic compounds like barium sulphate and some bismuth compounds thus are useful as radio-opaque constrast media for diagnostic use.

A large number of organic iodinated compounds are used as radio-opaque contrast media. These are administered either ways : (i) systemically i.e. orally or intravenously or (ii) by retrograde i.e. by mechanical means, backwardly for various diagnostic purpose. These compounds are useful for examination of gastrointestinal tract, kidney (urography) liver (cholecystography), gall bladder and bile duct, blood vessels of heart (angiography and cardiography), bronchial tract (bronchography) and that of urethra, vagina, etc. Discussion of these iodinated organic compounds is not covered in this book.

**Barium Sulphate :**
**$BaSO_4$**            Mol. Wt. 233.4

It contains 97.5 to 100.5% w/w $BaSO_4$.

**Preparation** : Barium sulphate for the Roentogen ray purpose (X-ray) is prepared by precipitating barium ions from cold dilute solutions of barium salt with dilute sulphuric acid.

$$Ba(OH)_2 + H_2SO_4 \longrightarrow BaSO_4 \downarrow + 2H_2O$$
$$BaCl_2 + H_2SO_4 \longrightarrow BaSO_4 \downarrow + 2HCl$$

The precipitated salt is thoroughly washed, dried and then screened. Industrial grade barium sulphate is a byproduct of many industries e.g. during the manufacture of $H_2O_2$ from $BaO_2.8H_2O$. It can also be prepared by the action of dilute $H_2SO_4$ on BaS (Barium sulphide).

**Properties :** It is a fine, white, odourless, tasteless and bulky powder that is free from grittiness. The salt is insoluble in water, organic solvents and dilute acids and alkalies. It is soluble in concentrated $H_2SO_4$.

$$BaSO_4 + H_2SO_4 \longrightarrow Ba(HSO_4)_2$$

Barium sulphate is so insoluble, that it shows very few reactions. It can be solubilised with $H_2SO_4$ or by fusing it with alkali carbonates. Once it is converted to a carbonate, it reacts with acids easily.

**Action and Uses :** It is used for preparation of barium sulphate compound powder and also as a contrast medium for X-ray examination of the alimentary tract. It is administered orally or by enema for examination of the colon. Dose is 200-400 g oral and 400-750 g by retrogate.

**Assay :** It is assayed gravimetrically.

### Barium Sulphate for Suspension :

**Syn :** Barium meal or 'shadow meal'.

It is a dry mixture of barium sulphate containing suitable colour, flavour, preservative and suspending or dispersing agent. It contains not less than 90% w/v of Barium sulphate.

**Action and Use :** It is used as a barium meal.

**Assay :** Barium sulphate for suspension is assayed by fusion of a known weight of compound with sodium carbonate and potassium carbonate at 100°C for fifteen minutes. It is cooled, suspended in water and decanted. The residue is washed with 2% sodium carbonate solution (until free from sulphate). Dilute hydrochloric acid is added followed by ammonium acetate and potassium dichromate and urea. The suspension is digested at 80-85°C for 16 hours and then filtered through sintered glass crucible. The residue washed with potassium dichromate solution followed by water and the contents weighed after drying at 105°C.

### Bismuth Compounds :

Bismuthyl nitrate and bismuthyl carbonate in 30-60 g as suspension in water used to be employed for examination of alimentary tract. These compounds have been replaced by other compounds.

## EXERCISE

1. Give properties of $\alpha$, $\beta$ and $\gamma$ radiations.
2. Define the terms 'radioactivity and 'radioisotope'. What is half life of radioactive compound ? Comment on the mode of measurement of radiations.
3. Explain the principle and working of scintillation counter.
4. Describe the working of Geiger-counter. What precautions are to be taken while handling radioactive material ?
5. Describe the various methods for measurement of radiations.
6. What are radio-opaque compounds ? Give method of preparation and uses of barium sulphate.
7. List the radioisotopes giving their uses in medicine.

# 18

# ANTIDOTES IN POISONING

Poisoning of the body can occur in various ways. Most commonly, poisoning occurs due to heavy metals present in the environment, which is getting richer in heavy metals or through metallic contamination of food and water. Many times, the metals are leached from utensils and cookwares leading to inadvertent poisoning. Poisoning can also be due to the insecticides or pesticides. Poisoning can be due to excessive use of drug (drug overdoses). Because of the wide scope of this topic, it has been decided to restrict discussion only to heavy metals and cyanide poisoning, and the antidotes used for them.

Antidotes are the agents which are used to reverse, stop or counteract the action of poisons. Antidotes can be classified on the basis of their mechanism of action as follows :

1. **Physiological antidote :** It acts by producing the effect opposite to that of poison, or counteracts the effect of poison physiologically.
2. **Chemical antidote :** It acts usually by combining with the poison and thus changing its chemical nature, so the poison cannot act any more.
3. **Mechanical antidotes :** Which usually acts by preventing the absorption of poison in the body or expelling out the poison by emesis or elimination through urine.

**Heavy Metals and their Antagonists :**

The common heavy metals which cause poisoning are, the salts of arsenic, lead, mercury, iron and cadmium. Heavy metal poisoning occurs due to intake of overdose or due to their incomplete metabolism in the body. Depending upon the content and type of heavy metal, the toxic effects manifest in the patients. The most widely adopted method is to use such heavy metal antagonist, which will specifically chelate or form complex with them.

The initial treatment in heavy metal poisoning into administer activated charcoal to adsorb the heavy metal or poison. This is followed by administrating compounds which produces emesis. This eliminates the possibility of any poison remaining in the stomach, being absorbed for circulation. Some inorganic compounds precipitate heavy metals and prevent their absorption. In case of poison being absorbed in body some effective organic antidotes are used in systemic heavy metal poisoning.

The inorganic pounds used as antidotes are as follows :

### Activated Charcoal :

**Preparation :** It is commercially obtained as a residue during destructive distillation of various organic matters or from burning organic materials in a special manner. The coarse material is powdered.

**Properties :** It occurs as a fine black, odourless, tasteless powder with smooth touch and free from gritty particles. It is almost insoluble in usual solvents. The fine powder offers more surface area for adsorbent properties.

**Action and Uses :** It is a general type of adsorbent used in poisoning. It not only adsorbs heavy metals, but also adsorbs drugs like hypnotics sedatives alkaloids, etc. and also gases like carbon monoxide, carbondioxide, nitrous oxide, etc. It is normally used in the ratio of 5:1 or 10:1 (charcoal to poison). It is administered in the form of tablets. It is also used in diarrhoea to adsorbs toxins.

### Kaolin :

This compound is already discussed under 'protective and adsorbents'.

**Action and Uses :** Kaolin is mainly used as adsorbent in treatment of food and alkaloidal poisoning as it absorbs toxins. Besides being an adsorbent, it is also used externally in preparation of kaolin poultice. For internal use it is the light kaolin which is commonly employed.

### Copper Sulphate :

Pharmaceutically, it is mainly use as emetic in a dose of 300 mg in 30 ml water. It acts as antidote in phosphorus poisoning. Externally it is used as astringent and also as a fungicide in 1 to 5% solution. It is an ingredient of Benedict's and Fehling's reagent.

### Magnesium Sulphate :

This compound is discussed under the topic 'saline cathartic'.

Magnesium sulphate besides acting as saline cathartic is used in treatment of barium and lead poisoning. These heavy metals get precipitated as insoluble sulphates. It thus acts as antidote in heavy metal poisoning.

### Sodium Phosphate :

This compound is also discussed under the chapter 'saline cathartics'.

Sodium phosphate is mainly used as an antidote for iron poisoning. It forms insoluble iron phosphate salt when administered orally.

Besides the above inorganic compounds, the following special organic compounds (official is B.P. 1988) are used as antidote in heavy metal poisoning.

**D-Penicillamine :** It is given in the form of tablets in Cu, Mg and Pb poisoning. Usual dose is 500 mg to 1.5 g per day in divided doses orally, depending upon individual metal poisoning. It forms complex with Cu, Hg, Zn and Rb and promotes its elimination through urine.

**Deferoxamine**: Deferrioxamine mesylate and its injection is official in B.P. 1988. It is mainly effective against $Fe^{++}$ ion. It is given in 500 mg by i.m. route in acute poisoning. Initial dose is 1 g followed by 500 mg as required. For chronic poisoning (thallassemia) it is given in 0.5 to 1 g per day.

**Dimercaprol**: Dimercaprol and its injection are official in B.P. 1988. It is given by deep i.m. injection in 1% solution in oil. The dose depends upon the nature and amount of metal poisoning. It forms a chelate between sulphadryl –SH group and metal. It is mainly effective against arsenic, gold and mercury poisoning. The metal complex is rapidly excreted.

**Calcium Disodium Edetate**: This compound and its infusion is official in B.P. 1988. This compound is effective in systemic poisoning of heavy metals. It is a universal type of antidote as it forms a chelate with many metals. It is mainly effective in lead poisoning wherein it replaces lead. It is given parenterally in 200 mg/ml by i.m. route. It should be used judiciously as it is a general antidote and shows side effects.

**Succimer**: It is a disulphydryl compound similar in action as of dimercaprol. It is orally active and is relatively nontoxic. It is effective in treatment of mercury, arsenic and lead poisoning.

## Cyanide Poisoning:

Cyanide Poisoning normally occurs accidently or when cyanide poison is taken intentionally for suicidal purpose. In cyanide poisoning, cyanide ion combines with ferric ion of cytochrome oxidase an, enzyme responsible for electron transfer reactions. This leads to stoppage of cellular respiration and metabolic reaction. Cyanide poisoning is usually fatal, if it is not treated immediately.

In cyanide poisoning, sodium nitrite and sodium thiosulphate injections are given to counteract the effects of cyanide poison. Sodium thiosulphate reacts with cyanide ions and converts into sodium thiocyanate which is less toxic than cyanide. While sodium nitrite reacts with ferrous iron of haemoglobin and converts into ferric iron of methanoglobin and thus reduces the concentration of cyanide ions.

**Sodium Nitrite :**

**Uses :** Medicinally, it is mainly used as antidote in cyanide and has a hypotensive effect. It has relaxant action on smooth muscles. It prevents rusting of surgical instruments and it is also used as food preservative.

**Sodium Thiosulphate :**

Sodium thiosulphate is specifically used as antidote in cyanide poisoning. Sodium thiosulphate injection (official) is used for the same purpose. The compound also shows cathartic action. It is a chemical used in photography and analytical laboratory.

## EXERCISE

1. Discuss the mechanism of actions of antidotes in poisoning. Outline the role of activated charcoal or kaolin in poisoning.
2. Describe the method of preparation and uses of the following inorganic compounds as antidotes :
   (a) Copper sulphate.
   (b) Sodium phosphate.
3. Give a brief account of the organic drugs used as antidote in poisoning,
4. Discuss the method of preparation, uses and assay of any two compounds used in cyanide poisoning.

■■■

# 19

# IDENTIFICATION TESTS FOR IONS AND RADICALS

Following are the identification tests for different ions/radicals as per 'India Pharmacopoeia'. Tests described in second edition (1966) and third edition (1985) are given below.

**ANIONS/RADICALS**

1. **Acetates : ($CH_3COO^-$)**
   1. When acetates are heated with equal quantity of oxalic acid; forms acetic acid which is recognised by its odour for e.g.
   
   $$2CH_3COONa + (COOH)_2 \xrightarrow{\Delta} 2CH_3COOH + COONa$$
   
   2. Acetates when mixed with sulphuric acid, followed by ethylalcohol and warmed, forms an ester, ethylacetate, recognised by its pleasant odour for e.g.
   
   $$CH_3COONa + C_2H_5OH \xrightarrow{H_2SO_4} CH_3COOC_2H_5 + H_2O + NaOH$$
   
   3. Neutral or slightly acidic solutions of acetate (alkali metal acetate or ammonium acetate) when treated with ferric chloride solution gives a red brown colour (acetate complex) which on boiling gives a red brown precipitate of basic iron acetate.
   
   $$3C_2H_3O_2^- + Fe^{+++} + 2H_2O \longrightarrow \underset{\text{Basic iron acetate}}{Fe(OH)_2(C_2H_3O_2)} \downarrow + 2CH_3COO^-$$
   
   On adding hydrochloric acid the colour of solution changes to yellow due to formation of ferric chloride.
   
   4. Acetates when heated with calcium oxide forms acetone. Acetone is detected when a filter paper moistened with 2% o-nitrobenzaldehyde solution and dried and again moistened with sodium hydroxide solution, is placed on the mouth of the test tube and it turns blue.
   
   5. Aqueous solution of acetates when treated with lanthanum nitrate solution followed by 2 drops of 0.1 N iodine and a drop of dilute ammonia, and boiled, gives blue precipitate or dark blue colour.

2. **Benzoates : ($C_6H_5COO^-$)**

   1. When benzoates are warmed gently with few drops of $H_2SO_4$, a white sublimate of benzoic acid is deposited on the wall of the test tube.

      $$2C_6H_5COONa + H_2SO_4 \xrightarrow{Warm} 2C_6H_5COOH + Na_2SO_4$$

   2. Aqueous solution of benzoates, when acidified with only a few drops of HCl, give a white precipitate of benzoic acid, which on filtration, washing and crystallization melts at about 120°C.

      $$C_6H_5COONa + HCl \longrightarrow C_6H_5COOH + NaCl$$

   3. Neutral solution of benzoates on treatment with ferric chloride solution gives a yellowish brownish precipitate of ferric benzoate which is soluble in organic solvents.

      $$3C_6H_5COO^- + Fe^{++} \longrightarrow Fe(C_6H_5COO)_3$$
      $$\text{Ferric benzoate}$$

3. **Bicarbonates : $\left(HCO_3^-\right)$**

   1. Aqueous solution of bicarbonates on boiling liberate $CO_2$, which when passed in calcium hydroxide solution gives a white precipitate of calcium carbonate.

      $$2NaHCO_3 \xrightarrow{Boil} Na_2CO_3 + CO_2 \uparrow + H_2O$$
      $$Ca(OH)_2 + CO_2 \xrightarrow{H_2O} CaCO_3 + H_2O$$

   2. When an aqueous solution of bicarbonate is treated with magnesium sulphate, no precipitate is formed, but on boiling, a white precipitate of magnesium carbonate is obtained (bicarbonate on heating is converted to carbonate which reacts with magnesium sulphate to forms basic magnesium carbonate.

      $$NaHCO_3 + MgSO_4 \longrightarrow \text{No reaction}$$
      $$NaHCO_3 \xrightarrow{Boil} Na_2CO_3$$
      $$5Na_2CO_3 + 5MgSO_4 \longrightarrow 4MgCO_3 \cdot Mg(OH)_2 \cdot 5H_2O \downarrow + CO_2 \uparrow$$

   3. Aqueous solution of carbonates on treatment with acetic acid liberates $CO_2$, which when passed in barium hydroxide solution gives a white precipitate of barium carbonate, which dissolves on addition of HCl, as it gets converted to barium chloride.

      $$NaHCO_3 + CH_3COOH \longrightarrow CH_3COONa + CO_2 \uparrow + H_2O$$
      $$Ba(OH)_2 + CO_2 \xrightarrow{H_2O} BaCO_3 \downarrow + H_2O$$
      $$BaCO_3 + 2HCl \longrightarrow BaCl_2 + CO_2 + H_2O$$

   4. Aqueous solution of bicarbonates on treatment with mercuric chloride solution produces a white precipitate of mercuric bicarbonate. It changes colour due to hydrolysis of mercuric hydroxide, which decomposes to give red mercuric oxide.

      $$2NaHCO_3 + HgCl_2 \longrightarrow Hg(HCO_3)_2 + 2NaCl$$
      $$Hg(HCO_3)_2 \longrightarrow Hg(OH)_2 + 2CO_2 \uparrow$$
      $$Hg(OH)_2 \longrightarrow HgO + H_2O$$

## 4. Bromides : (Br⁻)

1. When bromides are heated with sulphuric acid and strong oxidising agents like manganese, dioxide or potassium dichromate, vapours of bromine are formed, which imparts yellow colour to filter paper moistened with starch solution.

$$2Br^- + 4H^+ + MnO_2 \longrightarrow 2Mn^{++} + Br_2\uparrow + 2H_2O$$

$$6Br^- + 14H^+ + Cr_2O_7^{--} \longrightarrow 2Cr^{+++} + 3Br_2\uparrow + 7H_2O$$

2. Aqueous solution of bromides when acidified with nitric acid and treated with silver nitrate solution gives a curdy pale precipitate of silver bromide, which when separated by centrifugation, washed and treated with strong ammonia solution, dissolves slightly. It is insoluble in dilute ammonia solution or dilute nitric acid.

$$NaBr + AgNO_3 \xrightarrow{HNO_3} AgBr\downarrow + NaNO_3$$

$$AgBr + NH_3 \longrightarrow Ag(NH_3)_2^+ \; Br^- \text{ solution with difficulty}$$

3. Aqueous solution of bromides liberate bromine on treatment with chlorine solution, this liberated bromine gets dissolved in solvents chloroform and imparts reddish colour to chloroform layer. On addition of phenol solution to aqueous solution containing bromine a white precipitate of tribromophenol is formed.

$$2NaBr + Cl_2 \longrightarrow 2NaCl + Br_2 \text{ (soluble in chloroform and imparts colour)}$$

Br₂ + H₂O + [phenol] ⟶ [2,4,6-tribromophenol]

(2, 4, 6-tribromo phenol)

In testing of bromides in presence of iodides, the iodine is removed by boiling with aqueous solution of lead dioxide.

$$2I^- + 4H^+ + PbO_2 \longrightarrow Pb^{--} + 2H_2O + I_2 \uparrow \text{ removed by boiling}$$

## 5. Carbonates : $\left(CO_3^-\right)$

1. When carbonates, suspended/dissolved in water, are treated with acids (acetic acid, HCl etc.) gives effervescence due to formation of $CO_2$. These when passed in barium hydroxide solution gives white precipitate of barium carbonate. This on addition of hydrochloric acid, dissolves as it forms barium chloride.

$$Na_2CO_3 + 2CH_3COOH \longrightarrow 2CH_3COONa + CO_2 \uparrow H_2O$$

$$Ba(OH)_2 + CO_2 \longrightarrow BaCO_3 \downarrow$$

$$BaCO_3 + 2HCl \longrightarrow BaCl_2 + CO_2 \uparrow + H_2O$$

2. Aqueous solution of carbonates on treatment with magnesium sulphate solution gives a white precipitate of magnesium carbonate.

$$5Na_2CO_3 + 5MgSO_4 \longrightarrow 4MgCO_3 \cdot Mg(OH)_2 \cdot 5H_2O\uparrow$$

3. Solutions of carbonate produces a reddish brown precipitate of basic mercury carbonate on treatment with mercuric-chloride solution.

$$4HgCl_2 + 4Na_2CO_3 \xrightarrow{H_2O} HgCO_3 \cdot 3HgO + 3CO_2\downarrow\ 8NaCl$$

## 6. Chlorides : (Cl⁻)

1. Chlorides when heated with manganese dioxide and sulphuric acid, yields chlorine gas which can be recognised by its odour or by its action on starch-potassium iodide paper which turns blue. Chlorine liberates iodine from KI, which turns starch blue.

$$2NaCl + 2H_2SO_4 + MnO_2 \longrightarrow MnSO_4 + Na_2SO_4 + 2H_2O + Cl_2\uparrow$$

2. Aqueous solution of chloride when acidified with $HNO_3$ and treated with silver nitrate solution, gives a curdy white precipitate of silver chloride, which is insoluble in dilute nitric acid but dissolves in ammonia solution. On addition of nitric acid the precipitate reappears.

$$NaCl + AgNO_3 \longrightarrow AgCl\downarrow + NaNO_3$$
$$AgCl + 2NH_3 \longrightarrow [Ag(NH_3)_2]^+ Cl^-\ (clear\ solution)$$
$$Ag(NH_3)_2^+ Cl^- + HNO_3 \longrightarrow AgCl + (NH_4)_2NO_3$$

3. When sample containing chloride ion is treated with $K_2Cr_2O_7$ solution and $H_2SO_4$, and a paper moistened with diphenylcarbazide solution is placed over opening of the test tube, the paper turns violet.

## 7. Citrates :

1. Neutral solution of citrate on treatment with calcium chloride solution does not give any precipitate in cold, but on boiling gives a white precipitate of calcium citrate, which is soluble in acetic acid as it is converted to calcium acetate and citric acid.

```
        CH₂COONa                              CH₂COO        OOC—CH₂
         |                              boil        \Ca Ca/      |
    HO—C—COOH   + 3CaCl₂  ———→         HO—C—COO      OOC—C—OH
         |                                    |                  |
        CH₂COONa                             CH₂ COO Ca OOC——CH₂

      (Sodium citrate)                       (Calcium citrate)
                                                    | CH₃COOH
                                                    ↓
                                                    CH₂COOH
                                                    |
                          (CHCOO)₂ Ca  +  HO—C—COOH
                                                    |
                                                    CH₂COOH
                                                  (Citric acid)
```

2. Neutral solution of citrate on treatment with excess silver nitrate solution gives a white precipitate of silver citrate, which is soluble in nitric acid and in dilute ammonia solution. This ammonical solution on heating does not give silver mirror.

3. To alkali citrate solution when mercuric sulphate solution is added and heated, followed by solution of potassium permanganate, it gets decolourised and a white precipitate is obtained. The reaction involved can be written as follows :

(a) $2HgSO_4 + 2H_2O \longrightarrow Hg_2(OH)_2 + H_2SO_4$

(b)

$$\underset{\substack{\text{CH}_2\text{COOH} \\ | \\ \text{HO}-\text{C}-\text{COOH} \\ | \\ \text{CH}_2\text{COOH}}}{} + O_2 (KMnO_4) \xrightarrow{H^+} \underset{\substack{\text{CH}_2\text{COOH} \\ | \\ \text{C}=\text{O} \\ | \\ \text{CH}_2\text{COOH} \\ \text{acetone dicarboxylic acid}}}{}$$

4. When to aqueous solution is added two drops of $H_2SO_4$ and potassium permanganate solution and warmed till the $KMnO_4$ colour is discharged and then added few drops of solution of sodium nitroprusside in $H_2SO_4$ and 4 g of sulphamic acid and solution made alkaline with strong ammonia solution, a violet to violet blue colour is produced.

## 8. Iodides : (I⁻)

1. Aqueous solution of iodide when acidified with sulphuric acid and treated with potassium dichromate solution, and added chloroform and shaken, the chloroform layer becomes violet or red-violet. The potassium dichromate oxidises iodide to iodine, which dissolves in chloroform and imparts the colour.

$$6KI + K_2Cr_2O_7 + 7H_2SO_4 \longrightarrow K_2SO_4 + 2Cr(SO_4)_3 + 7H_2O + I_2$$

2. Solutions of iodides when treated with solution of potassium iodate and dilute acetic acid, liberates iodine, which imparts blue colour to starch solution, or if chloroform is added, imparts reddish violet colours to chloroform layer.

$$5KI + 6CH_3COOH + KIO_3 \longrightarrow 3I_2 + 6CH_2COOK + 3H_2O$$

3. Solution of iodide acidified with nitric acid and treated with silver nitrate solution, a curdy pale-yellow precipitate of silver iodide is obtained. This on separation, followed by washing water, and treatment with ammonia solution does not dissolves.

$$KI + AgNO_3 \xrightarrow{HNO_3} KNO_3 + AgI \text{ (insoluble in } NH_3)$$

4. When aqueous solution of iodide is treated with mercuric chloride solution, a dark red precipitate of mercuric iodide is obtained, which is slightly soluble in excess of reagent, but dissolves completely in excess of potassium iodide as it forms potassium mercuric iodide, which is soluble in water.

$$2KI + HgCl_2 \longrightarrow 2KCl + HgI_2 \text{ (red ppt.)}$$

$$HgI_2 + 2KI \longrightarrow [HgI_4]^{--} \text{ Potassium mercuric iodide}$$
$$\text{or } K_2HgI_4$$

## 9. Lactate :

1. When to the aqueous of solution of lactate added 1 ml bromine solution and 2 drops of 2 N $H_2SO_4$ and heated on water bath till yellow colour is discharged, and added 4 g of ammonium sulphate mixed well and treated with 4 drops of sodium nitroprusside solution in sulphuric acid, and then added strong ammonia solution without mixing and allowed to sand for 30 minutes; a dark green ring appears at the interface of the two liquids.

## 10. Nitrates : $\left(NO_3^-\right)$

1. Nitrates when heated with concentrated $H_2SO_4$ and copper liberates red fumes of nitrogen oxide.

$$2NO_3^- + Cu + 4H^+ \longrightarrow Cu^{++} + 2NO_2\uparrow + 2H_2O$$

2. Solutions of nitrate when carefully mixed with concentrated $H_2SO_4$, followed by crystal of brucine (alkaloid), a red colour is produced as alkaloid brucine is oxidised by nitric acid to a deep red coloured non-alkaloidal phenolic compound.

3. Aqueous solution of nitrate when treated with concentrated $H_2SO_4$ and cooled and to the inclined tube 1 drop of ferrous sulphate solution is added; a brown colour forms at the interface of the solutions ferrous sulphate and the acquisition. In presence of $H_2SO_4$ nitrates are reduced to NO, which combines with excess of ferrous ions to give brown ring.

$$NO_3^- + Fe^{++} + 4H^+ \longrightarrow NO + Fe^{+++} + 2H_2O$$

$$Fe^{++} + NO \longrightarrow [Fe(NO)]^{++} \dots \text{ (brown ring)}$$

4. When nitrate (solid) is added to a mixture of 2 drops of nitrobenzene and 4 drops of concentrated $H_2SO_4$ and kept for 5 minutes and then cooled in ice water and when to it is added slowly, 5 ml each of water, sodium hydroxide solution and acetone with continuous stirring, then allowed to stand; the upper layer shows an intense violet colour.

## 11. Phosphate : $\left(PO_4^{---}\right)$

1. Aqueous solution of phosphate (neutral, pH = 7) when treated with silver nitrate solution; a light yellow precipitate of silver orthophosphate is formed. This on heating does not change colour and is soluble in dilute ammonia and dilute nitric acid.

$$2HPO_4^{--} + 3\,Ag^+ \longrightarrow Ag_3PO_4 + H_2PO_4^-$$
$$\text{(yellow)}$$

2. When aqueous solution of phosphate is mixed with ammonical magnesium sulphate solution; a white crystalline precipitate is produced (magnesium orthophosphate).

$$HPO_4^{--} + Mg^{++} + NH_3 \xrightarrow{H_2O} MgNH_4PO_4 \cdot 6H_2O$$

3. When aqueous solution of phosphate is added to a mixture of equal volume of nitric acid and ammonium molybdate solution and warmed; a bright canary yellow precipitate of ammonium phosphomolybdate is formed.

$$HPO_4^{--} + 3NH_4^+ + 23H^+\ 12MnO_4^- \longrightarrow (NH_4)_3\,[P(MO_{12}O_{40})] + 12H_2O$$

## 12. Sulphates : $\left(SO_4^{--}\right)$

1. Aqueous solution of sulphate when acidified with HCl and treated with barium chloride solution gives a white precipitate of barium sulphate.

$$SO_4^{--} + Ba^{++} \longrightarrow BaSO_4 \downarrow$$

2. When aqueous solution of sulphate is treated with lead acetate solution; a white precipitate of lead sulphate is formed; which is soluble in ammonium acetate solution and also in sodium hydroxide solution.

$$Na_2SO_4 + (CH_3COO)_2Pb \longrightarrow PbSO_4 \downarrow + 2CH_3COONa$$

$$PbSO_4 + 4CH_3COO^- \longrightarrow [Pb(CH_3COO^-)_4]^{--} + SO_4^{--}$$
$$\text{soluble}$$

$$PbSO_4 + 3(OH)^- \longrightarrow HPbO_2^- + H_2O + SO_4^{--}$$
$$\text{soluble}$$

3. When the suspension obtained in test (1) of sulphate is treated with 2 drops of iodine solution; the suspension remains yellow or white. If sulphite or dithionate are present then iodine is decolourised.

## 13. Tartrates :

1. When tartrate is heated with concentrated $H_2SO_4$ on boiling water bath it chars rapidly and evolves carbon monoxide, which when ignited burns giving a blue flame.

2. Neutral solution of tartrate on treatment with excess of calcium chloride solution in cold, gives a white granular precipitate which is soluble in acetic acid.

3. When the solution of tartrate is neutralised with sodium hydroxide solution and treated with excess of silver nitrate solution a white precipitate (silver tartrate) is formed. This precipitate is soluble in nitric acid and also in ammonia solution. The ammonical solution when warmed, the silver ammonia complex is reduced to free silver, which forms silver mirror on the walls of the test tube.

(a) $KHC_4H_4O_6 + NaOH \longrightarrow KNa\ C_4H_4O_6 + H_2O$
(Sodium potassium tartrate)
neutral solution

(b) $KNaC_4H_4O_6 + 2AgNO_3 \longrightarrow Ag_2C_4H_4O_6 \downarrow + KNO_3 + NaNO_3$
(white precipitate)

(c) $Ag_2C_4H_4O_6 + 6NH_4OH \longrightarrow (NH_4)_2C_4H_4O_6 + 2Ag(NH_3)_2\ OH + 4H_2O$
(Clear solution)

(d) $2Ag(NH_3)_3OH \xrightarrow{\Delta} 2Ag\downarrow + 4NH_3 + H_2O_2$
(Silver mirro)

4. Aqueous solution of tartrate on treatment with 2 drops of ferrous sulphate and a drop of hydrogen peroxide gives a transient blue colour which changes to intense blue colour on dropwise addition of sodium hydroxide solution.

5. When to a tartrate salt, or 0.1 ml of aqueous solution, is added 2 drops of KBr solution, 2 drops of resorcinol solution and concentrated $H_2SO_4$ and heated on a water bath, a dark blue colour is produced, which changes to red when poured in water.

## CATIONS

### 14. Aluminium : ($Al^{+++}$)

1. Aqueous solution of aluminium salts when treated with dilute solution of ammonia, or ammonium sulphite forms a white gelatinous precipitate of aluminium hydroxide which is soluble in HCl.

(a) $Al^{+++} + 3NH_3 + 3H_2O \longrightarrow Al(OH)_3\downarrow + 3NH_4^+$

(b) $2Al^{+++} + 3S^- + 6H_2O \longrightarrow 2Al(OH)_3\downarrow + 3H_2S$

(c) $Al(OH)_3 + 3HCl \longrightarrow AlCl_3 + 3H_2O$

The precipitate of aluminium hydroxide so formed dissolves on further addition of sodium hydroxide solution as it forms sodium aluminate (soluble in water).

(a) $Al(OH)_3 + NaOH \longrightarrow AlO_2Na + 2H_2O$
(Sodium aluminate)

2. When aqueous solution of the salt is made just alkaline with dilute ammonia solution, and one drop of quinalizarine solution is added and heated to boiling, a reddish violet colour is produced due to formation complex of aluminium with quinalizarine.

3. Aqueous solution of aluminium salt when treated with few drops of ammonium acetate followed by few drops of mordent blue 3 solution produces intense blue colour due to complex formed with aluminium.

## 15. Ammonium : $(NH_4^+)$

1. When ammonium salt is heated with sodium hydroxide solution, it evolves ammonia which is recognised by its odour, it is confirmed when moist red litmus paper held over the fumes turns blue.

$$NH_4^+ + OH^- \longrightarrow NH_3\uparrow + H_2O$$

2. When aqueous solution is treated with light MgO and current of air is passed, the evolved gas is passed through 0.1 N HCl containing methyl red indicator, the colour of the solution changes to yellow (in acidic media methyl red has red colour, but in alkaline media it changes to yellow). To this solution when freshly prepared solution of sodium cobaltnitrite is added, it gives yellow precipitate of ammonium cobaltinitrite.

(a) $NH_4^+ + MgO \underset{}{\overset{air}{\rightleftharpoons}} NH_3\uparrow + Mg(OH)_2$

(b) HCl (methyl red) $\xrightarrow{\text{Excess } NH_3}$ NH₄Cl
 red (Colour of indicator turns yellow)

(c) $NH_4^+ + Na_3CO(NO_2)_6 \longrightarrow NH_4CO(NO_2)_6$
 (Sodium cobaltnitrate)
 (Yellow precipitate)

## 16. Antimony : (Sb, antimonous)

Slightly acidic solutions of antimony compounds when treated with hydrogen sulphide gives an organge coloured precipitate of antimony (III) sulphide. The precipitate is soluble in sodium hydroxide or in warm solution of hydrochloric acid.

(a) $2Sb^{+++} + 3S^- \longrightarrow Sb_2S_3\downarrow$ (antimony sulphide)

(b) $2Sb_2S_3 + 4OH^- \longrightarrow [Sb(OH)_4]^- + 3SbS^-$ (solution)

(c) $Sb_2S_3 + 8HCl \longrightarrow 2[SbCl_4]^- + 3H_2S\uparrow$ (solution)

## 17. Arsenic : (As, arsenous)

1. When solution of arsenous compound containing hydrochloric acid treated with hydrogen sulphide gives a yellow precipitate, soluble in solution of sodium hydroxide and solution of ammonium carbonate.

   (a) $2AsCl_3 + 3S^{--} \longrightarrow As_2S_3\downarrow + 6Cl^-$

   (b) $As_2S_3 + 6OH^- \longrightarrow AsO_3^{---} + AsS_3^{---} + 3H_2O$ (solution)

   (c) $As_2S_3 + 3CO_3^{--} \longrightarrow AsO_3^{---} + AsS_3^{---} + 3CO_2$

2. When prescribed solution of arsenic is heated with equal quality of hypophosphorous reagent on water bath, it gives gives a brown precipitate.

## 18. Barium : ($Ba^{++}$)

1. When barium salts are heated in nonluminous flame, it imparts yellowish-green colour to flame. When this is viewed through green glass, the flame appears blue.

2. Barium salts when dissolved in dilute HCl and treated with dilute sulphuric acid, gives a white precipitate of barium sulphate.

   $Ba^{++} + SO_4^{--} \longrightarrow BaSO_4 \downarrow$

## 19. Bismuth : ($Bi^{++}$)

1. To a solution of bismuth salt, when $H_2S$ is added, a brownish black precipitate of Bismuth sulphide, which is insoluble in solution of sodium hydroxide, dilute HCl, but soluble in warm nitric acid is formed.

   $2BiO^+ + 3HS^- + H^+ \longrightarrow Bi_2S_3\downarrow + 2H_2O$

2. A solution of bismuth salt is prepared in 2 N HCl, boiled cooled and filtered (if necessary). When 1 ml of this solution is diluted with 20 ml water, a white or slightly yellowish precipitate of bismuth oxychloride appears. On addition of 2 drops of sodium sulphide solution, a brown precipitate of bismuth sulphide is produced.

   $Bi^{+++} + 3HCl \longrightarrow BiCl_3$ (clear solution)

   $BiCl_3 + 4H_2O \rightleftharpoons BiOCl + 2H^+ + 2Cl^-$
   (bismuth oxychloride)

   $Bi^{+++} + 3Na_2S \longrightarrow Bi_2S_3\downarrow$ (Bismuth sulphide)

3. Solution of bismuth salt on treatment with KI solution yields a dark brown precipitate of bismuth iodide ($BiI_3$), which is soluble in excess of reagent giving a yellowish brown solution. This solution on dilution with water gives an orange-red precipitate of basic bismuth iodide (BiOI).

   (a) $BiO^+ + 3I^- + 2H^+ \longrightarrow BiI_3 + H_2O$
   Bismuth iodide

   (b) $BiI_3 + I^+ \longrightarrow [BiI_4] -$ soluble in water

4. Solution of bismuth salt is prepared in 2N nitric acid, by boiling, cooling and filtering (if required). When this solution is treated with solution of thiourea, it gives a orange-yellow colour or precipitate. On addition of sodium fluoride solution, the solution is not decolourised in thirty minutes.

## 20. Calcium : ($Ca^{++}$)

1. When solution of calcium salt is prepared with minimum amount of HCl, neutralised with sodium hydroxide solution and treated with ammonium carbonate solution gives a white precipitate of $CaCO_3$. On boiling and cooling the amorphous precipitate of $CaCO_3$ becomes crystalline. The precipitate is very sparingly soluble in ammonium chloride solution.

$$Ca^{++} + CO_3^{--} \longrightarrow CaCO_3\downarrow$$

2. When ammonium oxalate solution is added to a solution of calcium salt, a white precipitate of calcium oxalate is obtained. This precipitate is sparingly soluble in dilute acetic acid but dissolves in hydrochloric acid, forming calcium chloride and oxalic acid).

$$Ca^{++} + C_2O_4^{--} \longrightarrow CaC_2O_4\downarrow \xrightarrow{2\,HCl} CaCl_2 + H_2C_2O_4$$

(Oxalate)                                                                      Oxalic acid

3. Concentrated solution of calcium salts on treatment with potassium chromate solution gives a yellow crystalline precipitate of calcium chromate on shaking. On dilution with water the precipitate dissolves.

$$2Ca^{++} + 2CrO_4^{-} \longrightarrow 2CaCrO_4\downarrow$$

4. When an solution of calcium salt is acidified with glacial acetic acid or solution prepared in dilute acetic acid, and treated with few drops of potassium ferrocyanide solution, the salt solution remains clear (as it forms double calcium compound $CaK_2[Fe(CN)]_3$ slowly, which otherwise precipitates). On addition of ammonium chloride it gives a white precipitate which may be formulated as ($CaNH_4KFe(CN)_6$), which is less soluble. The exact composition of second precipitate depends on amount of ammonium ions.

$$Ca^{++} + 2K^+ + Fe(CN)_6^{----} \longrightarrow CaK_2[Fe(CN)]_6 \xrightarrow{NH_4^+} CaNH_4KFe(CN)_6$$

## 21. Ferric Salts : ($Fe^{+++}$)

1. Solution of ferric salt on treatment with aqueous solution of ammonium salt of nitrosopenyl hydroxylamine ($C_6H_5N(NO))OH$ gives a reddish brown precipitate of nitrosophenylhydroxylamine ferric complex.

2. When an aqueous solution of ferric salt is acidified with dilute HCl and treated with ammonium thiocyante, the solution acquires a blood red colour due to formation of ferric thiocynate. On addition of ether and shaking, the ether layer becomes pink as the complex is extracted by ether. But on addition of mercuric chloride the colour is

discharged as the initially formed ferric thiocynate forms a complex with excess of thiocynate ions.

(a) $Fe^{+++} + NCS^- \longrightarrow [Fe(NCS)]^{++}$ blood red colour.

(b) $[Fe(NCS)]^{++} + HgCl_2 + 3NCS \longrightarrow Hg(NCS)_4^{--}$

3. When aqueous solution of ferric salt is treated with solution of potassium ferrocyanide an intense blue precipitate of ferri ferrocyanide; is formed, which is insoluble in dilute HCl.

$$4Fe^{+++} + 3K_4 Fe(CN)_6 \longrightarrow Fe_4[Fe(CN)_6]_3 \downarrow + 12K$$
(Prussian blue)

4. Strongly acidified solutions of ferric salts with acetic acid, on treatment with solution of 8-hydroxy-7-iodoquinoline-5-sulphonic acid give a stable green colour as the ferric iron is complexed by the reagent.

## 22. Ferrous Salts : ($Fe^{++}$)

1. Solution of ferrous salts on treatment with solution of potassium ferrocyanide gives a white precipitate, which due to oxidation on exposure to air, is converted to a blue precipitate

    (a) $Fe^{++} + 2K^+ + [Fe(CN)_6]^{4-} \longrightarrow K_2Fe[Fe(CN)_6] \downarrow$ + white

    (b) $4K_2Fe[Fe(CN)_6] + 4H^+ + O_2 \longrightarrow 4K Fe[Fe(CN)_6] \downarrow + 4K^+ + 2H_2O$
    Blue colour

2. When an aqueous solution of ferrous salt is treated with potassium ferrocyanide solution, a dark blue precipitate is obtained which is insoluble in dilute HCl, but is decomposed by sodium hydroxide solution.

    (a) $3Fe^{++} + 2[Fe(CN)_6]^{---} \longrightarrow Fe_3[Fe(CN)_6]_2 \downarrow$

    (b) $Fe_3[Fe(CN)_6]_2 + 8NaOH \longrightarrow 2Na_4(Fe(CN)_6) + 2Fe(OH)_2 \downarrow$

3. When ferrous salt solution is treated with sodium hydroxide solution, a dark green precipitate of mixed ferrous hydroxide is formed, which on filtration and exposure to air becomes reddish brown as it is oxidised to mixed ferric hydroxide.

    (a) $Fe^{++} + 2OH \longrightarrow Fe(OH)_2 \downarrow$

    (b) $4Fe(OH)_2 + 2H_2O + O_2 \longrightarrow 4Fe(OH)_3 \downarrow$

4. A strongly acidified solution of ferrous salt with dilute $H_2SO_4$, when treated with solution of 1 : 10-phenanthroline gives a intense red colour due to formation of ferrous phenanthroline complex. When slight excess of ceric ammonium sulphate is added the colour is discharged as ferrous ion is oxidised to ferric form.

(a) $Fe^{++} + 3C_{12}H_8N_2 \longrightarrow (C_{12}H_8N_2)_3 Fe^{++}$
(Red colour)

(b) $(C_{12}H_8N_2) Fe^{++} + Ce^{++++} \longrightarrow 3C_{12}H_8N_2 + Fe^{+++} + Ce^{+++}$

23. **Lead : ($Pb^{++}$)**

1. Concentrated solution of lead salts with HCl gives a white-precipitate of lead chloride, which dissolves on boiling but redeposites on cooling.

$Pb^{++} + 2Cl^- \longrightarrow PbCl_2 \downarrow$

2. Solution of lead salts in moderately acidic media reacts with $H_2S$ and gives black precipitate of lead sulphide, which is insoluble in dilute HCl and solution of ammonium sulphide but soluble in hot nitric acid.

(a) $Pb^{++} + S^{--} \longrightarrow PbS \downarrow$

(b) $3PbS + 8H^+ + 2NO_3^- \longrightarrow 3Pb^{++} + 2NO\uparrow + 4H_2O + 3S\downarrow$

3. Solution of lead salts, when treated with sulphuric acid yields white precipitate of lead sulphate, which is insoluble in water, practically insoluble in $H_2SO_4$ but soluble in ammonium acetate solution.

(a) $Pb^{++} + SO_4^{--} \longrightarrow PbSO_4 \downarrow$

(b) $PbSO_4 + 4C_2H_3O_2^- \longrightarrow [Pb(C_2H_3O)_4]^{--} + SO_4^{--}$
(acetate)

4. Solution of lead salts in dilute acetic acid when treated with potassium chromate solution gives yellow precipitate of lead chromate, which is soluble in dilute solution of NaOH as it forms plumbites.

(a) $Pb^{++} + CrO_4^{--} \longrightarrow PbCrO_4 \downarrow$

(b) $PbCrO_4 + 3(OH)^- \longrightarrow HPbO_2^- + CrO_4^{--} + H_2O$

5. When solution of lead salt in dilute acetic acid is treated with KI solution gives a yellow precipitate of lead iodide, which on boiling and cooling is converted into yellow shining plates.

$Pb^{++} + 2I^- \longrightarrow PbI_2 \downarrow$

6. Solution of lead salt when treated with solution of potassium cyanide and made alkaline with ammonia a brick red colour is produced. The above solution on shaking with solution of lead free diphenylthiocarbazone (dithizone), the complex of lead formed dissolves in chloroform, and the chloroform layer acquires brick-red colour.

$$2S=C{\overset{NH.\ NH.\ C_6H_5}{\underset{N=N.\ C_6H_5}{\Large\diagup\kern-1em\diagdown}}} + Pb \rightarrow$$

(Lead dithzone complex)

## 24. Magnesium ($Mg^{++}$)

1. Solution of magnesium salt when treated with solution of ammonium carbonate on boiling gives white precipitate of basic magnesium carbonate, but in presence of ammonium salts like ammonium chloride no precipitate is produced as the ammonium ion converts the carbonate ion to bicarbonate.

   (a) $5Mg^{++} + 5CO_3^{--} + 6H_2O \longrightarrow 4MgCO_3 \cdot Mg(OH)_2 \cdot 5H_2O\downarrow + CO_2\uparrow$

   (b) $CO_3^{--} + NH_4^{+} \longrightarrow NH_3 + NCO_3^{-}$

   (Magnesium carbonate is not precipitated)

2. When an aqueous solution of magnesium salt is made alkaline with ammonia; a white precipitate of $Mg(OH)_2$ is formed. It disappears on addition of ammonium chloride solution (as the concentration of hydroxide ion is depressed by excess of $NH_4$ ions produced by $NH_4Cl$). On addition of solution of disodium hydrogen phosphate a white precipitate of magnesium ammonium phosphate is obtained.

   (a) $Mg^{++} + 2NH_4OH \rightleftharpoons Mg(OH)_2 \xrightarrow{2NH_4^+} Mg^{++} + 2NH_3 + 2H_2O$

   (b) $Mg^{++} + NH_3 + 6H_2O + HPO_4^{--} \longrightarrow MgNH_4PO_4 \cdot 6H_2O\downarrow$

3. Solution of magnesium salts when treated with solution of NaOH and diphenylcarbazide, gives a pink precipitate probably due to adsorption.

4. When aqueous solution of salt is treated with sodium hydroxide solution a gelatinous precipitate of $Mg(OH)_2$ is formed which is insoluble in excess of reagent but dissolves in solution of ammonium chloride.

   $Mg^{++} + 2OH^- \longrightarrow Mg(OH)_2 \downarrow \xrightarrow{2NH_4^+} Mg^{++} + 2NH_3 + 2H_2O$

5. When a neutral or slightly acidic solution of magnesium salt is treated with titan yellow solution and made just alkaline with 0.1N NaOH solution, bright red turbidity develops which settles down as bright red precipitate.

## 25. Potassium : ($K^+$)

1. Potassium salt moistened with HCl and taken on a platinium wire, when held in a bunsen flame gives a violet colour to flame.

2. Concentrated solutions of salt when treated with perchloric acid gives a white crystalline precipitate of potassium perchlorate.

$$K^+ + ClO_4^- \longrightarrow KClO_4 \downarrow$$

3. Aqueous solution of salt acidified with acetic acid when treated with freshly prepared solution of sodium cobalt nitrite [$Na_3CO(NO_2)_6$] gives a orange-yellow precipitate of potassium cobaltinitrite.

$$3K^+ + [Na_3CO(NO_2)_6]^{--} \longrightarrow K_3[CO(NO_2)_6] \downarrow$$

4. When solution of sodium carbonate is added to the solution of potassium salt, no precipitate is obtained. On further addition of sodium sulphide solution to the above still no precipitate is obtained. The above solution on cooling in ice water when treated with tartaric acid solution and allowed to stand gives a white precipitate of potassium hydrogen tartrate.

$$K^+ + Na_2CO_3 \longrightarrow \text{no reaction} \xrightarrow{Na_2S} \text{no reaction} \xrightarrow[+ \text{ tartaric acid}]{\text{Cooled}}$$

$$\longrightarrow KHC_4H_4O_6 \downarrow$$

5. Aqueous solution of potassium salts on treatment with sodium tetraphenylboron solution gives a white precipitate of potassium tetraphenylboron.

$$K^+ + Na[B(C_6H_5)_4] \longrightarrow K[B(C_6H_5)_4] \downarrow + Na^+$$

6. Potassium salts when ignited, cooled and dissolved in minimum quantity of water and treated with platinic chloride and HCl, gives a yellow crystalline precipitate of potassium chloroplatinate, which on ignition gives KCl and platinum.

$$2K^+ + H_2PtCl_6 \longrightarrow K_2PtCl_6 \downarrow \xrightarrow{\Delta} KCl + Pt \downarrow$$

## 26. Silver : ($Ag^+$)

1. Aqueous solution of silver salt when treated with few drops of dilute HCl gives a curdy white precipitate of silver chloride which is soluble in dilute ammonia solution (due to formation of silver ammoniate), but on further addition of potassium iodide solution gives a yellow precipitate of silver iodide.

$$Ag^+ + {}^-Cl \longrightarrow AgCl \downarrow \xrightarrow{2NH_3} Ag(NH_3)_2^+ \; Cl^- \xrightarrow{KI} AgI \downarrow + 2NH_3 + Cl^-$$

(Clear solution)

2. Solution of silver salt on treatment with potassium chromate solution gives a red precipitate of silver chromate which is soluble in dilute nitric acid (as silver is converted to silver nitrate).

$$2Ag^+ + CrO_4^- \longrightarrow Ag_2CrO_4\downarrow \xrightarrow{2HNO_3} 2AgNO_3 + CrO_4^{--}$$

(Clear solution)

## 27. Sodium : ($Na^+$)

1. Sodium salt moistened with HCl when taken on a platinum wire and held on a bunsen flame, imparts a yellow colour to the flame.

2. When sodium salt solution is boiled with potassium carbonate solution no precipitate is obtained. But if potassium antimonate solution is added to the above, boiled solution and sides of the test tube rubbed with a glass rod forms a dense white precipitate of disodium antimonate.

$$4Na^+ + 2KH_2SbO_4 \longrightarrow 2Na_2H_2SbO_4 + 2K^+$$

3. Aqueous solution of sodium salt when acidified with acetic acid and treated with magnesium uranylacetate solution gives a yellow crystalline precipitate of triple acetate.

$$Na^+ + 3UO_2(C_2H_3O_2)_2 \cdot Mg(C_2H_3O_2)_2 \xrightarrow{\frac{CH_2COOH}{H_2O}} NaMg(UO_2)_3(C_2H_3O_2)_9 \cdot 6H_2O\downarrow$$

## 28. Zinc : ($Zn^{++}$)

1. When a solution of zinc salts is made basified with dilute NaOH solution gives a white precipitate of zinc hydroxide which dissolves in excess of sodium hydroxide solution as it forms zinkate which is soluble. This solution on addition of ammonium chloride solution remains clear (as it forms tetra ammonium zinc hydroxide which is soluble). To the above is added few drops of sodium sulphide solution, forming a white precipitate of zinc sulphide.

    (a) $Zn^{++} + 2(OH)^- \longrightarrow Zn(OH)_2 \xrightarrow{Excess\ NaOH} Na_2ZnO_2 + 2H_2O$

    (Sod. zinkate)

    (b) $ZnO_2^{--} + 4NH_4^+ \longrightarrow [Zn(NH_3)_4(OH)_2^-] \xrightarrow{Na_2S} ZnS\downarrow$

2. Solutions of zinc salt when treated with solution of potassium ferrocyanide gives a white precipitate of zinc ferrocyanide, which is insoluble in hydrochloric acid.

$$2Zn^{++} + [Fe(CN)_6]^- \dashrightarrow Zn_2[Fe(CN)_6]\downarrow$$

3. Aqueous solution of the salt when acidified with dilute $H_2SO_4$ and treated with one drop of copper sulphate solution, followed by ammonium mercury thiocynate solution gives a violet precipitate (zinc ion complex).

## EXERCISE

1. Give identification tests with chemical reactions for the following ions/radicals :

    (a) Bromide,

    (b) Carbonate,

    (c) Acetate,

    (d) Silver,

    (e) Magnesium and

    (f) Calcium.

2. Describe the tests to distinguish the following ions/radicals :

    (i) Ferrous and ferric ion,

    (ii) Carbonate and bicarbonate,

    (iii) Iodide and bromide.

3. Outline the tests for identification of sodium and potassium ions.

4. Give identification tests for the following radicals :

    (a) Lactate,

    (b) Citrate,

    (c) Salicylate and

    (d) Oxalate.

5. Describe the use of following reagents in identification tests :

    (a) Quinalizarin,

    (b) Silvernitrate,

    (c) Diphenylthiocarbazone and

    (d) Ammonium molybdate.

6. Give the chemical reactions involved in the identification tests in the following :

   (a) Solution of ferric iron on treatment with potassium ferrocyanide or ferricyanide solution.

   (b) Neutral solution of citrate with silver nitrate reagent.

   (c) Solution of calcium salt with potassium chromate solution.

   (d) Solution of p-aminosalicylate on treatment with ferric chloride solution.

   (e) Treatment of borate with ethyl alcohol and a drop of sulphuric acid followed by heating.

■■■

# APPENDIX

## DEFINITIONS OF COMMONLY USED TERMS

**Acid :** A substance that ionizes in aqueous solution to yield a hydronium ion as one of the ions on a substance that donates proton or accepts electron. The strength of an acid depends upon the degree of ionization.

**Acidimetry :** The titration of free bases or those formed from the hydrolysis of salts of weak acids with a standard acid.

**Alkalimetry :** The titration of free acids or those formed by the hydrolysis of salts of weak bases with a standard alkali.

**Amphoteric :** A substance having the ability to react with either acid or base.

**Amorphous :** A substance having no definite shape or size, and which is coarse in nature.

**Anion :** An ion or a radical having a negative charge.

**Atomic number :** The number of protons in the nucleus of an atom.

**Atomic weight :** The weight of an atom with reference to the oxygen atom as 16.00.

**Base :** A substance that ionizes in an aqueous solution to yield hydroxide ion as one of the ion or as substance that possesses at least a lone pair of electrons or which accepts a proton. The strength of base depends upon the degree of ionization.

**Buffer solution :** A solution which resists changes in hydrogen ion concentration, upon the addition of small amounts of acid or alkali.

**Catalyst :** A substance which alters the rate of reaction (increasing or decreasing) and which remains unchanged and can be received at the end of the reaction.

**Cation :** An ion or radical having a positive charge.

**Combining weight :** The atomic weight of an element or radical, divided by the valency of the element or radical.

**Complex ion :** An ion which contains more than one element in a complex-combined form.

**Decrepitation :** A process of cracking or splitting when heated.

**Delequescence :** A process in which a substance absorbs sufficient water to form a liquid.

**Efflorescence :** Loss of a water molecule from a crystalline substance.

**Equilibrium :** A point at which the forward and reverse reaction rates are equal.

**Equivalent weight (of acid) :** Is that weight of it which contains one atom of replaceable hydrogen ion. For base, is that weight of it which contains one replaceable hydroxyl group i.e. 17.008 g of ionizable hydroxyl.

(Of oxidant mole reductant) is the molecular weight divided by the number of electrons which 1 mol of substance gains or loses in the reaction.

**Hydration :** Association of one or more molecules of water with an ion or molecule or compound.

**Hydrolysis :** A reaction involving double decomposition in which water is one of the reactants.

**Hygroscopic :** A substance that has the ability to absorb water from the atmosphere or air.

**Hypertonic :** A solution having an osmotic pressure higher than another solution, with which it is compared.

**Hypotonic :** A solution having an osmotic pressure lower than another solution, with which it is compared.

**Indicator paper :** A paper impregnated with a solution of an indicator which shows a change of colour at a certain hydrogen ion concentration.

**Ionization constant :** It is a ratio of the produce of concentration in moles of the anions and cations of an electrolyte, divided by the concentration in moles of the undissociated electrolyte. The constant remains the same under standard conditions of temperature, pressure, etc.

**Ionization potential :** It is the energy required to convert a neutral atom from its lower most energy level to form a positive ion.

**Isotonic :** A solution having the same osmotic pressure as that of body fluids.

$K_a$ : Ionization constant of acid.

$K_b$ : Ionization constant of base.

**Molar solution :** A solution containing one mole (molecular weight in g) per thousand ml of solution.

**Neutralization :** A chemical reaction in which an acid and a base react to form water and salt.

**Normal solution :** A solution containing one gram equivalent weight per thousand ml of solution.

**Osmosis :** A process wherein certain constituents of a solution diffuse through a semipermeable membrane.

**Oxidation :** The process which results in the loss of one or more electrons by atoms or ions.

**Oxidising agent :** A substance which brings oxidation by accepting an electron.

**pH :** Negative log of hydrogen ion concentration.

**Periodic Law :** A periodic variations in physical and chemical properties, when elements are arranged in the order of their atomic weights or atomic number.

$pK_a$ = The negative log of $K_a$.

$pK_b$ = The negative log of $K_b$.

**Polymorph :** A state wherein the substance exists in two or more crystalline forms.

**Reduction :** The process which results in the gain of one or more electrons by atoms or ions.

**Reducing agent :** A substance which brings about reduction by donating an electron.

**Reversible reaction :** It is process of reaction in which the reaction products react with each other to form the original substances.

**Solute :** A substance (the component of the solution) which is dissolved in a solvent.

**Solvent :** A substance (the component of the solution) which dissolves solute.

**Valency electrons :** The electrons present in the outermost shell of the atom of an element, which are gained, lost or shared in chemical reaction.

## International Atomic Weights of some Elements

| Element | Symbol | Atomic No. | Atomic Weight |
|---|---|---|---|
| Aluminium | Al | 13 | 26.98 |
| Antimony | Sb | 51 | 121.75 |
| Barium | Ba | 56 | 137.36 |
| Bismuth | Bi | 83 | 209.98 |
| Boron | B | 5 | 10.81 |
| Bromine | Br | 35 | 79.904 |
| Cadmium | Cd | 48 | 112.41 |
| Calcium | Ca | 20 | 40.08 |
| Carbon | C | 6 | 12.011 |
| Chlorine | Cl | 17 | 35.453 |
| Chromium | Cr | 24 | 51.966 |
| Cobalt | Co | 27 | 58.933 |
| Copper | Cu | 29 | 63.54 |
| Fluorine | F | 9 | 18.998 |
| Gold | Au | 79 | 196.966 |
| Hydrogen | H | 1 | 1.008 |
| Iodine | I | 53 | 126.94 |
| Lead | Pb | 82 | 207.2 |
| Lithium | Li | 3 | 6.940 |
| Magnesium | Mg | 12 | 24.35 |
| Mercury | Hg | 80 | 200.59 |
| Nickel | Ni | 28 | 58.71 |
| Nitrogen | N | 7 | 14.00 |
| Oxygen | O | 8 | 15.999 |
| Phosphorus | P | 15 | 30.97 |
| Potassium | K | 19 | 39.098 |
| Silicon | Si | 14 | 28.098 |
| Silver | Ag | 47 | 107.86 |
| Sodium | Na | 11 | 22.989 |
| Strontium | Sr | 38 | 87.63 |
| Sulphur | S | 16 | 32.06 |
| Tin | Sn | 50 | 118.69 |
| Zinc | Zn | 30 | 65.38 |

# INDEX

Absorbents, 9.1
Acidifying Agents, 6.1
Acidity, 3.4
Acidosis, 13.13
Activated Charcoals, 18.3
Agents, 8.4
Alkality, 3.4
Alkalosis, 13.13
Aluminium Chloride, 9.25
Aluminium Sulphate, 9.25
Aluminium Subaccetate Solution, 9.26
Alpha particles, 17.2
Alum, 9.26
Aluminium Glycinate, 8.5
Aluminium Hydroxide gel, 8.3
Aluminium Hydroxide gel Dried, 8.4
Aluminium Hydroxide Tablets, 8.4
Aluminium Phosphate, 8.4
Ammonia Solution, 6.12, 12.6
Ammonia Solution Strong, 6.12
Ammonium Acitate, 12.2
Ammonium Carbonate, 12.2, 12.6
Ammonia Chloride, 12.1
Ammonium Solution, 12.6
Antacids, 7.2
Anti Action of Mechanisms, 7.1
Anti oxidants, 7.2
Anti Selection, 7.2
Anticartes Agents, 10.1

Antimicrobial Agents, 9.6
Antimony Potassium Tartrate, 12.4
Applications of Radioisotopes, 17.7
Aromatic spirit of Ammonia, 12.6
Arrhenius Theory, 6.1
Ash, 3.4
Astringents, 9.6
Barium Sulphate, 17.8
Behaviour, 5.2
Bismuth Compounds, 8.11
Bismuth Subcarbonate, 8.12
Bismuth Subgallate, 8.12
Bismuth Subnitrate, 8.12
Bita Particles, 17.2
Bleaching Powder, 17.1
Borax, 9.12
Boric Acid, 9.11
Bronstead and Lowry Theory, 6.2
Buffer Action, 6.4
Buffer Capacity, 6.4
Buffer Physiological, 6.5
Buffer Solution, 6.3
Buffer Standard, 6.5
Calamine, 9.3
Calamine Cream, 9.4
Calamine Lotion, 9.4
Calamine Ointment, 9.4
Calcium Acetate, 16.3
Calcium Carbonate, 16.4

Calcium Chloride, 16.5
Calcium Compound, 8.5
Calcium Glycerophosphate, 16.13
Calcium Glyconate, 16.4
Calcium Hydroxide, 16.6
Calcium Lactate, 16.6
Calcium Levulinate, 16.7
Calcium Mandelate, 16.13
Calcium Pantothenate, 16.12
Calcium PAS, 16.12
Calcium Phosphate, 16.10
Calcium Sodium Edetate, 16.14
Calcium Sodium Lactate, 16.13
Calcium Sulphate, 16.12
Calomel, 8.17
Carbondioxide, 11.3
Chlorinated Lime, 17.1
Cleaning Agents, 10.2
Colligativ Properties, 5.5
Copper Sulphate, 12.5
Cyanide Poisoning, 19.2
Decomposition, 3.2
Dental Products, 10.1
Desentising Agents, 10.4
Effect of Impurities, 3.3
Errors in Analysis, 2.1
Expectorants, 12.6
Extracellular Electrolytes, 13.1
FerricAmmonium Citrate, 14.2
Ferrous Fumurate, 14.3
Ferrous Gluconate, 14.4

Ferrous Incompatibilities, 14.5
Ferrous Succinate, 14.5
Ferrous Sulphate, 14.5, 14.6
Handling of materials, 17.7
Hardness of water, 4.3
Hydration, 4.2
Hydrochloric Acid, 6.10
Hydrogen Peroxide, 9.6
Hypophosphorus Acid, 14.1, 7.3
Identification :
    Acetates, 19.2
    Aluminiu, 19.12
    Ammonium, 19.12
    Antimony, 19.13
    Arsenic, 19.13
    Barium, 19.14
    Bicarbonate, 19.4
    Bismuth, 19.10
    Bromide, 19.4
    Calcium, 19.15
    Carbonate, 19.4
    Chloride, 19.4
    Citrate, 19.4
    Ferric Salt, 19.10
    Iodides, 19.7
    Lactates, 19.7
    Lead, 19.12
    Magnessium, 19.13
    Phosphate, 19.8
    Potassium, 19.6
    Silver, 19.7
    Sodium, 19.7
    Sulphate, 19.6
    Tartrate, 19.7
    Zinc, 19.8
Inhalants, 11.1
Inderterminate Errors, 2.2

Iodine, 15.1, 15.2
Iodine Compounds, 15.3
Iodine Solution, 9.12, 9.13
Ion Compounds, 14.1
Kaolin, 8.12, 18.12
Lewis Theory, 6.2
Limit test for Arsenic, 3.10, 3.11
Limit test for Heavy-metals, 3.8
Limit test for Iron, 3.8
Limit test for Lead, 3.9, 3.10
Limit test for Sulphate, 3.5, 3.6
Limit test of Chloride, 8.6
Magnesium Carbonate, 8.6
Magnesium Compound, 8.7
Magnesium Hydroxide, 8.6
Magnesium Oxide, 8.8
Magnesium Trisillicate, 3.6, 18.3
Magnesium Sulphate, 8.14, 18.2
Major Anions, 13.5
Major cations, 13.3
Mercury Compounds, 9.22
Mercury Oxide, 9.22
Method of softening Water, 4.6
Mild Silver protein, 9.8
Milk of Magnesia, 8.6
Molar Solution, 5.3
Molar Solution, 5.3
Nessler's cylinder, 3.5
Nitrous Oxide, 11.5
Oral Dehydration Salts, 13.5
Osmotic pressures, 5.6

Oxygen, 11.6
Prepreslion of freezing point, 5.4
Percent Solution, 5.2
Permisible, 3.2
pH , POH, 6.4
Phosphoric Acid, 6.8
Phosphorus Acid, 7.2
Physico Chemical Constants, 3.3
Poisoning Antidotes, 18.2
Polishing Agents, 10.2
Potassium Acitate, 13.14
Potassium Bitartrate, 8.16
Potassium Chloride, 13.8
Potassium Citrate, 13.9
Potassium Hydroxide, 6.8
Potassium Iodide, 12.3
Potassium Permagnate, 9.8
Precipitated Sulphur, 9.28
Preparation of solution for test, 3.4
Protectives, 9.1
Pumice, 10.3
Purified water, 4.4
Q. Test, 2.4
Quality Control , 1.1
Radiation Materials, 17.4
Radiation measurements, 17.4
Radiation properties, 17.3
Radio activity, 17.3
Radio Isotopes, 17.2
Radio Opaque Media, 17.7
Radioactive Iodine, 15.6

Radio active Decay, 17.2
Rejection of Results, 2.4
Relative Errors, 2.1
Rounding of figures, 2.5
Saline Cathartics, 8.14
Silver nitrate, 9.14
Significant figures, 2.4
Sodium Bicarbonate, 13.15
Sodium Borate, 9.14
Sodium Carbonate, 6.12
Sodium Chloride, 13.5
Sodium Chloride Hypertonic, 13.7
Sodium Chloride Injection, 13.7
Sodium Compound, 8.12
Sodium Fluoride, 10.3
Sodium Hydroxide, 6.13
Sodium hypo-chloride, 9.20
Sodium Lactate, 13.14
Sodium Metabisulphide, 7.5
Sodium Nitrate, 7.5, 19.1
Sodium Perborate, 7.6

Sodium Phosphate, 7.5
Sodium Potassium tartrate, 8.6
Sodium Thiosulphate, 7.6, 19.2
Solubility of 31, 5.1
Solubility Product Principle, 5.3
Sources of Impurities, 3.1
Source, 2.1
Storage Conditions, 3.2
Strong Silver Protein, 9.22
Sublimed Sulphur, 9.29
Sulphur, 9.29
Sulphur Ointment9
Sulphur Dioxide, 7.3
Talc, 9.2
Test for purity, 3.3
Titanium Dioxide, 9.3
Water, 4.1
Water for Injection, 4.7
Zinc Chloride, 9.27
Zinc Sulphate, 9.28

■■■

# BIBLIOGRAPHY

1. A Text book of Quantitative Inorganic Chemistry by A.I. Vogel, Third Ed., The English Language Book Society, Longman, London.

2. Bentley and Driver's Text Book of Pharmaceutical Chemistry. Ed., by L.M. Artherden, 8th Ed., Oxford University Press, London.

3. British Pharmacopoeia 1988, Her Majesty's stationery Office, London.

4. Impurities in Pharmaceutical Substances by M. L. Schroff, and B.M. Mithal, Second Ed., A.K. Schroff, Sahpuram, Armuganeri.

5. Inorganic Medicinal and Pharmaceutical Chemistry by J.H. Block E.B. Roche, T.O. Soine and C.O., Wilson, 1974, Lea and Febiger, Philadelphia.

6. Modern Inorganic Pharmaceutical Chemistry By C.A. Discher 1964 John Wiley and Sons Inc. New York.

7. Pharmaceutical Chemistry Vol. I by L.G. Chatten, 1969, Marcel Dekker Ltd., 14 Crufurd Rise, Mainden head, Berkshire, England.

8. Pharmaceutical Chemistry Vol. I and II by M.L. Schroff, 1st Ed. 1969, A.K. Schroff, National Book Centre, P-76 Sundar Mohan Avenue, Calcutta.

9. Pharmacopoeia of India, Third Ed., 1985, Ministry of Health Govt., of India, New Delhi.

10. Pharmacopoeia of India, Supplement 1975, Ministry of Health, Govt. of India, New Delhi.

11. Quantitative Pharmaceutical Chemistry, 6th Edition, 1967, Genkins. Knevel, Digang Mc Graw Hill Book Company, New York.

12. Remington's Pharmaceutical Sciences. Fifteenth Ed., 1975, Mack Publishing Company, Easton Pennsylvania.

13. Roger's Inorganic Pharmaceutical Chemistry by T.O. Soine and C.O. Wilson, Seventh Ed., 1961, Lea and Febiger. Philadelphia.

14. The Quantitative Analysis of Drugs by D.C. Garret, 3rd Ed., Chapman and Hall Ltd., 11, New Felter Lane, London.

15. Theoretical Pharmaceutical Chemistry, 2nd Edition, 1950. Lyons and Appleyard Sir Issac Pitman and Sons Ltd., London.

16. United States Pharmacopoeia, Nineteenth Revision, United States, Pharmacopoeial Convention, Inc. 12601, Twinbrook Parkway Rockville, Md. 20852.

■■■